Also by Newt Gingrich

Gettysburg co-authored by William Forstchen
Lessons Learned the Hard Way: A Personal Report
Renewing American Civilization
1945 co-authored by William Forstchen
To Renew America
Contract with America: The Bold Plan to Change the Nation
Window of Opportunity: A Blueprint for the Future
Saving Lives and Saving Money
Winning The Future

To Larry

your friend

Newt

The Art of Transformation

Newt Gingrich and Nancy Desmond

CHT PRESS
The Center for Health Transformation
1425 K Street, NW, Suite 450
Washington, D.C. 20005
www.healthtransformation.net

CHT
PRESS

INAUGURAL PUBLICATION
FIRST EDITION/FIRST PRINTING

ISBN : 1-933966-00-9

DEDICATION

To the members of the Center for Health Transformation, who have made our transformational work possible and who have contributed so much to our understanding of the art of transformation.

CONTENTS

Authors' Foreword

In November 1994, the Republican Party took control of the U.S. House of Representatives for the first time in forty years.

Many saw it as the result of a short and well-executed campaign. Others thought it was a fluke resulting from an intersection of unplanned or unexpected variables.

But as part of the team involved in igniting what many called the Republican Revolution, we knew it was no accident. It was the result of many years of effort, built on a planning and leadership model as well as on a set of critical principles, rules, and habits that we believed—and subsequently proved—could create a remarkable transformation.

Five years later, moving from the public to the private sector, the authors embarked on a new endeavor. We believed that the same transformational model that brought about victory in 1994, along with the lessons we learned along the way, could be applied to the private sector and to a private/public partnership to create a 21st century in which all Americans live in greater freedom, health, prosperity, and safety.

With the help of our clients at the Gingrich Group and our members at the Center for Health Transformation, the transformation model has been refined and expanded.

This book is the first in a series designed to train a critical mass of civic, industry, and government leaders who are interested in not only transforming their own lives, organizations, or industries, but in creating a better future for all Americans.

The Art of Transformation: Fifteen Key Steps

Within a leadership model of Listen, Learn, Help, Lead:

1. Scan the environment (past, present, future) to assess the need and opportunity for transformation, apply the lessons of history, and ask yourself if this requires management (reform) or transformational leadership (fundamental change). Always try to find a management answer, as transformation is so big and takes so long.

2. Recognize that the decision to advocate and develop a transformational future is inherently a moral decision, and that you have asserted the right or necessity to make it. The burden is ultimately on you.

3. If you decide that the situation requires transformation either to meet a threat or develop an opportunity, be prepared for a long, serious, complex process.

4. Create a vision of the ideal future and present it to others for their reaction. Improve the vision as you listen.

5. Build a collaboration of core leaders that will change and grow, and which will be at the heart of building the movement. This can be within your company or across a community.

6. Define the mission, key metrics, and the strategies needed to close the gap between your ideal future and today.

7. Create structures, processes, and doctrines that maximize communication, mutual learning, and synergy but allow for decentralized decision-making and leadership.

8. Constantly communicate the vision and the moral imperative in order to get buy-in and grow the movement.

9. Constantly train and grow a critical mass of leaders.

10. Constantly identify and communicate proven solutions that help people understand and believe the vision.

11. Whenever possible, achieve small wins so morale keeps growing and the possibility of transformation seems more real.

12. Create definable, delegatable projects with clear metrics that help fulfill the strategies and make the transition to the new vision. Recruit leaders for those projects.

13. Move to the sound of the guns in order to constantly leverage new opportunities to drive the transformation. Recognize that real change involves doing new things and that doing new things is very hard. The transformational leader learns more than teaches and helps more than orders.

14. Throughout implementation, engage in constant metrics-led leadership and management, in tandem with a focus on systems thinking and quality.

15. Whenever possible, have fun and include others. Share every victory and success. This is hard and the team needs to grow into it so the leader is gradually surrounded and overshadowed by a much larger, very engaged team of leaders.

ACKNOWLEDGEMENTS

This book would not have been possible without the support of many people.

First, we'd like to thank our team, our members, and our clients from the Center for Health Transformation and the Gingrich Group, who helped develop many of these ideas.

In particular, we are grateful to Laura Linn, who worked closely with us in reviewing the book and in pulling together many of the transcripts, graphs, and documents that enriched the manuscript. In addition, we are grateful to Melissa Ferguson, Rob Egge, Jim Frogue, Wayne Oliver, Sarah Murphy, Megan Meehan, Amy Nyhuis, Jenny Blackham, and Katie Harman; without their contributions at the Center for Health Transformation, this book would not have been possible.

We also owe many thanks to three members of the CHT team who made special contributions to the book: Scott Cotter, who helped with many of the details related to contracts, website presence, and copyrighting; David Merritt, who helped coordinate the preparation of the testimony appearing in the Appendix of the book; and CHT fellow Vince Haley, who helped with the editing of the chapter on government transformation.

We are especially grateful to Kathy Lubbers and Sylvia Garcia, who managed the book editing and publishing process. Our gratitude also goes out to the other members of the Gingrich Communications team, including Joe DeSantis, Jessica Gavora, and Chris Davis.

We are indebted to the many people who reviewed and offered edits to the book, including Rick Tyler of Gingrich Communications and Steve Hanser, whose guidance, support, and review of this manuscript were invaluable.

Sonya Harrison, Bess Kelly, and Amy Pearman, as always, helped orchestrate busy schedules and conflicting priorities in order to ensure the timely completion of this project. Thanks also to Jackie Cushman and Oliver Logan, who provided IT support throughout the months of work.

As always, we are grateful to Randy Evans and Stefan Passantino for their advice and counsel and to Joe Gaylord for his years of wisdom and creativity, which contributed to many of the ideas and principles included in this book.

Our editor, Rowena Itchon, did an amazing job, as did Paula Currall, who did our copyediting and fact-checking, and Robin Krauss, who handled the graphic design. We are also grateful to Brandi Laughey, who patiently worked with us to bring to life the cover design we envisioned.

Many people throughout the years helped teach us the lessons included in the book, including Generals Donn Starry and Don Morelli, who first taught us to think of systematic transformation; Peter Drucker and W. Edwards Deming, who taught us many of the principles and lessons that are at the heart of *The Art of Transformation;* and President Ronald Reagan, from whom we learned so much about the kind of courage, leadership, and communications that can transform the world.

We are grateful to them and to the many other leaders included in this book, both for what they added to our work and, more important, for what they have contributed to America and to the world through their leadership and wisdom.

Our spouses, Callista and Denny, and our entire families, as always, served as both our inspiration and the wind beneath our wings.

PART ONE

Today's Age of Transformation

Why Transformation Will Be Everyone's Job
in the 21st Century

America is entering the greatest and most complex period of challenge since April 1861 when the first shots were fired from Fort Sumter and the Civil War began.

The Great Depression was simpler.

The Second World War was simpler.

The Cold War was simpler.

Each of these problems was huge and affected the entire country. But each was singularly definable.

Today America is confronting:

- An extraordinary scale of scientific change (four to seven times as much in the next twenty-five years as in the last quarter century).

- The first two great economic competitors—China and India. Not since 1840 have we confronted economic powerhouses that can truly challenge our own.

If America is to succeed and remain the most prosperous, powerful, and freest nation in the world, we Americans must transform many of our fundamental institutions, including education, healthcare, litigation, regulation, taxation, and our energy policy.

Our efforts to be competitive will be made even more complicated by the effects of the demographic revolution. The Baby Boomers will live longer than any generation in human history and as a result, will have tremendous consequences for work, retirement, and health-care. Moreover, the scale of immigration combined with the hostility to American values among our intellectual and news media elites will put great pressure on sustaining American civilization and maintaining a common civic culture.

All of these concerns at home will be operating within a world that is threatened by four major developments:

1. The long war with the Irreconcilable Wing of Islam. This irreconcilable wing of Islam aims to destroy our civilization and is willing and eager to kill millions of Americans to do so;

2. The rise of aggressive dictatorships seeking nuclear and biological weapons while openly threatening to use them to defeat the United States and our allies;

3. The emergence of an anti-American coalition of dictators who feel threatened by our insistence on human rights and freedom. Hugo Chavez of Venezuela and Fidel Castro of Cuba are aligning to reach out to dictators worldwide to form a coalition of tyrants with the goal to dominate votes in the UN General Assembly;

4. The emergence of China as a world power with systematic, diplomatic, and economic reach across the entire planet (from shops in Africa, to pipelines in Sudan, to diplomatic efforts in Bolivia and Venezuela, to the Shanghai Cooperative Association effort that unites the dictators of central Asia).

Our efforts to meet these challenges will be hampered by the obvious fact that our great bureaucracies are now obsolete and simply cannot operate at the speed, flexibility, and effectiveness demanded by the information age in a global society.

Our generation is facing a more complex and demanding set of challenges than any generation since Abraham Lincoln.

In April 1861, Lincoln called for 75,000 volunteers for 90 days. Little did he know he was entering a war that would last four years, kill

660,000 Americans (the most in our history by a huge margin), force the government to go off the gold standard and issue paperback money (greenbacks which we still carry), build a transcontinental railroad to keep California in the union, adopt a draft and then have to send 10,000 federal troops into New York City to suppress anti-draft riots that were destroying the city.

Just as Lincoln could not know how hard and complex his challenge would be, we do not fully understand how hard and complex our challenge will be.

If our children and grandchildren are to inherit from us an America that is as free, prosperous, and safe as the country our parents worked and fought to give us, then we will have to have the courage to transform many of our institutions, businesses, and professions to meet the challenges of the 21st century.

The Choice: Reform or Transformation

Reform is a process of improving an existing system. Transformation is a method of visualizing a new system, culture, process, and structure, and migrating the current system to the new.

Reform involves much less change and is much less difficult. It requires a lot less learning and a lot less effort. Transformation is difficult and demanding. It is by definition a journey into a new and different system, with new and different rules and principles.

Reform can improve most activities. If the system or organization can survive and succeed with only marginal changes, then reform is the answer. Transformation is needed when we face a challenge so great that our current organization cannot meet it, or when we have a goal so different that the current system cannot achieve it.

America has reached that moment in time.

We believe reform will decline and transformation will dramatically increase. The pace of change in the world will give us no choice.

By contrast, imagine being the head of a stagecoach company in 1840. Railroads were very few and very slow. There was still a vast amount of America that could profitably be served by stagecoach. We would have been right to focus on reform.

We might have bought new and streamlined stagecoaches, used the latest axle grease product to minimize friction, applied the new method of changing horses at the way station, and invested in the new breed of horses that could pull faster and longer—these were all reforms that might have given our stagecoach company an advantage over our competitors or a greater profit margin.

However, by 1870, it would have become obvious that no amount of reforms on our stagecoach company would keep us in business. We would have had to start thinking through a transformation in America's transportation system.

In modern times we have seen the managements of major companies fail to recognize that they had reached a transformational point in the lives of their businesses.

After airline deregulation in 1978, it was obvious that a new world of price competition and greater passenger choice was dawning. The highly leveraged, unionized, comfortably managed airlines of the regulatory era were about to face unending upheaval and competition. None of the existing major airlines or their unions could bring themselves to think transformationally.

Along came Southwest Airlines. It was designed from the ground up to be a lean, low-cost, highly competitive system. As costs per passenger mile have dropped from 23 cents to 12 cents, the dominant airlines of 1978 have gone through a slow, reluctant, and agonizing change that has resulted in either bankruptcy or extinction. Southwest has continued to thrive and is now one of the largest domestic airlines.

When transformation is the only thing that will work, focusing on reform is ruinous. By focusing on reform, the leadership wastes its time and energy on projects that, even if they succeed, will prove at best inadequate and at worst detrimental. When transformation is needed but ignored, the organization becomes steadily weaker and more demoralized.

The 1983 "Nation at Risk" report warned that American education had collapsed to the point that it was a genuine threat to our future. Since then, there have been unending efforts to reform education. These efforts have failed because reform of the bureaucratic, unionized, credentialed, state curriculum–controlled, obsolete industrial-era system will never produce results adequate for the 21st century.

What is needed is a focus on transformation into a 21st century intelligent, effective learning system that would be dramatically different in its principles, systems, and practices than the inherited 19th and early 20th century education bureaucracy.

We have to assess our organizations and professions and determine whether we can achieve our goals and meet the challenges we face within the context of the current approach. If we can, then we can survive with a focus on reform.

However, for those organizations that need transformation—and for America—this book provides many of the principles, practices, and tools that can make that journey successful.

Four Key Questions

1. What is the current reality?
2. What is our definition of success?
3. Can we get there within the current reality?
4. If not, what is the transformational system that needs to be developed?

Transformation in the 21st Century

For government and industries still clinging to a 20th century model, transformation is a necessity. The only other option is decay.

In the 21st century there will be more change in scientific knowledge in the next twenty-five years than in the past one hundred years. We are exceeding by four to seven times the rate of change of the past twenty-five years. This means that by even the most conservative estimate, we will experience between 2005 and 2030 the scale of change experienced between 1905 and 2005.

More scientists are alive today than in all of human history combined. And instead of sharing knowledge at the rate of the printing press and mail delivery, scientists are sharing knowledge through the Internet and the cell phone, resulting in the highest rate of information transmission than at any time in history. This explosion of knowledge is moving from laboratory to market by a venture capital/licensing/royalty system of unprecedented power and ability.

Moreover, the potential for production is being radically expanded by the rise of China and India as the lowest-cost production leaders. The dominant model of the 21st century will be more choices of higher quality at lower cost. In any area or industry where that is not happening, such as government, healthcare, and education, transformation must occur if America is to continue to lead the world.

> **Moore's Law** is a rule of thumb in the computer industry about the growth of computing power over time. Attributed to Gordon E. Moore, the co-founder of Intel, it states that the growth of computing power per dollar follows an empirical exponential law. Moore originally proposed a 12-month doubling and, later, a 24-month period.

Drivers of change fueled by Moore's Law will increase knowledge and productivity worldwide—virtually guaranteeing continuous downward pricing pressures in information technology, communications, nano-scale science and technology, quantum mechanics, and biology.

Indeed, we are entering a period similar to what America experienced between 1873 and 1896 when there were advancements in steel, electricity, electric light, steamships, and the telephone. The introduction of commercial refrigerator cars for railroads and ships, for example, meant that Texas ranchers could deliver their beef anywhere, which resulted in the collapse of food prices. Similarly, the constant and steady explosion of productivity will continue to reduce the cost of many products today.

The profound changes we will experience from 2005 to 2030 will require at least seven significant transformations:

1. National security
2. Health and healthcare
3. Education in general and math and science in particular
4. Government management
5. Taxation
6. Litigation
7. Energy and the environment

Against the backdrop of scientific change, four other trends are creating a perfect storm that will demand transformation.

1. The aging demographics of our society will present new challenges that will be impossible to address within a 20th century framework. Take Medicare, for example. Unless we dramatically transform our current healthcare system into one that focuses on health and wellness and is capable of rapidly adopting proven technologies and best practices to save lives and money, the cost in human lives and suffering will be unsustainable.

> According to the U.S. Centers for Disease Control, the proportion of the U.S. population over 65 is projected to increase from 12.4 percent in 2000 to 19.6 percent by 2030—an increase from approximately 35 million in 2000 to an estimated 71 million in 2030. The number of people over 80 is expected to increase from 9.3 million in 2000 to 19.5 million in 2030.

2. We are undergoing vast cultural changes, many of which are driven by immigration and by the very nature of a technology-rich world. Our hospitals

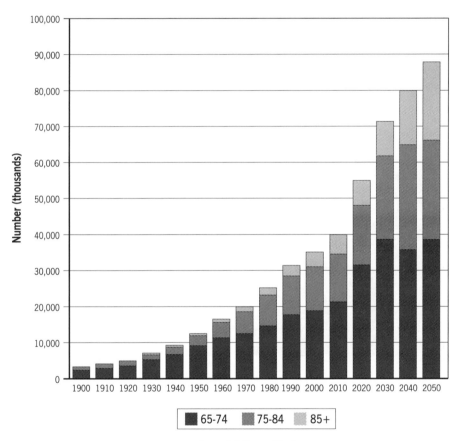

Older Population by Age: 1900-2050

Source: U.S. Bureau of the Census

Number of Medicare Beneficiaries

The number of people Medicare serves will nearly double by 2030

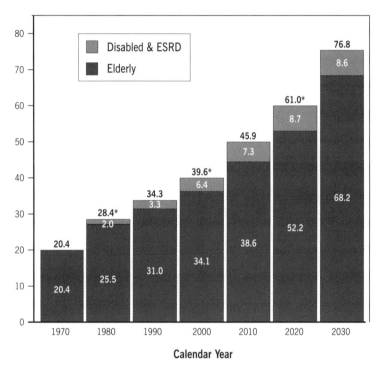

Calendar Year

* Numbers may not sum due to rounding
Source: Centers for Medicare and Medicaid Services, Office of the Actuary

are drowning under the cost of caring for illegal immigrants who are uninsured and who use emergency rooms rather than doctors' offices for primary care; our schools are struggling to deal with an influx of students who don't speak English and who are often transient.

3. The global market is making it increasingly difficult for us to succeed without transforming our tax laws, our educational system (particularly science and math), and our litigation system.

4. The threat of a terrorist attack, or a biological or engineered pandemic, is making the absence of an effective public health network and the slow adoption of technologies more and more dangerous and unacceptable.

As Americans, it is as if we are sitting on a houseboat watching these four waves descend upon us, wondering if we can re-make our houseboat into a sailboat in time to navigate the approaching waves. The changing environment will require America to undergo profound transformations if we want our children and grandchildren to continue to live in the most productive economy in the world.

We must transform or fall behind. It's that simple.

The Scale and Implications of the 21st Century Transformation

We are not on the edge of an information age with a single learnable set of principles. We are in the middle of an ongoing series of changes that will force us to continue adapting for the rest of our lifetimes.

We will continue to be inundated with discoveries, inventions, and entrepreneurs with startup companies creating new goods and services. The new products and services created by this Age of Transformation are providing vast opportunities for improving everyday life.

They are also creating a constant churning and changing that can be both exhilarating and exhausting.

For those who ask when the change will stop and when we will return to a more tranquil existence, the answer is *never*.

The earliest observations of this vast change were Kenneth Boulding's *The Meaning of the Twentieth Century* (1964), Peter Drucker's *The Age of Discontinuity* (1969), Alvin and Heidi Toffler's *Future Shock* (1970), and the Tofflers' far more useful and analytical *The Third Wave* (1980). These commentators all understood that the industrial era was being replaced by something new and profound. As Drucker's title indicates, these futurists were not sure what would come out on the other end, but they were sure it would not simply be a more powerful industrial era.

> "We are the final generation of an old civilization and the first generation of a new one, and much of our personal confusion, anguish, and disorientation can be traced directly to the conflict within us and within our political institutions—between the dying Second Wave civilization and the emergent Third Wave civilization that is thundering to take its place."
> *Alvin Toffler*
> *The Third Wave, 1980*

Computing is a key element in transformation. The first computer with a transistor, Tradic, was built in 1955 and had only 800 transistors. The Pentium II chip has 7.5 million transistors. Within fifteen to twenty years there will be a chip with one trillion transistors. However you graph that scale of change, it is enormous—and its implications are huge.

Yet focusing only on computer power understates the scale of change. Communications capabilities are going to continue to expand dramatically, and that may have as big an impact as computing power. From 1984 to 2003, the number of households with a computer grew from 8.2 million to 61.8 million—a seven-fold increase. Meanwhile, from 1989 to 2003, the percentage of households with Internet connections grew from 15 percent to nearly 55 percent. The Pew Institute reports that, by the end of 2005, 70 percent of adults had Internet access.

Tradic 1955
Source: thinkquest.org

A 2005 report from the U.S. Census Bureau showed that 40 percent of adults used the Internet to obtain news, weather, or sports information in 2003—a sharp increase from only 7 percent six years earlier. The report also

Households with a Computer and Internet Access: 1984-2003

(in percent)

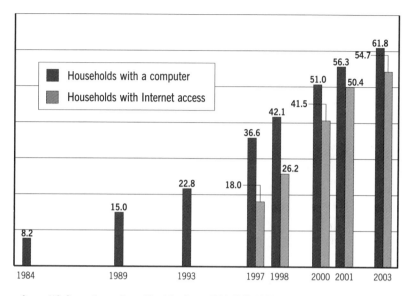

Source: U.S. Census Bureau, Current Population Survey, 1984, 1989, 1993, 1997, 1998, 2000, 2001, 2003.

showed that in 2003, nearly half (47 percent) of adults used the Internet to find information on products or services. And about one-third (32 percent) purchased a product or service online, compared with only 2 percent of adults who shopped online in 1997.

In a measure of how interpersonal communications are changing, more than half of adults (55 percent) used e-mail or instant messaging in 2003, a dramatic increase from the 12 percent who did so in 1997.

Think back to a world without Google, eBay, Amazon, or Travelocity. For most of us these services have become an indispensable part of daily life.

Moreover, our world is being expanded by the continuing development of the cell phone into a universal utility with voice, Internet, credit card, and television applications all in one. This is an area in which Europe, Korea, and Japan are ahead of us, and requires that we review and change some of our policies.

**Population 18 Years and Older Using the Internet for a Specific Task:
1997, 2001 and 2003** *(in percent)*

	0% 10% 20% 30% 40% 50% 60% 70% 80%
Total using Internet	22.1 / 55.3 / 59.5
E-mail	11.5 / 48.6 / 54.5
Information on products or services	41.7 / 46.5
News, weather, sports information	7.2 / 37.4 / 40.1
Information on government/ health services	11.5 / 26.4 / 32.8
Purchase products or services	2.1 / 25.7 / 32.3

■ 1997
■ 2001
▫ 2003

Source: U.S. Census Bureau

A 2005 report by the Pew Internet Project reported that 134 million American adults have cell phones and that 27 percent of them reported using the text message feature on those phones within the past month. The report also noted that the proliferation of cell phones and the spread of text messaging are changing patterns of communication for many Americans, especially younger Americans, creating a new perception of what it means to be present with someone else and about what it means to be in conversation with them. Indeed, according to the Pew Project, for some cell phone users, the stream of conversation hardly ever ends.

When it comes to entertainment, we have almost as many options on our cell phones as we do in our living rooms. Cell phones today allow us to access the Internet, watch TV, and watch full-motion video on demand.

But beyond social and entertainment capabilities, cell phones are constantly expanding their utility in a variety of other areas, including healthcare. For example, one company has recently introduced a diabetes phone with a built-in glucose monitor that allows people with diabetes to check their blood glucose level and automatically have the results transmitted to their doctor's office. The phone can even be programmed to call users to remind them to check their glucose levels.

Focusing on computers and communications is only the first step toward understanding the nature of the 21st century. An even bigger area of change will be our understanding of biology and the development of new medicines and diagnostic tools.

In the next decade, the Human Genome Project will teach us more about humans than at any time in medical history. The development of new technologies (largely a function of physics and mathematics) will increase our understanding of the human brain in ways previously unimaginable. From Alzheimer's disease, to Parkinson's disease, to schizophrenia, there will be virtually no aspect of our understanding of the human brain and human nervous system that can not be transformed in the next two decades.

Beyond traditional biology, there are still more extraordinary breakthroughs to come. Nanotechnology may be one of the most powerful new areas of knowledge. Nanotechnology is the science of designing machines and systems at the level of molecules and atoms. This is also the level at which most of the biological activities that define our health occur. It may be possible to build or grow small systems that would clean out human arteries. We would be able to simply drink several million of them in a glass of orange juice.

It may be possible to grow carbon storage tubes so small that hydrogen could be safely stored without refrigeration. This would enable the creation of a hydrogen fuel cell technology that would have dramatic implications for the economy and the environment. Nanotechnology is already emerging with commercial applications and will be at least as powerful as space or computing in its implications for new tools and capabilities.

We are also on the edge of a series of materials technology breakthroughs that will continue to change how we build things, how much they weigh, and how much stress and punishment they can take. These new materials may make possible a one-hour flight from New York to Tokyo, an ultra lightweight car with virtually no environmental impact, and a host of other possibilities.

We are on the verge of creating intelligent synthetic environments that will revolutionize how we learn and how we plan. Designing a building or an organization in the synthetic world before you decide to do it for real will become increasingly sophisticated. The opportunities for education will be unending.

These examples are merely indicators of the scale and complexity of the changes that are almost certainly coming in the next twenty to thirty years. They should make clear why this is an Age of Transformation. No individual and no country will fully understand all the changes as they occur, nor will they be able to adapt to them flawlessly during this time. However, individuals, companies, and nations that recognize these large trends and are able to learn and adjust rapidly to them will have enormous advantages.

21st Century Trends

Forty-five years after Boulding's first explanation of the coming change, and forty years after Drucker taught us how to think about discontinuity, there are some key trends that must be considered as business, political, and government leaders think through the appropriate policies for the 21st century. This section will outline a number of those trends. However, it should first be noted that there are two overarching general rules: (1) the core pattern of the 21st century, as mentioned earlier, is more choices of higher quality at lower cost; and (2) there will constantly be more changes coming.

Today there are more scientists, engineers, and entrepreneurs than in all of previous human history. Markets continue to shift away from the smokestack industries and toward new models. Moreover, there is a growing world market in which more entrepreneurs of more nationalities are competing for a bigger share of the world marketplace. This growing momentum of change simply means that no knowledge or reform will be guaranteed to last for very long. Just as we become good at one thing, it will be challenged by an emerging new idea or achievement from a direction we haven't considered.

We first presented a version of this list of trends six years ago as future trends. Today, in many industries and areas of society, they are embedded in the way we do business. Other areas, like healthcare, education, and government bureaucracies, continue to block these movements. Yet even in those areas, it is just a matter of time—accelerated by the demands of the American people—until these trends gain recognition and acceptance.

A Customer-Centered Personalized System

Amazon and other systems allow us to select precisely the books or movies we want and, after a while, they sense our tastes and begin to present us with products that may interest us.

We know personal Social Security Plus accounts are workable because of our experience with IRAs and 401(k)s. The same can be said for personalized education and customized healthcare.

As Alvin Toffler pointed out, this is an era of de-massification. New technologies and discoveries have made it possible for us to have greater customization without higher cost. People today can receive news stories via e-mail based only on what they want to read. We go to the paint store and a computerized system can create a paint color that exactly matches a fabric or object in our house. The computerized paint color does not cost the consumer a dime more than the standard mass-produced color; the news stories can be obtained for free.

In the future, medicine will become more personalized. We will be able to use an individual's genetic predisposition and other factors such as age and sex to determine exactly what drug or treatment will work best. It is likely that drugs will become as customized as our paint and news are today.

Anything that is not personalized and responsive to changes in the individual, and which does not provide the customer with information about cost and quality, will rapidly find itself replaced by something that meets that standard of expectation.

Electronic Systems That Provide Access to Information Anywhere, Anytime

Customer access twenty-four hours a day, seven days a week, will become the standard for almost everything. ATMs symbolize this emerging customer convenience standard. We can get cash any time, anywhere.

By contrast, the majority of today's schools combine an agricultural-era ten-month school year (with the summer off for harvesting) with an industrial-era model: fifty-minute class sessions, a foreman at the front of the room facing the class, a factory-style schedule with a Monday through Friday work week. Yet learning outside the school system is embedded in the computer and on the Internet and is available on demand with a great deal of customization for each learner. It's a clear indication of how out of step our educational system is with today's society.

In healthcare, we see a similar disconnect, as the paper-based system in most hospitals and doctor's offices is incompatible with our 21st century society. Indeed, with time, the demand for access to medical records from anywhere in the world will drive the need for an inter-operable electronic system, as our mobile population begins to realize that there is a solution to the inconvenience of healthcare's archaic paper system. Safety concerns will add to the demand for change—in fact, the loss of victims' paper medical records during Hurricane Katrina served as a wake-up call for many regarding the need to move rapidly from paper to electronic records.

Convenience as a Requirement

With the growing use of online shopping, consumers are beginning to demand similar convenience in all aspects of life, including government.

With more than one-third of Americans already ordering products and services online, it is clear that the 21st century model is one of easy access to cost and quality information.

People are starting to carry these attitudes into their dealings with bureaucracies and will increasingly demand more convenience and ready access to information from organizations in all areas of life, including healthcare providers and educational institutions.

Finally, as voters Americans will increasingly favor politicians who work to make their lives easier and more convenient.

Convergence of Technologies

The various computation and communication technologies are converging. Cell phones, computers, land-lines, mobile systems, satellite, and cable are coming together into a unified system that will dramatically expand both capabilities and convenience.

Companies that figure out how to bundle services and converge technologies will rapidly replace those that don't.

Expert System Empowered Processes and Networks

When we look up an airline reservation on the Internet, we are dealing with an expert system. In virtually all Internet shopping we are asking questions of such a system.

The ability to deal with individual sales and individual tastes is a function of the growing capacity of expert systems and the power to share information through information networks. These capabilities will revolutionize healthcare, education, and government.

Delaying the adoption of expert systems can be costly not only financially but also in terms of human lives. Due to a lack of expert systems, it currently takes seventeen years for a new best practice to reach the doctor's office, meaning that countless Americans suffer and die because they don't benefit from existing clinical practices that could have saved their lives. In addition, thousands of Americans die each year due to medication errors that could have been prevented if an expert system of e-prescribing had been used. As Americans become more aware of what the failure to adopt expert systems is costing them, the public demand for transformation to a 21st century system will drown out the arguments from those who oppose it.

If it can be codified and standardized, it should be done by an expert system rather than by a human being. That is a simple rule to apply to every activity, in both the private and public sector.

Disappearance of Middlemen

This is one of the most powerful trends of the Age of Transformation. In the commercial world, where competition and profit margins force change, it is clear that customers are served better from very flat hierarchies, with very few people in the middle. In many industries, the middleman is being replaced by the individual customer armed with new technology. Consider the plight of travel agents in the wake of Travelocity, or gas station attendants now that self-service pumps are nearly ubiquitous (with the exception of New Jersey and Oregon, the last two remaining states that continue to believe that allowing people to pump their own gas will likely result in gas stations being set on fire by incompetent customers).

In the protected guilds (medicine, education, law, and groups that use political power to slow change) and in government there are still very large numbers of middlemen. This will be one of the most profitable areas for political and government leaders to explore.

In a 21st century system, the customer should be foremost and every unnecessary layer should be eliminated to create a more agile, rapidly changing, customer-centered, less expensive system.

New, Unexpected Sources of Change

Many of the most innovative ideas over the last thirty years have come from unexpected places, from unexpected people. Anyone can have a good idea—the key is to focus on the power of the idea rather than the pedigree of the inventor. Bill Gates's creation of Microsoft and Steve Jobs's invention of Apple, iPod, and Pixar are examples of uncredentialed entrepreneurs creating a future without any elite's certification or approval.

Blogs are another example of this. Almost anyone can start a blog—and more and more people are going to blogs (often set up by non-experts), to get information and news. This has had a remarkable impact on the power of the traditional media.

Blog Activity, January 13–March 21, 2005	
Internet users who have created blogs	9%
Internet users who read blogs	25%
Men who have created blogs	11%
Women who have created blogs	8%
Young adults (18-29) who have created blogs	19%

This rising success of ideas from uncredentialed sources directly challenges much of the peer review assumptions of the scientific community, much of the screening for consultants used by government, much of the credentialing done by education and medicine, and much of the contractor certification done by government. This trend requires us to look widely for the newest ideas, products, and services, and requires testing by trial and error more than by credentialing or traditional assumptions.

A Shift of Resources from Lesser Opportunity to Greater Opportunity

One of the most powerful engines driving the American economy has been the rise of a venture capitalist movement that allocates investments to new opportunities and grows those opportunities better than any other economy in the world. There is as yet no comparable government capacity to shift resources to new startups and to empower government entrepreneurs. There are countless efforts to reform and modernize bureaucracies, but that is exactly the wrong strategy. Venture capitalists very seldom put new money into old corporate bureaucracies.

Even many of the established corporations are creating their own startups to prepare the environment and conditions for big breakthroughs. We need a doctrine for a venture capitalist/entrepreneurial model of government in defense, education, and healthcare. This doctrine should focus on opportunities, not maintaining the status quo and solving its associated problems.

It is the nature of politics, government, and large bureaucracies to focus on problems (schools that fail, hospitals that are too expensive, people living in poverty) when the real breakthroughs come from focusing on opportunities (new models of learning that work, new approaches to health and healthcare that lower the cost of hospitals, ways to get people to work so they are no longer in poverty).

Venture capitalists are very good at shifting their attention away from problem zones toward opportunity zones. Similarly, the organizations that flourish will be those that focus on new 21st century solutions rather than trying to figure out how to manage problems within a 20th century context.

The Rapid Development of Better, Less Expensive Products, Leading to a Continued Process of Replacement

Goods and services are continuously replaced as their successors literally push them out the door. The adoption of more capable, less expensive goods and services—and in some cases revolutionary replacements (as the mimeograph by the Xerox and as traditional mail by the fax machine and e-mail)—is creating a sense of impermanence that is changing our notion of ownership.

One example is the shrinking of the music CD market as a result of the ability to download music from the Internet. From 2000 to 2004, the sales of music CDs dropped 14.7 percent as more and more people began downloading music onto their iPods. The shift has not only impacted sales of music CDs, but it is also creating a shift in the music industry, where the new medium is making it easier to introduce new artists. The individual consumer is in essence taking part in a much earlier phase of "star" development, and the longevity and stability "stars" enjoyed due to a limited list of consumer choices is likely to erode.

Intelligent Risk-Taking as an Important Element of Success

Entrepreneurs and venture capitalists have a surprisingly high tolerance for intelligent failure. They praise those who take risks, even if they fail, over those who avoid risks, even if they avoid failure. To innovate and change at the rate today's world requires, government and large bureaucratic organizations and businesses will have to shift their attitudes dramatically. Historically, it is far more dangerous for a bureaucrat to take a risk than it is to do nothing. Bureaucracies tend to reward (with retirement and peace of mind) serving time. There are virtual-

> "Anyone who has never made a mistake has never tried anything new."
>
> *Albert Einstein*

ly no rewards for taking risks. Yet in areas of science, technology, and entrepreneurship, the great breakthroughs often involve a series of failures. Consider Thomas Edison's thousands of failed experiments in inventing the electric light (an estimated 49,000 experiments).

Instituting a culture of trying and rewarding success, while tolerating intelligent failure, will be part of the shift as organizations adjust to what it will take to survive in the 21st century.

Constant Breakthroughs That Force Ongoing Dramatic Change

The accelerated rate of discoveries and breakthroughs in the 21st century will force organizations to constantly change. Before Disney World existed, it would have been hard to imagine how many millions would travel to Orlando. Before the Super Bowl became a cultural event, it was hard to imagine how much of the country would stop for an entire evening. Before faxes, we did not need them, and before e-mail, no one knew how helpful it would become.

One of the key differences between the private sector and the public sector or industries protected or closely controlled by the public sector is the speed of accepting new products and creating new expectations. The public sector tends to insist on either avoiding the new altogether or using it to prop up the old.

> "If Thomas Edison invented electric light today . . . Dan Rather would report it on CBS News as 'the candle-making industry was threatened today.' We would get a story explaining that electricity kills. There would be interviews with five candle-makers. At least three politicians would pass a bill banning electricity."
>
> *Renewing American Civilization, 1993*

For two generations we have tried to get computers into the classroom, with minimal results. That's because we have been approaching the opportunity backward: the key is to get the classroom into the computer and the computer into the child's home, so learning becomes personal and 24/7. This is a

Degree of Electronic Health Record (EHR) Implementation, by Practice Size, 2005

	Degree of Implementation				
Number of FTE physicians in practice	Fully implemented for all physicians in all locations	Implementation in process	Implementation planned in next 12 months	Implementation planned in next 13-24 months	Not implemented and no plans to implement in next 24 months
5 or lower	10.4	10.3	12.6	18.9	47.8
6-10	13.6	11.8	15.9	21.4	37.8
11-20	13.9	20.7	20.0	18.4	27.0
21 or more	11.0	28.5	15.7	24.2	20.2
All practices*	11.5	12.7	14.2	19.8	41.8

Source: The information in this exhibit is derived from authors' own analyses.

Note: FTE is full-time equivalent.

* Percentage of all practices that have fully implemented an EHR for all physicians in all locations in the raw data was 15.0 percent, corrected to 11.5 percent after weighting to correct for having oversampled larger practices.

Health Affairs, 2005, Vol. 24, No. 5

transformational shift from bureaucratic education to personalized learning.

Many doctors still resist the information technologies that promise to revolutionize health and healthcare, to lower administrative costs, and to dramatically decrease unnecessary deaths and illnesses. In the true free-market sector, competition and the customer force change. In government and government-protected guilds, the innovations are distorted to prop up the old, and the public (that is, the customer) suffers from higher expense and less-effective goods and services.

Speed

In today's world we get frustrated waiting a few seconds for an ATM to check our bank account balance from an account possibly thousands of miles away, register a withdrawal, record and update the balance, and deliver the cash into our hands. And if we are in a foreign country, we may have to wait a few more extra seconds to receive the cash in euros, yen, or pesos.

And yet, many of us accept the long delays in our current healthcare system. A study by Balas and Boren (2000) shows that on average it takes about seventeen years for new knowledge generated by randomized controlled trials to be implemented at a doctor's office. This means that your doctor is likely to use an obsolete approach to cure disease and that you have a greater risk of not being cured than you should. This is increasingly unacceptable. We will see a growing demand for technologies and processes that speed up that adoption rate, despite the opposition of those who cling to the 20th century model of practicing medicine.

Quality and Lean Thinking

Whether it is the earlier model of quality espoused by W. Edwards Deming or the more recent concept of lean thinking advocated by James Womack and Daniel Jones, it is clear that a systematic model of thinking through production and value creates more profitable, less expensive processes. Companies that have followed these approaches have had remarkable success in producing better products at lower expense, yet it is almost never used by people who want to rethink government.

If government and its major activities (health and education) had experienced the same revolution in productivity, convenience, and effectiveness as the private sector, we would be in a different world today. If the principles of removing waste that we see in the Toyota Production System were implemented in all levels of government, those bureaucracies would be much more productive and much less expensive.

Increased Transparency

Thanks to the Internet, it is much easier for the public to access information about the cost and quality of goods and services. Public demand for such access will intensify and will impact those organizations and industries that have resisted sharing such information in the past, including government, education, and healthcare providers. This will ultimately change the pricing structure and increase competition and accountability for organizations across the board.

The right to know cost and quality information is not only transforming the private sector but is also even beginning to impact the more transformational parts of our government entities. The state of Florida recently set up two healthcare–related websites. One publicizes hospital information such as infection rates, and the other displays prescription drug prices. (http://www.floridacomparecare.gov/ and http://www.myfloridarx.com/). In time, the public's growing demand for access to information will result in more state governments following Florida's lead, which will, over time and combined with the right incentives, drive up quality while driving down prices.

Continuous Partnering—Some Permanent, Some Temporary

No company or government can possibly understand all the changes in today's Age of Transformation. Moreover, new ideas are emerging with great speed. As a result, we simply don't have the time to develop in-house expertise and stay up-to-date on skill sets outside our own specialties. It is generally more profitable to partner with experts than to try to build expertise in non-core areas.

Partnering allows everyone to focus on what they do best while working as a team toward a common goal. Yet, despite being a dominant organizing system of 21st century private sector organizations, this system is prohibited throughout most of government and education. The result is a lack of both efficiency and quality.

Cost Crashes

As a result of the preceding trends, a major pattern of the 21st century will be continuing, and in many cases steep, declines in cost. In that respect, Wal-Mart's continuous pressure to lower prices and therefore to lower costs is in many ways a model for the 21st century. An ATM is dramatically cheaper than a bank teller. A direct-dial phone call is much less expensive than an operator-assisted call. Both are examples of technologies following the natural pattern of more choices of higher quality at lower cost.

The NPD Consumer Electronics Price Watch reported a 31 percent decline in collective cost for the most frequently purchased consumer electronics between January 2003 and November 2004.

During that same period, the cost of DVD recorders plummeted 51 percent!

The rise of Internet businesses such as Travelocity or Priceline allows online shoppers to get four airline tickets for the price of one. In fact, from the deregulation of the airlines in 1978 to 2005, the price per passenger mile dropped from $.23 to $.12 in constant dollars. That is, you travel today for about half of what it cost you to travel twenty-five years ago.

Domestic Airline Yield Adjusted for Inflation (2004 dollars)

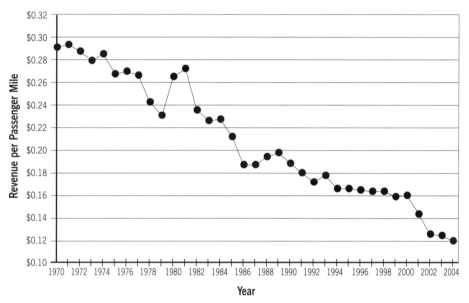

Source: Statement of Stephen Morrison and Clifford Winston, hearing before the Subcommittee on Aviation, Committee on Transportation and Infrastructure, September 28, 2005

In Madison, Wisconsin, an online real estate cooperative has lowered the cost of selling or buying a house by 97 percent. In 2005, home sales that would have incurred $17 million in agent fees under the old system were handled for only $300,000. This particular system was created by two housewives in their homes working part-time.

We have not even begun to realize how much costs will decline, particularly in health and healthcare, education and learning, defense procurement, and government administration. We also have not yet learned to think in terms of purchasing power instead of salary. Yet huge changes are likely in both purchasing power and behavior for citizens and government.

Those who are aggressive and alert will find remarkable savings by moving to the optimum cost crashes faster than anyone else. As a result, they will dramatically expand their purchasing power.

There exists today no model at the Congressional Budget Office or the Office of Management and Budget for this kind of continuous cost decline. No state government has a budget office with this kind of model. The result is that governments do not seek to develop the kind of programs that could provide greater service with greater convenience at lower cost. Developing this new model of budgeting is one of the greatest challenges in transforming government.

These trends, which are already impacting our everyday lives, illuminate the possibilities a 21st century leader should consider. They can be refined, expanded, and improved, but they identify how different a 21st century system is from the bureaucratic-industrial system of the 20th century, which remains at the heart of contemporary government and areas where government has maximum control, such as healthcare and education.

4

Understanding Transformation

Large-scale change requires transformation, not reform. The two are vastly different. Transformation is a major systems change, while reform is about making marginal improvements to the existing system.

Making a better horse and buggy was reforming. Inventing the internal combustion engine was transforming. Instituting longer hours for bank tellers was reforming. Inventing the automatic teller machine was transforming. The difference between reforming a 20th century system and moving to a 21st century system can be represented by the following graphic:

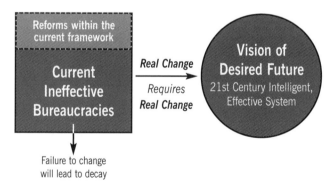

Rather than change, most bureaucracies prefer the comfortable routine of explaining failure

Making marginal changes to the 20th century system rather than moving to a 21st century system will not only fail to create a better future—it will lead to decay. At its core, the 20th century system is hopelessly flawed because it is based on outdated principles. Every effort at reform simply makes the current system more complicated and leads the entrenched forces of the past to modify their behavior just enough to protect their self-interests regardless of what the new system requires. What is necessary is the migration to a whole new system, built on a new vision and on 21st century principles.

When we first showed this model to Bob Kerrey, former senator from Nebraska and now president of the New School University in New York City, he noted that this was the right model for thinking about transformation but that managing the actual process would look very different. He made the point that large systems actually do not jump from one state to another. Rather, they migrate over time. Furthermore, some aspects of the past are effective and useful and need to be retained, while the new is gradually added and the ineffective parts of the past are gradually dropped. He pointed out that some things we are currently doing fit within the 21st century model. We want to retain, improve, and use these as bridges to take us to a 21st century system. His comments led us to modify our model to the following:

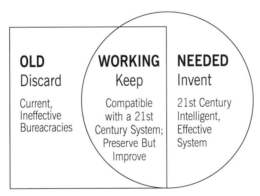

(With thanks to Senator Bob Kerrey for helping to develop this model)
©2006 Center for Health Transformation

Politics is almost always about reforming and almost never about transforming. The old interest groups and the old arguments dominate politicians, their staffs, and the news media. Interest groups and lobbyists focus on making reforms to the current system, not on creating a whole new system. Reporters and columnists tend to make their living by writing about today. Seldom is the focus on transformation, but rather on arguments about whether to spend more or less to prop up failed programs.

Today's powerful interest groups are based on the guilds and structures of the past. Invariably they absorb all the available money from government, making it impossible to invest in creating a future that demands new structures. Bureaucracies compound the problem. Career bureaucrats generally focus on the status quo. They are unlikely to invent a new system that might be controversial and that will disrupt the structure that provides them with job security and insulates them from the changes that impact the private sector.

Despite the natural forces that protect the past and prop up existing institutions, it is possible, through transformational leadership, to develop and implement substantial change. When, in 1994, Republicans won control of the House of Representatives for the first time in forty years, we instituted the first outside audit in the 206-year history of the House. We created the THOMAS system so House activities would be online and available to the world free of charge. We established term limits for committee chairmen so new members could bring new ideas to positions of authority on a regular basis.

In one amusing example of change, we eliminated the House iceman, who had daily brought ice to House offices and to committee hearing rooms and replaced him with refrigerators. It had been at least fifty years since icemen had delivered ice to American houses, but until we took over, the taxpayer was still funding the delivery of ice to the people's House. These were real changes that helped create a more modern, more transparent, and more accountable House of Representatives.

Transforming: The Creation of Large-Scale Change

The standards and requirements of the past century will be vastly different from the 21st century. The key to the 20th century was production engineering geared to consumer choice. If we could produce more products at a price our customers could afford, we would own a bigger share of the market.

The key to the 21st century is market making. It is about entrepreneurs creatively meeting customer needs with new and better values. It is being able to bring more choices of higher quality at lower cost. It means paying constant attention to the totality of our system. In the case of systems that are tightly regulated by government, like healthcare, it means fundamentally reshaping how government interacts with the marketplace, in order to transform government from being the largest inhibitor of quality to being its largest advocate.

One example of how government can support quality is the recent demonstration project undertaken by the Centers for Medicare and Medicaid Services to increase Medicare payments to hospitals that improve their quality of in-patient care. Results from the first year already reflect significant improvement in the quality of care in the five clinical areas involved in the project: Acute Myocardial Infarction (AMI), Coronary Artery Bypass Graft (CABG), Community Acquired Pneumonia (CAP), Heart Failure (HF), and Hip and Knee Replacement (HIP).

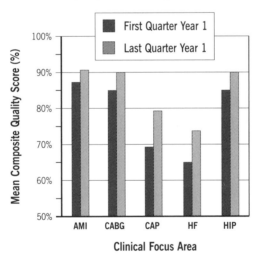

Year 1
Quality Improvements by Clinical Focus Area

Displayed with permission of Modern Healthcare.
Copyright Crain Communication, Inc. 2005

Crossing the Watershed

The transformation to a 21st century model requires a series of changes on a scale that is much like crossing a watershed. A watershed is the area of land from which water drains into a single point.

A ridge of higher ground generally forms the boundary between two watersheds, and the terrain on either side of the boundary tends to be very different. For example, consider what we encounter in Washington State.

As clouds come in off the Pacific Ocean and travel up the mountainside, they dump all their rain. As a result, on the western side of the mountain we have a temperate rainforest, the Olympia Rainforest, that creates on the eastern side of the mountain a rain shadow, where residents get only three to five inches of rain per year. On the western side, people carry raincoats; on the eastern side, canteens. One side has huge trees that require lots of moisture. The other side has scrub country and a totally different ecosystem. It is not a marginal difference.

Watersheds

Rainforest
Bring your raincoat

Desert
Bring your canteen

Copyright 2005, The Center for Health Transformation.

A good example of crossing a watershed is the story of AT&T and the telephone industry at the turn of the 20th century.

Vail - AT&T Watershed

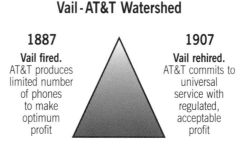

1887
Vail fired.
AT&T produces limited number of phones to make optimum profit

1907
Vail rehired.
AT&T commits to universal service with regulated, acceptable profit

Theodore Vail became president of AT&T in 1885, having previously served as president of the Railway Express, a branch of the U.S. Post Office. Vail was a public-spirited, intelligent man who grew to believe that the telephone was so important that every American should have one, and that AT&T's pricing should be structured accordingly. His vision proved to be at odds with the AT&T board, who believed that they should sell the number of phones that optimized return on investment, even if that meant 40 percent of the people in America would be unable to afford a telephone. Vail was fired as president in 1887 but was kept on the board of directors.

In the following years many small companies took advantage of the large market of customers demanding phone service below the price offered by AT&T. By 1900 there were 2,500 phone companies. However, they had no commonality. In fact, doctors in small towns often had two phones in their homes or in their offices—one was the AT&T phone for the rich people and the other was whatever the local phone company was for the poor people. They had to have both phones because the various systems couldn't talk to each other.

By 1907, the last remaining privately held big phone company in the world was AT&T. Every other government in the world had nationalized its phone company. The AT&T board, which realized that Vail's vision twenty years earlier had been correct and that the choice was to voluntarily become a universal system or be nationalized by government, asked Vail to return as president. Vail accepted, under the condition that the board would agree to create public utility commissions, become a regulated monopoly, and earn a reasonable profit based on everybody having a phone. In 1909, Vail announced that the company was going to provide nationwide service with the unprecedented creation of a coast-to-coast phone system.

This was an enormous revolution and is a great example of transformation. On one side we have a private-sector, profit-optimizing, and market-limiting system; on the other side a public-focused, profit-making, but different system with a different set of rules.

Multiple Crossings

Often we can't create transformation in one jump. Rather than cross one giant mountain, we must instead traverse a mountain chain.

Even if we see only one mountain in front of us, we're likely to find another just over the top.

The early development of the auto industry is a good example of crossing a series of watersheds.

Series of Watersheds: Ford / Sloan Example

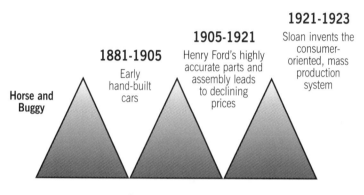

1921-1923
Sloan invents the consumer-oriented, mass production system

1905-1921
Henry Ford's highly accurate parts and assembly leads to declining prices

1881-1905
Early hand-built cars

Horse and Buggy

Recommended Reading:
James Womack, *The Machine That Changed the World*
Peter Drucker, *The Concept of the Corporation*
Alfred Sloan, *Adventures of a White Collar Man* and *My Years with General Motors*

Copyright 2005 The Center for Health Transformation

The first transformation was from the horse and buggy to the automobile. The early hand-built cars were toys for the rich and for mechanics and hobbyists. Each one was unique, with non-interchangeable parts. The next great breakthrough came when Henry Ford designed interchangeable parts, which led Ford to his second breakthrough, the assembly line. The result was an explosion in productivity and lowering of costs. However, when Ford began his revolution in productivity, Americans were, for the most part, still riding horses or walking. In that setting, Ford had a very straightforward idea—he would have the longest possible production run to bring down cost over time by manufacturing as many identical cars as possible.

Ford had a social contract behind his industrial contract. The social contract was that he would expand access by giving Americans a reliable, inexpensive, transportation device. The result was the one-size-fits-all Model T that came in only one color: black. By using the assembly line and creating only one model, he brought down the cost of the Model T every year. He then produced the Model A, a bigger, more powerful version of the Model T, which was produced using the same model of uniform engineering-driven manufacturing.

The Model A was merely a reform. It was larger and more powerful, but every car was still exactly the same and available only in black. It was about this time that General Motors hired Alfred Sloan to try to save the dying enterprise. Sloan, an MIT-educated engineer who designed refrigerators for consumers, brought a consumer focus to the automobile industry. What Sloan did was transform GM.

Rather than focus on how to produce cars and compete with Ford on production efficiencies, he started to think about the American customer. Sloan believed, in 1921, that Americans would get richer and would want to show off their success. Sloan developed a new social contract that moved the automobile from simple transportation to status symbol and luxury item.

Sloan pioneered the concept of the annual model; it was not a manufacturing strategy, but a marketing strategy that had economic and manufacturing components. Traveling to a different part of America for one week every quarter, Sloan personally sold cars to better understand his customers. By answering their questions, he got the earliest indicators of how people's tastes were changing. Where Ford had pioneered the lowest-cost production run, Sloan pioneered the customer-defined manufacturing process. Each was a great breakthrough for its era, and each was uniquely right for its time, but they were vastly different and based on different social contracts.

Sloan came up with three ideas that changed the automobile world, all of which Ford thought were totally wrong. First, the concept of a new annual model. Second, the strategy to price his cars above Ford's, not below. And third, the invention of the used car lot, allowing customers to trade in their old car for a newer one. By 1927, General Motors had replaced Ford as the largest car company in the world. As the result of a deliberate social strategy executed as an economic strategy, in six years Sloan took GM from the edge of bankruptcy to the dominant industrial corporation in the world.

America couldn't have jumped from horse and buggy to GM's luxury cars. We couldn't even have jumped from early cars to General Motors. Sloan's right design for the 1920s would have been wrong in 1905. Ford's design in 1905 was right, but he failed to adapt to the new model that was needed when people began to see the car as a "vehicle" for social status as well as for transportation.

By the 1960s, the quality ideas developed by Dr. W. Edwards Deming and Joseph M. Juran spurred another transformation when they increased productivity and lowered cost through the Toyota Production System. The concept of worker involvement in eliminating waste and systematically seeking more effective ways to be productive proved to be as great a revolution in production capability as the original design of mass production under Ford. (We will further explore the evolution of quality and systems thinking in a later chapter, as it is central to our planning and leadership model and many of the principles included in this book.)

The history of the automobile is an example of crossing a series of watersheds. It took many different changes to arrive at today's modern mass-production, consumer-oriented, multi-choice system of automobiles. It involved major systems change, not just marginal improvements of the current system.

Welfare reform is a modern-day example of crossing a watershed in politics and government. It took from 1970, when then governor Ronald Reagan proposed welfare reform, until 1996 for welfare to be transformed. For many years we heard that welfare could never be reformed. In fact, that was true—it had to be completely transformed. We had to create a whole new vision of a better future, one in which independence replaced dependency, opportunity replaced poverty, responsibility replaced irresponsibility, self-sufficiency replaced helplessness, and caring replaced caretaking.

Over time more and more Americans heard and believed in that vision. By 1996, after a twenty-six-year effort, the American people had made their decision. Driven by the overwhelming sentiment of the people, welfare reform was passed by Congress three times. The first two times President Bill Clinton vetoed it, but, following the wide circulation of a report noting that 92 percent of Americans favored changing the system (including 88 percent of those on welfare), it was clear that he would have a hard time vetoing it and being re-elected. The third time Congress passed it, President Clinton signed the bill.

A watershed was crossed. Welfare workers moved from being advocates of dependency to counselors of opportunity. The welfare rolls shrank by 60 percent. Child abuse declined, spousal abuse was reduced, teen pregnancy rates fell, marriage increased, and income went up for those who left welfare for school and work. Yet the transformation is far from complete—other watersheds lie ahead. Transformation of Medicaid, education, workers' compensation, the culture of dependency and self-limitation, among others, will also be needed if we are to replace the 20th century system of welfare with a 21st century model of opportunity and responsibility.

As the history of the automobile and the telephone illustrate, once the majority of people cross over the intellectual mountain range to a better future, they usually do not want to go back to the old system. In essence, each mountaintop represents a concept that, once accepted, affords climbers a glorious view of the benefits as they travel to the valley below, where they are confronted with another mountain until they have crossed the range. That process is transformation one conceptual challenge at a time. Once across the range, it is intellectually impossible to turn back.

Transformation vs. Reform
Two Approaches to Saving Lives from Deadly Prescription Errors

REFORMING:
Florida House and Senate passed Section 45.42 on May 23, 2003. "A written prescription for a medicinal drug issued by a healthcare practitioner licensed by law to prescribe such a drug **must be legibly printed...**"

TRANSFORMING:
In February 2003, the Rhode Island Quality Institute teamed up with SureScripts to launch a state-wide electronic prescribing program to achieve 100 percent electronic prescription writing in the state of Rhode Island.

PART TWO

Principles of Transformation

5

The Power—and Rejection—of Proven Principles

President Ronald Reagan used to say that people were wrong to suggest there were not simple answers. He asserted that there were simple truths, but they often led to very hard decisions. People want to avoid hard decisions, so they ignore or reject the simple truths. Their search for complexity is in fact a method of avoiding the hard choices.

Most Americans have learned the simple truth that diet and exercise work. It is just very hard for us to follow that truth and implement it in our daily lives. We know that if we watch what we eat and drink and make sure to exercise regularly, we will weigh less and be healthier. Yet it is hard to follow these simple principles day after day. There is always an excuse for a few more calories or a little less exercise.

The Baby Boomers are just starting to learn that regular exercise will extend their lives and minimize illness. If one has better genetics it is possible to worry less about diet and exercise—and if we do everything right but are unlucky, we may still have severe problems. Yet on balance there is statistically no question that consistent exercise for most people will both extend life and improve its quality.

Similarly, it is a fact that students who go to class, pay attention, and do their homework will learn more and do better than students who ignore learning. This is not totally true—very smart people may be able to do better than others with less effort—but in general, students who work harder and study more tend to do better than those who do not.

Despite the facts and the data, people find it hard to follow principles that work. It somehow seems to go against a deeply ingrained part of human nature that causes us to engage in self-destructive or less-productive behaviors just because we "want to." In a sense, this is the story of Adam and Eve in the Garden of Eden. Even in Paradise, we could not follow the rules.

What is true for individuals is also true for organizations, societies, and governments. There are principles that work, and there is objective evidence that those principles work, but we avoid learning them. Consider a few facts.

In 1960, Ghana and South Korea had the same per capita income. Today South Korea is one of the wealthiest countries in the world and has a very dynamic technology- and science-based sector of its economy. Ghana is still very poor, and its people continue to be trapped in a largely pre-modern world.

Twenty years ago Germany had a much bigger economy per person than did Ireland. Ireland, partly because of British colonial policy and of local patterns, had long lagged behind Western Europe in productivity and income. Following two decades of education reform, tax cuts, foreign investment, and infrastructure development, Ireland developed dramatically.

During the same two decades, Germany followed union-endorsed, bureaucratic, welfare-state policies. The result is that Ireland today has a larger economy per person than Germany, and the Bundesbank reports that the gap is likely to widen in Ireland's favor.

There are clearly policies that work: the rule of law, lower tax rates, a learning system that succeeds, foreign investment that brings the best new ideas and most productive methods into society, and the creation of new companies and jobs. These are among the keys to dramatic increases in productivity and prosperity.

If we want people to live better and longer, we have to learn from the countries that have succeeded and also from those that have failed. The differences are stark and stunning. The lessons to be learned are clear and vivid.

People live better and have more choices in the United States, Japan, Taiwan, South Korea, Australia, New Zealand, Singapore, Hong Kong, Israel, and Europe. At the other extreme, most of sub-Saharan Africa, virtually all of the Arab world, and most of Latin America (in approximately that order) continue to avoid the lessons of productivity and prosperity. The rest of the world tends to fall between those two groups.

We are faced with a 21st century of First, Second, and Third Worlds. There is a First World that obeys the rules of productivity and prosperity and encourages the culture of achievement. This world is stunningly successful and growing more so. There is no dominant race in the First World; European, Asian, and New World countries are in this group. There are also a few countries at the cusp—Chile, Turkey, Thailand, and portions of India and China

There is a 21st century Second World that moves back and forth between modern and antiquated approaches. The most modern parts of Latin America (the Brazilian upper middle class, much of the urban parts of Colombia, many people in Mexico) are in this Second World. Russia was in the Second World moving toward the First until President Vladimir Putin and his former KGB cronies began replacing the rule of law with government autocracy and a preference for control over progress.

Finally, the most entrenched cultures of poverty and despair in the Third World show very few signs of learning the lessons that will achieve productivity and prosperity. The evidence we have today shows that some power structures and cultures continue to reject these lessons. These are robber cultures in which the powerful sustain themselves at the expense of everyone else. These are cultures of corruption, lawlessness, and exploitation; cultures in which the powerful prey upon the weak; and cultures whose very identities are often wrapped up in behaviors that destroy productivity and prosperity.

As a general principle, when we encounter those who actively reject the principles of productivity and prosperity, we are almost certainly encountering a culture in which the winners believe they will lose status and resources if their societies begin to modernize. They prefer being the most powerful in a very poor community to being less powerful in a much more prosperous community. The rejection of opportunity and a better future is as powerful and restricting in a poor neighborhood in America as it is in sub-Saharan Africa, or in the most oppressed slums of Latin America or the repressed societies of the Arab world.

Our failure to help those trapped in poverty both at home and abroad is largely a function of our inability to come to grips with the power of the old winners: the entrenched elite of a country or community, the union bosses, the bureaucracies of education, the doctors resistant to electronic health records and modern systems of quality.

Everywhere we turn, we find people who might need transformational change but are afraid it will cost them power, influence, or wealth. They prefer decaying and underachieving with the known system rather than risking the loss of status or power.

Fascinatingly, the modern academic Left (and its echo chamber of students in the news media and its celebrants in Hollywood) seems to be ideologically incapable of analyzing and learning the lessons of over half a century of rising productivity and prosperity. They consistently fail to objectively review the facts of the sixty years since the Second World War. For half a century this rejection of productivity, of the rule of law, of free markets, and of entrepreneurial behavior has driven academia and the news media to fundamentally misreport reality and misprescribe policy changes. Even worse, Hollywood has become the proponent of an anti-productivity and anti-prosperity culture by glorifying destruction and decadence and mocking the solid behaviors and principles that lead to achievement.

The transformational principles presented in this book are meant literally as principles. They are not mere suggestions but are rather a cookbook of how to think through and apply transformation to an organization, a profession, or the government. What we outline in this book works. It has worked historically. It is working now. But for it to work, we have to apply the principles and methodically work at mastering the art of transformation.

This is a gourmet cookbook. Short-order cookbooks are simple. Follow the recipe and it will almost certainly provide a decent meal. Being a gourmet chef is far more complex. Ingredients and a recipe in the hands of a first-time cook will produce a startlingly different meal than the same ingredients and recipe in the hands of a master chef.

However, even the finest master chef cannot produce a boiled egg if he refuses to put the egg in boiling water. There are basic principles upon which the master chef innovates and improvises.

Similarly, we are going to outline a set of principles that we believe will enable you to undertake substantial projects of transformation. We believe that if you follow these principles and master them, you will be successful at transformation.

Principles do work.

Policies do work.

The art of transformation is learnable.

In the next two chapters we will introduce what we believe from our own experiences are some of the key principles for succeeding in any transformational effort.

6

Principles of Transformation

There are a number of key principles that we consider central to both designing and leading transformation. While many were first developed while we were in politics and government, they have proven to be just as applicable to organizations and entities in the private sector seeking to lead or leverage today's Age of Transformation.

Principle One
A RIGHT vision
- Vision becomes the attracting and organizing common reference.
- Our vision must be functionally accurate as well as sound right—we must "walk the talk."

The first principle is developing a vision that, if implemented, would accomplish what we are trying to achieve. To create transformation, leaders must spend a lot of time thinking, rethinking, and constantly strengthening their vision details and principles. Since vision becomes the attracting and organizing common reference, getting it right is essential. Our team should be able to look at our vision statement and understand where we are collectively going and how we are measuring ourselves. Without a clear vision, we cannot distinguish activity from progress. It's like jumping into a car and driving all day in order to cover six hundred miles. If we're driving in the wrong direction—or around in circles—our activity report will look good: we drove six hundred miles in one day. But our progress report will show absolutely nothing. In fact, we could be six hundred miles farther away from our goal.

It is vital to ask ourselves every day: how do I distinguish activity from progress? Truly effective people spend remarkably little time on random activity. They spend their energy on progress, and they are relentless in ensuring that almost everything they do is related to their vision.

Since what we do should be built around our vision, that vision can't be a slogan that sounds catchy but means little. We have to be able to write out a vision statement, vision details, and the key metrics related to that vision to define how we live out each day. If we can't do that, we need to rethink our vision.

Principle Two
Real change requires real change
  • New results require new ideas, new actions, and sometimes new structures and new cultures.

If transformation is the goal, we have to be committed to adopting new ideas and new actions. Much of the time, transformation also involves changing both structures and cultures.

When W. Edwards Deming was brought in to help transform corporations, he refused to work with them unless the CEO was directly involved. He knew that without a real commitment from the highest level, transformation was impossible. The fact is real change can happen only if the person at the top is invested and leading the charge.

Principle Three
Focus on solutions, not problems
  • Look for and adopt what is already working.

America, at its best, is a country that cares about finding solutions, not about studying and dissecting problems. It's an important model to remember and to carry with us as we define our strategies for driving transformation.

In most areas where we want to create solutions, there are existing fact-based models of success that can be learned from and built upon. At the Center for Health Transformation, one of our major strategies is to constantly find proven solutions and share them with a wide range of leaders and decision-makers. This is important for two reasons. First, it allows us to implement projects that have already been proven, which is much easier than inventing something totally new. Second, providing concrete proof that something works increases the likelihood that leaders of risk-averse organizations, such as government and large bureaucracies, will consider adopting them.

Transformation requires us to identify proven solutions, modify them to meet our needs, then accelerate their adoption across the system.

Principle Four
Focus on large changes that really make a difference
- Lions have to distinguish between antelope and chipmunks. If they spend their time on the wrong thing, they will starve to death.
- Define your antelope—don't get distracted by the chipmunks.

It is very important, if the goal is to get big change, to focus on big things. Lions can't afford to hunt chipmunks because, even if they catch them, they starve to death. Lions have to hunt antelope and zebras.

Ronald Reagan understood this principle. Reagan got up every morning and had three antelope on his agenda: defeat the Soviet Empire, renew American economic growth by cutting taxes and regulations, and rebuild American civic culture so people were proud to be Americans. Those were the three things he worked on.

He would walk into the Oval Office each day, and hundreds of chipmunks would come rushing in. (Of course, a federal chipmunk could be $10 billion, which points out that one person's chipmunk will be another person's antelope.) Reagan would listen patiently to each chipmunk—because he was a very pleasant man—and would then say, "That's terrific. Have you met Jim Baker?" Jim Baker, his chief of staff, became the largest chipmunk collector in the world.

Reagan was stunningly good at this. Much of the criticism he occasionally received about not being serious or not paying attention was because he was amazingly disciplined about shuffling the chipmunks away from himself. According to former secretary of state George Shultz, you could understand Reagan's true intelligence and focus if you watched how he handled the Soviet Union, one of his three antelope.

Reagan read all the briefing material, studied all the intelligence reports, and conducted personal interviews with people who knew Soviet Union president Mikhail Gorbachev before going to the first summit. When Shultz suggested that the first meeting include only Reagan, Gorbachev, and a translator, the rest of the White House staff was stunned. They did not grasp that the Reagan they watched each day deflecting all the chipmunks would be very different when dealing with the antelope. Shultz understood this and knew that Reagan had been a labor leader in the 1940s and had even led a strike in Hollywood—he knew how to negotiate. He had also been thinking about and studying the Soviet Union since 1947. Most important, he had done his homework.

The first summit proved Shultz right and ended up being a stunning example of leadership. It took place in Switzerland in the middle of winter. Reagan arrived first and, when Gorbachev arrived, he came outside to greet him, walking briskly down the steps, wearing no overcoat. Gorbachev was bundled up in a Russian coat and hat, and clumsily got out of the car—because you can't help but look awkward getting out of a car in a big Russian coat and hat. Reagan helped him out of the car and then took his arm to escort him up the stairs.

On television you saw a trim, elegant, athletic Reagan assisting a bundled-up Gorbachev. The fact that Gorbachev was twenty years younger was suddenly either forgotten or irrelevant. The image was that Reagan was strong and in charge, and it set the tone for the summit. All this was a carefully planned strategy, not an accident. These opening two minutes defined their relationship. Reagan was confident, competent, and able. Yet it's doubtful that those two minutes would have unfolded as they did had Reagan not known, in the days before the event, that the next twenty-two chipmunks were not as important as thinking through the opening two minutes of his first meeting with Gorbachev.

It's one of the key lessons that Reagan taught us. Whether we are talking about our profession, our company, or our own career, we have to know what our antelope are. We have to decide what the two, three, or four things are that, if we solved them, would truly change our world. And we also have to know what is necessary rather than desirable. When leading transformation, we must focus first and foremost on doing what is necessary not what is desirable.

Once we've decided what our antelope are, we then have to focus on those and delegate the chipmunks to someone else. Even if it seems that there is no one to whom the chipmunks can be delegated, people can be trained with amazing speed if we assign things to them, encourage them, and then get out of their way.

Principle Five
"Yes, if…" not "No, because …"
- Approach new ideas by saying "yes, if" rather than "no, because."
- Rather than rejecting a solution, think about the conditions under which it would work or be acceptable.

When dealing with large-scale change, one of the most important principles is to learn to say "yes, if," rather than "no, because." The psychological difference between the two is amazing.

"Yes, if" completely changes the conversation and our receptiveness. It helps open us to possibilities that we would otherwise dismiss and helps us think more broadly about the conditions under which we could agree to a new idea. "No, because" encourages us to cling to the status quo.

If we can create an environment where everyone starts by saying "yes, if," we can change the dialogue from one of automatically rejecting new ideas to one of thinking through how we can adopt transformational ideas and solutions.

Principle Six
Concentrate on marketing instead of on selling
- Marketing is better than selling.
- Marketing is listening to your audience's needs and utilizing your skills to fill their needs.
- Selling is convincing people to think they need what you are offering.
- Marketing lasts longer than selling and builds much greater loyalty.
- Focus on meeting or exceeding customer needs.

Marketing involves offering a solution to people's problems. Selling is having a product we're trying to convince someone to buy.

Selling means that we are asking the customer to solve our problem (i.e., how we can profit from this particular product) rather than solving the customer's problem. Even if we're good at sales and can convince customers to buy a product that doesn't meet their needs, we end up with a customer who has learned not to let us in the door again.

Whether a healthcare provider serving patients, a vendor dealing with a customer, a group dealing with political figures, or an organization trying to drive large-scale change, what we really want to figure out is what the customer's needs are and how we are going to meet those needs. Marketing consistently lasts longer than selling because we are meeting someone's needs. It also makes it much easier to make the next appointment. And it's absolutely essential if we are trying to build a network of allies and collaborators.

When Alfred Sloan was rebuilding General Motors, he would go out every quarter and work a week as a salesman on a car lot. He was the head of the biggest industrial company in the world and he would sell cars one week every three months, going to a different region of the country each quarter. He did this because he believed that listening to customers ask questions told him more about where the auto industry was going than any other thing he did.

Every conversation is an opportunity to let people tell us their interests, so that we begin to understand their needs. We can then start meeting their needs, which is what marketing is about.

Principle Seven
Incentives work
   • Change should be incentive-pulled, not punishment-driven.
   • Punishers get fired.

Incentives really work. People voluntarily change their behavior for incentives. Organizations seeking transformation need to think about what the incentives are that can move the system—and their team—in the right direction.

People respond better to an incentive system because they are in charge—they are making the decision about whether they want to earn an incentive. No one is trying to force them. People do not like to be pushed, which is why, in a punishment-based system, they tend to rebel and try to figure out how to game the system.

Incentive-pulled versus punishment-driven systems are vastly different approaches and yield vastly different responses. Even in secret police states, where people are threatened with torture and jail, there are huge black markets because people will inherently try to pursue their own interests even if they must defy authority to do so.

Tying incentives to metrics is a key strategy for getting our team (or others we're trying to change) focused on what we're trying to accomplish during implementation. Assigning projects with clear goals and metrics and then tying financial and other rewards to the attainment of those goals can dramatically impact success and create very high-tempo teams.

Consider the difference when government road projects tie financial rewards to outcomes. On one hand we have the Boston Big Dig, where financial rewards were tied to ongoing activities rather than defined outcomes. The Big Dig, even with the slow pace allowed by the government-approved plan, came in seven years late and cost more than five times the amount budgeted by the federal government—$14.6 billion dollars rather than $2.6 billion dollars. Its price tag ended up being more than double the cost of the Panama Canal, in today's dollars!

On the other hand, we have the Santa Monica Freeway project, a road construction initiative undertaken after the devastating destruction in California from the 1994 earthquake. Potential bidders were informed that if their work was completed after the established due date, they would be penalized, and if the work was completed prior to the due date, they would receive bonuses. The penalty/bonus incentive for the Santa Monica project was set at $200,000 per day.

The contractors were required to submit bids that included not only a price for the work, but also a projected due date of completion. It was mandated that the completion date had to be no more than 140 days. Motivated by the incentive structure, the selected contractor ended up completing the job in 66 days—74 days ahead of schedule —and reaped a bonus of about $14.5 million. Despite the bonus, the early completion was determined to have saved the Los Angeles economy as much as $34 million.

Principle Eight
Deep / mid / near campaigns
  • Design for
        Deep campaigns (three to eight years): 10 percent
        Mid campaigns (one to two years): 20 percent
        Near campaigns (immediate): 70 percent
  • Always focus on the deep campaign first to learn how to shape
    near and mid campaigns.

We always try to design at three levels simultaneously. This is a page
from the Army's design in the 1980s. Leaders have to pay attention at
all three levels: deep, mid, and near. Usually, deep is six to eight years:
what we want to accomplish that is really big, is worth a lot of work,
and will get us to a big change. Leaders should spend 10 percent of
their time there.

Mid campaigns focus on the next few years. Leaders should spend
about 20 percent of their time there.

Near-term campaigns are where leaders spend the majority of their
time. Near is immediate, what we are doing today and over the next
year. Seventy percent of a leader's time should be focused here.

Under this principle, a leader working 50 weeks at 40 hours a week—
2,000 hours annually—should spend 200 hours or 10 percent of that
time on long-term plans. For 200 hours a year, the leader has to
become removed from the day-to-day fray and concentrate on the
deep campaign. Since many leaders work more than 2,000 hours a
year, they should devote proportionately more time to planning
deep.

The top people in an organization need to be thinking three to eight
years out. Failing to do this is like driving a car and not looking far
enough ahead to avoid hitting the person in front of us. The more
complex we are, the farther out we have to look. If we are flying a 747,
we have to look farther than someone driving a car. Someone driving
a car has to look farther out than someone walking. A different level
of speed or complexity requires a different level of advance planning
and foresight.

The Republican congressional victory in 1994 can be traced back to a project that began in December 1978. At that time, the House Republican Party had been in the minority for twenty-four years and there was no plan to create a majority. The Planning Committee, established in December 1978, focused on trying to achieve a majority. It failed every two years, but kept coming back to the core challenge of building a big enough system that House Republicans could compete directly with the dominant House Democrats for control of the Congress.

A key moment came in a planning retreat in August 1989. For thirty-five years, there had been a consistent track record of failure. The eighteen-day retreat in 1989 laid out the framework for the Republican victory in 1994. It took a lot of things working right to make it happen, but without the planning during those eighteen days, the victory of 1994 would almost certainly not have happened.

It's important to work each day within the context of the deep campaign. If we don't know where we are going in the long run, it is impossible to make the right decision today. Once we define the deep, we can then come back through mid and then get to today's decisions. It comes back to the distinction between activity and progress.

When we think through the deep and mid terms, we begin making smarter decisions every day. We know what not to invest in, what not to train people in, what not to reward, and we begin to have a much more rapid rate of change than what would have occurred had we concentrated only on the near term.

Principle Nine
Plan back from victory
  • It is very important to plan back from victory rather than forward from the present.

If we plan forward from where we are, we will never plan big enough changes. We will instead make incremental changes to the current system and think we have made amazing progress.

We need to define what victory is and then plan back from there.

For example, it's unlikely the Republicans would have gained control of Congress in 1994 had we not set that up as our definition of victory. Our goal was to become the majority party that was elected by the American people because they shared our vision and supported our agenda. To do that, we needed to have a contract that candidates across the country agreed to, which we would present six weeks prior to the election. To do that, we would need to get agreement by Republican candidates. To do that, we would have to meet with them, listen to them, and find a way to meet their needs. Prior to holding those meetings, we would need to have an initial draft. To create the initial draft, we would have to have a number of working groups, each tasked with creating one of the ten contract items.

This gives you an idea of what we mean by planning back from victory. Yet even this is a simplified version to illustrate the principle. In reality, this was only the final phase of a campaign that had started several years earlier and involved many other components that had brought us to this point in 1994, including the recruitment and training of candidates that would be able to lead and communicate the Contract with America.

This was a completely different approach from merely looking at how many congressional seats we had and deciding how to hold on to those seats or how to add a few to our existing number. And it yielded totally different results. The only way to lead transformation is to start by defining success and to then plan back from our vision of the ideal future.

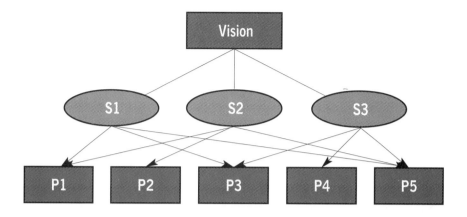

Principle Ten

Build a matrix

- Design projects that advance as many strategies as possible.
- Get the most bang for your buck.

A key to maximizing impact is building a matrix. The goal is to develop projects that actually fulfill a number of strategies. The more strategies a project fulfills, the more effective that project can be in maximizing our reach and resources. High-impact leaders design projects to fulfill several strategies and key metrics. The illustration above provides an example of how a vision is translated into strategies (S1, S2, S3), which then lead to projects (P1, P2, P3, P4, P5) that fulfill a number of the strategies.

In the Age of Transformation, we can't do things individually. We can't do them sequentially. We don't have enough time. We have to learn how to pull things together so we are getting two, three, or four things done simultaneously, using time as effectively and productively as possible.

Principle Eleven

Take context into account

- Everything is in the context of current opportunities and cultural history, and is often country- or region-specific.

This seems obvious but from our experience it is not. Great leaders understand instinctively the context in which they are operating. As we mentioned earlier, both internal and external environments are key to creating a strategic plan. But the context of what is happening each day will impact how we implement that plan, and may indicate that our strategies need to change or need to be prioritized differently.

Consider our attempt to advance 21st century health consumerism by getting health savings accounts adopted. The approach we may have otherwise taken was superseded when it became clear that there was a real opportunity to get health savings accounts included in the Medicare reform bill. Other efforts and activities were tabled in favor of what we saw as a unique moment in time that could—and proved to—be a dramatic lever for accelerating health transformation. Had we merely stuck with our plans for the month, rather than understanding the context and seizing the opportunity to focus on this important issue, we would have lost a rare opportunity.

Principle Twelve
Move to the sound of the guns
- Quickly recognize and move to key opportunities and challenges.
- The greatest potential for change exists at times of crisis.

As we design transformational change, it's important to build in a level of flexibility that allows us to move to the sound of the guns, which means being able to rapidly move to the most vital place we can make a difference.

Very often, decisive moments develop unexpectedly and necessitate a sudden shift in focus. Effective leaders intuit when they can make a decisive difference and shift their schedules and plans to meet the opportunity or challenge created by the sudden "firing of the guns."

Moving quickly to the decisive point is vital for two very different reasons. First, if the event is vital, the most effective and capable people in the organization should be ensuring success. Presumably those people are the top leadership. Second, the rest of the organization learns by watching the behavior of the senior leadership. If these people are focused on reality and are flexible in shifting time and resources to meet the new challenges, then more junior members of the team will learn the same habits.

Successfully moving to the sound of the guns as a habit requires creating a monitoring system that allows us to discern the presence of a crisis—since the greatest leverage for change exists at times of crisis—and then being able to quickly move to that crisis. Further explanation of this principle can be found in Chapter Ten, in our discussion of implementation.

Principle Thirteen
Operate within an OODA loop model
  • Adopt a rapid cycle of Observe-Orient-Decide-Act.

The OODA loop, which is a model for improving the speed of decision-making, is the American military's biggest innovation in the last generation. It was originally developed by retired Air Force colonel John Boyd, who had been asked to help design the F-16 fighter plane. He analyzed the experience of the American F-86 fighter in the Korean War. The Soviet-built MiG-15 could dive better, climb better, and turn better than the American plane. Yet the Americans held a commanding twelve to one advantage in shooting down the Soviet plane. Why? The hydraulics on the MiG-15 changed too slowly, which made it impossible for the MiG pilot to keep up with the American pilot as long as the latter was constantly changing his actions. If the American pilot stayed in the same mode (diving, climbing, turning) then the MiG pilot could compete successfully. However if the American pilot shifted his plane from mode to mode quickly, the MiG pilot would rapidly find himself falling behind and getting out of synchronization with his competitor. After a few minutes the MiG pilot's nerve would break and he would turn and head for home. At that point the American pilot had victory in hand.

Boyd analyzed this data and concluded that the side that most quickly observes a fact, orients itself to the meaning of that fact, decides based on that meaning, and acts based on that decision—and then loops back to observe—will always beat its opponent.

Boyd developed a six-hour lecture that carried his audiences through the history of warfare, emphasizing the advantage of the side that could observe-orient-decide-act faster. He eventually convinced much of the American military that this OODA-loop model was exactly right. In many ways, Boyd's insights became the foundation for the modern high-tempo, stunningly fast, and precise American military.

Boyd's model also applies to any attempt to lead large-scale change. If we can quickly and accurately figure out what the problem is,

Boyd's OODA "Loop" Sketch

Adapted from "The Essence of Winning and Losing" John R. Boyd, January 1996

determine a solution, make the decision, act on it, and then come back to see if it is working, we will get dramatically better results. It's a model that is almost universally applicable in any kind of information or competitive system.

Principle Fourteen
Plans should reflect future reality
- Try to design arguments and policies for which, over time, reality reinforces your point.

Plans ought to reflect future reality. This may seem obvious, but it means we have to think deeply about the future.

President Reagan was successful because he understood that we not only had to be allied with the core beliefs of the American people, but we also had to be flowing with the natural stream of history.

President Reagan understood the long sweep of future developments because he had lived them in his own life.

President Reagan also understood the power of humans to change things. He had been born into a world with czars, emperors, and kings. He was a young adult when that world had been replaced with the rise of Imperial Japan, Fascist Italy, the Soviet Union, and Nazi Germany. As a mature adult he participated in a world war that eliminated three of the four great dictatorships but further entrenched the Soviet Union and set the stage for the rise of Mao and Communist China. Reagan understood the importance of thinking about patterns of historic change because he had lived through them and been shaped by them.

> "In my life's journey over these past eight decades, I have seen the human race through a period of unparalleled tumult and triumph. I have seen the birth of Communism and the death of Communism. I have witnessed the bloody futility of two world wars, Korea, Vietnam, and the Persian Gulf. I have seen Germany united, divided, and united again. I have seen television grow from a parlor novelty to become the most powerful vehicle of communication in history. As a boy I saw streets filled with Model-Ts; as a man I have met men who walked on the moon. I have not only seen, but lived the marvels of what historians have called the 'American Century.' But while I take inspiration from the past, like most Americans, I live for the future."
>
> *Ronald Reagan*

Changing demographics, such as the aging of the Baby Boomers, will greatly impact the future economy, in particular long-term care and healthcare costs. Moreover, people will increasingly be living beyond the age of eighty. This can be either an amazing opportunity or a daunting challenge.

Learning about the patterns of aging, the shifting economic considerations of retirement in the 21st century, and the wishes and expectations of the Baby Boomers is a useful investment in what will inevitably be a significant issue for the next thirty years. More people will retire and live longer with more resources (and greater demands) than ever before in human history. It's one of the many patterns of long-term reality that should help shape our planning.

Principle Fifteen
Plan for exponential industries
  • Consider the areas of computing, biology, and communications
    as you make your plans.

As we have discussed, computing, biology, and communications are
areas of exponential growth. In planning the future, every organization should take these three areas into consideration. The future will
be vastly different from today and, as we plan our deep campaign, we
need to recognize what that world will most likely resemble. Of
course, we can't know with certainty all the details, but there are
things we can assume with some level of confidence.

Predictable exponential growth is enormously powerful. For example, Moore's Law asserts that the amount of computing per dollar
doubles every sixteen months. This turns out to be a hundred-fold
increase in computing power per dollar per decade. That means the
amount of computing power you buy for $1 in year one is 100 times
as much in year 10 and 10,000 times as much in year 20. By year 50
computing power per dollar has gone up by 10,000,000,000 (ten billion) times. Since fifty years is the lifespan of a nuclear-powered aircraft carrier, this trend poses huge implications for designing continuous improvement into modern warships.

The ability of exponential change to create waves of capability and to
have implications for most activities is something planners find difficult to take into account. The power of an exponential change is felt
over time as it accelerates and deepens.

For example, in healthcare, it is inconceivable that in ten years we
would not have electronic medical records, expert systems that
check against prescription errors, and same-day payment through
electronic funds transfer. The technologies already exist to do these
things. Once they are adopted universally, there will be major implications for how doctors practice, for the role of pharmacists, and
even for the future of the insurance industry.

We need to think through what block modernization of health facilities would entail. What would a truly information-rich facility look
like? As an example, there is a robot in a VA hospital in North Carolina

that delivers medicine. It costs $5 an hour—and it works. It is stunningly accurate at delivering the right medicine all over the hospital.

In this decade we will be able to access wireless systems that will carry more information than we currently get from a broadband cable or from an ISDN line. That will have a dramatic impact on the way medicine is practiced.

In the area of biology, the volume of information that we are going to learn about human beings, how we function, and our personal health patterns is accelerating so dramatically that it is going to change virtually everything.

We are already able to test for risk factors in many areas. As the practice of medicine catches up with scientific discovery, we will know about our likelihood for various diseases, receive information about nutrition and lifestyle changes that can prevent their development, find out what specific individualized drugs or treatments are best for us given our profile, and hence avoid or delay illness and various chronic conditions. That's all coming. The challenge is taking it from the lab and getting it into the hands of the everyday person, which gets us back to computing and communications.

The importance of computing can be seen in the rise of Wal-Mart, where lowest everyday price is a function of lowest everyday cost. We can trace a large part of Wal-Mart's success to a trip Sam Walton took to Japan, where he observed what the Japanese were doing with computing. He came back and made a huge investment in information technology. As a result, Wal-Mart had the most expensive information system in retail—and they reaped huge savings from it. It has allowed them to have a real-time understanding of what products are selling and a real-time approach to managing their supply chain. This has been the heart of their success.

In the future, the person or organization that bets on computing, communications, and biology is going to have a big advantage over those who ignore the scale of change in these areas. In our planning, we have to consistently look for exponential developments that might affect our lives and our organizations.

Principle Sixteen
Major changes will come from outside your industry
- Concept of sustaining vs. disruptive technologies
- Sustaining: improvements in the current system
- Disruptive: radically new way of doing things or a way of doing new things

Transforming an industry, an organization, or a career requires constant scanning outside the immediate environment of that industry. Many of the big changes that affect us will not be from within our profession or industry. Therefore we have to scan the external environment constantly and broadly. We have to ask what we're trying to solve and then look for someone who has already solved it.

In areas where adoption of information technology is slow, such as healthcare, looking at other, more modernized industries can help us not only solve our current problems but also better understand what our own industry will probably look like in the future. Bar-coding was used in grocery stores for decades before it was finally adopted for use in hospitals to reduce medication errors.

The technology to make doctors' appointments online or to use the Internet to check out the cost and quality of specific procedures by hospital or doctor is now possible, but not widely available. Yet 93 percent of the American people believe they have the right to know information about the cost and quality of healthcare providers, making it a certainty that access to such information will be a part of the future. The hospital or doctor who does not prepare for that future is being foolish and unrealistic.

Disruptive versus sustaining technologies

As Clayton Christensen pointed out in his book, *The Innovator's Dilemma,* technologies can be either disruptive or sustaining. A disruptive technology is a new technological innovation, product, or service that eventually overturns the existing dominant technology. It often initially performs worse than the leading technology according to existing measures, but comes to dominate the market by either filling a role that the older technology could not fill or by making performance improvements until it displaces the current technology. By contrast, sustaining technology refers to the successive incremental improvements to performance that market incumbents incorporate into their existing product

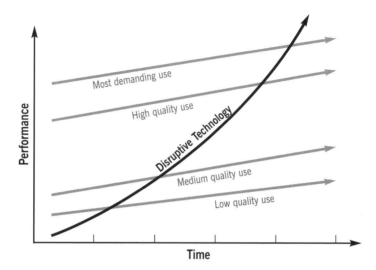

Wikipedia contributors. Disruptive Technology Graph. Wikipedia, The Free Encyclopedia. October 18, 2005, 11:10. Available at: http://en.Wikipedia.org/wiki/Image:Disruptivetechnology.gif. Accessed June 12, 2006.

"Low-end disruption" occurs when the rate at which products improve exceeds the rate at which customers can learn and adopt the new performance. Therefore, at some point the performance of the product overshoots the needs of certain customer segments. At this time, a disruptive technology may enter the market and provide a product that has lower performance than the incumbent but which exceeds the requirements of certain segments, thereby gaining a foothold in the market.

Market leaders often cannot afford to introduce disruptive technologies and instead wait until the market is large and/or the technology is advanced and more reliable. Some companies, often those who are the most innovative, invest in a separate company or division to develop disruptive innovations, while their main division continues to focus on their dominant product.

If we had gone to IBM in the 1970s and said we wanted a better mainframe computer, IBM could have created it. They were in the business of creating big, powerful, expensive computers. All of the IBM senior salespeople were making their money by simply selling three or four giant mainframes a year. They could not internally accommodate small, weak computing. It took Steve Jobs to come along and build the Apple personal computer in his garage. Initially, only enthusiasts and hobbyists bought it. However as the personal computer got better and better, more people wanted one. When it became a big enough market, IBM could introduce an IBM PC. But because of their size and business model, they could not afford to introduce it when it was disruptive.

An example of a disruptive technology that at first filled a niche and then began to replace the dominant technology is the hydraulic shovel, which was invented in 1947. Steam shovels were very big, very heavy, and able to move huge volumes of dirt. They were capable of building the Panama Canal or a high-rise office building. Hydraulic shovels were much smaller and weaker. The inventors had to ask themselves if there was a market. It turned out that if someone had a job that required digging with a pick and shovel, an otherwise weak hydraulic shovel was very powerful. The first market for the hydraulic shovel, which came to be known as a backhoe, was for laying water pipes or a sewer pipe. Over time they built bigger and better backhoes, and one day they took over the bottom third of the steam shovel market.

All of this is important to understand when leading a transformation because the American people are constantly looking for new solutions and new ways to improve what they are doing. In many cases, small companies with new solutions, often outside an industry, will provide the greatest opportunities, particularly if the new technology can be applied to or adapted for our particular niche. Even if we are not willing to assume the risk of investing a great deal in a new solution that offers great potential, being able to launch small test projects using them—or at the very least keeping an eye on their progress—is crucial to leading the future.

Principle Seventeen
Benchmark the obvious in the world around you
   • Constantly learn from the successes and solutions of others.
   • Learn from those within your industry and outside your industry.

We live in a world of continuous improvement and constant innovation. We do not have to hire expensive consultants to find breakthroughs that will provoke serious thought about our own business, profession, or activity. We merely need to open our eyes to the emerging commercial realities.

An obvious example of sudden commercial success is the iPod—a relatively inexpensive product that provides a new level of portability and choice for the user. Cell phones with cameras are increasingly ubiquitous and declining in price while improving in quality. GoogleEarth is an amazing new system of capability at virtually no cost. What do these and other new breakthroughs mean for our future?

If we simply benchmark the obvious in an age of dramatic change, we will find many new ways to develop breakthroughs in our own professions, organizations, and activities. Furthermore, we will be better able to explain the realities and the possibilities of transformation—and get people to believe in what we're saying—if we describe real changes that they are experiencing in their own lives.

Principle Eighteen
Shift from planning to anticipatory leadership
- Plans cannot be static.
- Our plans must allow for flexibility and be able to change with the shifting opportunities and realities.
- Thoughtful experimentation must replace bureaucratic analysis and risk-averse delay.

Change on this scale will require a profound shift from the planning patterns of the industrial era. The scale of change will be so great and so unpredictable that it will be impossible to create a static plan or execute an orderly, predictable implementation. An information-age system is going to have to be capable of a very rapid response to partial breakthroughs and maintain a constant effort to anticipate and move toward glimmerings of the future.

The industrial-era model of planning assumes a stable world in which the planner can study, learn, analyze, plan, and then implement. It is very powerful when mobilizing stable systems of capability (building navies or creating mass-produced consumer automobiles). This system is now much too slow and risk-averse for the speed and complexity of the emerging information age and global economy.

The Wright brothers understood that they did not know how to fly. Their answer was to engage in systematic experimentation that slowly but surely led to successful powered, manned flight. The bureaucratic model studies too long, tries to plan too much, and leaves too little opportunity for "intelligent failure."

The entire process of government acquisition has to be rethought to move it from slow, risk-averse, and mistake-avoiding systems that guarantee obsolescence to a new model of delegated, thoughtful experimentation. Entrepreneurial success in an age of transformational change is more a function of focused intelligent failure and a deep commitment to try and try again.

Principle Nineteen
Acquire allies and partners
- We cannot validate ourselves.
- We must have validating allies who have an interest in achieving the vision.
- In large public policy change, we are coordinating coalitions and building collaborations, not managing direct activities.
- What is our allies' self-interest? How do they win? How is this vision going to positively impact them?

We need to create a series of alliances with people or groups who will validate us and will help work toward achieving our vision. This means building and coordinating a coalition. In our definition, a coalition is when we give A what they need in order to get permission from A to give B what they need in order to get permission from B to give C what they need. The result is that the four of us are now working for the same goal. This doesn't mean that A necessarily agrees with the goal of B, but A is willing for B to reach their goal if A in turn reaches their goal. Coalition members don't have to necessarily agree with every one of the strategies, but they should be aware of them.

Coordinating coalitions is key to large-scale change in a political system because any big change requires more energy and more effort than any single group can bring to bear. We have to have a coalition of groups that are collectively working to get something done.

To take it a step further, we believe that the coalitions we are coordinating also must become part of a collaboration. We want to produce a vision that will mean a better future for every coalition partner. This involves using the planning and leadership model discussed in Chapter Three, with a major focus on listening, learning, helping, and leading.

At the Center for Health Transformation, part of our vision is to become a collaboration of leaders, which means not only collaborating with our allies but helping them to assume a leadership role in creating and communicating the 21st Century Intelligent Health System we envision. The idea of a collaboration of leaders is just as important as the idea of this system, since both the quality of the system and the ability to create it are dependent upon having a real collaboration of leaders.

Organizations should look both internally and externally for allies, particularly those who offer substantial distribution channels. AARP is a good example. They could be a valuable ally for almost any group, particularly when it comes to healthcare. Recent reports indicate that AARP has 35 million dues-paying members. As an example of their reach, in the state of Montana there are 950,000 people, including children. Approximately 350,000 of them pay dues to AARP. AARP is also one of the two or three highest-valued brands in America.

Imagine the clout AARP has when they look among their own membership for allies who can help communicate a message. Any member of Congress who has held a town hall meeting or paid attention to the phone calls that come into his or her congressional and district offices is well aware of the ability of AARP to mobilize their internal allies. Imagine if AARP also pulls in their suppliers and vendors. The impact is stunning.

We divide our stakeholders or allies into four categories based on the role they will play: leaders, those who will work with us to actively lead the transformation; implementers, those who will implement the solutions; participants, those who will participate with us but not lead or implement; and passive supporters, those who passively support what we are doing but won't actively participate. We also evaluate allies according to their importance in achieving our goals, with the different levels receiving different degrees of time, attention, and involvement.

Stakeholder Category	Level of Desired Involvement
Indispensable: those without whom we lose	Involve early, often, and deeply in both design and implementation; buy-in and approval of plan vital
Key: any group or individual whose buy-in or support makes success more likely, but is not decisive	Involve in design and implementation; buy-in and approval of plan desirable
Helpful: can be helpful but not strong enough to be key	Involve in ways that help (import knowledge/export work); assign helping rather than approving role
Volunteer: those who want to help and don't hurt us but are not likely to have much impact	Involve at low cost in less direct manner, generally to spread the word

The key to success is spending the most time and energy with the groups at the highest level and finding a way to keep those at the lowest levels supportive and enthusiastic without expending a great deal of time or resources—such as through mass electronic communications and the creation of self-organizing groups.

Principle Twenty
Focus on collaboration, not control
- Collaboration is key to transformation.
- Collaboration is more decentralized and requires great clarity in communications.

Collaboration, not control, is key to a successful transformation. Transformation requires buy-in and support from many outside allies. Precisely because we need allies and partners, we must cultivate a model of consistent collaboration that enables us to work with many people.

Collaboration is inherently more decentralized and complex than a controlled system. In order to collaborate, we have to be very clear about the mutually agreed goals and we have to identify and discuss the metrics that will be used to measure achievement of those goals.

Because we have to rely on people beyond our control, a lot more focus is needed on clarity of communication, including the communication of our metrics of success. In collaboration we have to be supportive of our allies and partners, who may have other goals in addition to the ones we share with them. We also have to remember that they are engaged for their own reasons and have their own agendas.

Collaboration requires more emphasis on supportive communications, praise, trust, team building, and emotional reinforcement because we are creating human ties to bond people who are not part of the same organization and rewarded or punished in the same hierarchy. Because people in collaborations tend to be geographically dispersed and have many distractions, it is even more important to have clear, effective communications.

We discovered while organizing the Conservative Opportunity Society among the House Republicans in the 1980s that we had to require members to meet once a week to sustain commitment to our goals. We had to routinely (usually quarterly) have day-long meetings to develop plans, learn from the projects under way, and rebuild enthusiasm and commitment. It was important that staff participate so they could understand our mission, but staff attendance was always conditional on member participation to retain a system of loyalty and engagement among members.

We have to make more investments in the early stages of collaboration than are required in a single organization, but in the long run we garner vastly more energy and resources through the collaborative process.

Principle Twenty-one
Design a system that can constantly evolve
   • Build in room for failure.
   • Plan for change, not perfect execution.
   • Be aware of the need to constantly evolve.

Any large-scale change involves having to solve hundreds of problems, most of which occur just as we solve the preceding problem. Change on this scale demands a system that is designed for iteration and failure as the project evolves. When the Wright brothers invented the airplane, they planned for failure. They knew that there would be many attempts to get the airplane to fly before they were successful. Every time they left Dayton for Kitty Hawk, they took lots of extra wood because their expectation was that they were going to wreck the plane. They often wrecked it six times a day, only to rebuild it and try again.

Compare that to the Smithsonian Institution, which got a contract for $50,000 to build an airplane. Scientists studied the project for a long time and then decided they would launch it from a catapult over the Potomac. The airplane crashed into the Potomac. The Wright brothers reckoned their plane would crash five or six times a day; the Smithsonian scientists believed they could successfully fly it on the first attempt.

The Smithsonian approach to building an airplane was typical of large corporations and government organizations. They typically study a project for a very long time because they want to get it exactly right. The fact is, they won't get it exactly right. They would be better off if they just started moving, knowing that things would be changing constantly, and that it will be impossible to ensure a perfect launch no matter how long they study the situation.

In the next quarter century, change will be constant, and nothing will be exactly as we planned when we started. Unless we create a permanently evolving system, we will be unable to keep up with the transformation. The answer is not to try to plan for perfection but to design for change.

Principle Twenty-two
The "too hard" box
- Create a "too hard" box to place problems that are too hard to solve immediately.
- Deal with problems in the "too hard" box by breaking them down into smaller, manageable projects.

John Reichart recently wrote a National Defense University paper noting that in the mid-1980s, biological warfare was considered too difficult to solve. As a consequence, it didn't go in the "in" box or the "out" box—it went in the "too hard" box. It's an important concept involving two elements. First, we need to have a "too hard" box that we are aware of and pay attention to. If something is vital but too hard to figure out immediately, we need to put it in the "too hard" box. However, we can't just decide that something is too hard and ignore it. If we really have to convince the political system to think differently in order to get to the rules, regulations, and financing structures that we need, then—even though it seems too hard—we need to figure out how to do it.

Second, everything we encounter that strikes us as too hard should be examined. Those that are really necessary have to go into the "too hard" box. And, most important, the things we've put in the "too hard" box have to be broken down into a series of steps that fit in the "in" box.

Principle Twenty-three
Define the social contract that you and your organization will fulfill
  • Transformation is about changing lives.
  • What is our contract with our customers, employees, and the American public?

Large-scale change almost always involves a social contract. Henry Ford's goal was for every one of his employees to be able to afford a Model T. Thomas Edison envisioned changing the lives of everyday Americans through electricity. Theodore Vail wanted every American to have a telephone. In America, improving the life of the individual is at the heart of creating transformation.

Transformation is always about changing the lives of people. Those who seek to lead transformation have to define what their social contract is with their workforce, their customers, and the American public. That contract has to be a part of the vision we communicate and the moral cause that defines us.

Principle Twenty-four
Use systems thinking, not linear thinking
  • Understand the whole, not just the parts.

• Identify patterns and root causes.
• Focus on the long-term, not just tactics.
• What are the key leverage points?

To understand large-scale change, we have to use systems thinking, which is so important that we will devote an entire chapter to it later in the book. Linear thinking, which looks at a simple cause-and-effect relationship in an isolated event, is inadequate if our goal is to understand or lead a transformation.

We live in a complex world system in which all the sub-systems overlap and affect each other. Systems thinking is a way of understanding change by understanding the relationships among sub-systems.

Systems thinking allows us to identify patterns and root causes, so that we understand the geographically or temporally distant changes that led to an event. By unraveling the patterns and the processes, we are able to determine the places at which making a change will impact the cycle that created an event. If the event was positive, we can act to accelerate or strengthen its occurrence; if negative, we can act to prevent or lessen its future occurrence.

Take our approach to diabetes, which is a stunning example of our failure to use systems thinking. The CDC has estimated that one out of three Americans born in the year 2000 will develop diabetes in his or her lifetime. If you're Hispanic, it's worse: one in two. Diabetes, meanwhile, is the fifth deadliest disease in America and the primary cause of end-stage renal disease, adult blindness, and non-traumatic lower limb amputations. It is estimated to cost Americans $132 billion annually and accounts for one of every four dollars of Medicare spending.

The Impact of Diabetes in America

Every 24 hours, there are...

• 4,100 new cases of diabetes diagnosed

• 230 diabetes-related amputations

• 120 Americans who enter end-state renal disease programs

• 55 new cases of diabetes-related blindness

Source: CDC

We know that obesity, diet, and inactivity are the major factors linked to Type Two diabetes, which accounts for 90 to 95 percent of all cases of diabetes. However, we continue to focus our efforts on treating diabetes once it has occurred rather than intervening earlier in the cycle to prevent obesity by requiring physical education in schools, mandating healthy school lunches, and removing unhealthy snacks from school vending machines. And schools are just one place in the system where action could break the cycle. The epidemic of obesity and diabetes could also be stemmed by anti-obesity efforts in the medical community, the family, the restaurant business, and other areas. Instead, families continue to give children unhealthy snacks and tolerate their inactivity, physicians tend to avoid discussing obesity and diabetes risks, and fast-food restaurants continue to focus on high-calorie foods.

Meanwhile, studies show that only 45 percent of diabetics receive the standard of care they need. We have been slow to tie incentives or rewards to physician performance or to change the medical culture to ensure delivery of proven best standards of care. Instead, we focus on paying for amputations and dialysis that could have, in many cases, been prevented had we acted earlier.

All of this is symptomatic of our failure to concentrate on dealing with the root causes or early phases of illnesses like diabetes, as opposed to waiting and dealing with a crisis once it has occurred. In addition to allowing us to understand and address root causes, systems thinking also focuses our attention on the long-term versus the tactical. As we design transformational change, systems thinking compels us to concentrate on the interactions between various parts of the system—and between systems—that can move us more quickly toward the desired outcome. It also focuses us on the ripple effects that are likely to occur as a result of an event or an action we undertake. Every action has unintended consequences, but systems thinking provides a framework for us to understand and even begin to anticipate those consequences.

Finally, and perhaps most important, by using systems thinking we can begin to identify key leverage points where a small act can have a profound impact, which is one of the keys to mastering the art of transformation.

[See Appendix B for an example of the mind-mapping approach we use at the Center for Health Transformation to think systemically and broadly, rather than in a linear manner, during brainstorming sessions.]

Principle Twenty-five
Plan for second- and third-order effects
 • Recognize and think through the second- and third-order effects of any change or breakthrough.
 • Society is transformed in second- and third-order effects.
 • Recognize glimmerings and the effects they might have.

Transformational changes have dramatic and enduring impacts beyond the initial place and time they occur. They create a ripple effect and produce second- and third-order effects that are outside the primary change.

Technology breakthroughs initially replace earlier technologies. However, as a critical mass of people adopt the new technology, the impact is felt in other unrelated systems. It is in these second- and third-order changes that technological revolutions transform society.

For example, in the late 1800s, the railroad train (itself a second-order effect of the steam engine) was invented and rapidly replaced the horse-drawn carriage. A second-order effect of the invention of the train was a dramatic increase in travel. Once a critical mass of people began to use the train, another effect occurred. That effect, which proved to dramatically transform American society, was the migration of people away from the industrial cities where they worked and into the suburbs.

No one in the middle of the 18th century knew that the steam engine would lead to the transcontinental railroad and that American society would be transformed. Even today, the breakthroughs that will change the world cannot be predicted. However, the better we become at quickly recognizing potential changes and breakthroughs and understanding their second-order effects, the intersections of opportunity, and their benefits for society, the more adept we will be at both preparing for and helping shape the future.

Principle Twenty-six
Plan and celebrate small victories
- While we need to know what our antelope are, it is also important to plan small victories, related to our antelope, along the way.
- We need to consciously define projects, tasks, and milestones, work to successfully complete those, and then celebrate those achievements.

In 1994, the House Republicans created the Contract with America. The Contract was made up of ten major changes that we promised to bring to the floor of the House for a vote within our first hundred days in office. After we took control of the House, we immediately went to work to do just as we promised. We planned for and held a huge celebration at the end of the hundred days to recognize the important milestone. We also, however, learned the importance of planning events and celebrations along the way, to commemorate the completion of each of the ten items. (In fact, the contract we used as a prop each time to mark off the items as they were completed is now part of the Smithsonian collection.)

Stopping to celebrate along the way was absolutely critical to maintaining the morale of our team members, who worked under constant pressure and an unending workload. It was also critical for our external allies, who, after forty years of the old regime, were starved for proof that this Congress would be different. (So exhausting was the pace kept during those hundred days that, at the conclusion, the hallways of Congress were filled with people proudly wearing pins that said "I Survived the First 100 Days.")

Transformation is a very hard, very long process, and having small projects and key milestones along the way is absolutely essential, not only from an operational perspective but also from a morale perspective. In the midst of a long and arduous battle, a key strategy for keeping the troops engaged, committed, and enthusiastic is to plan for short-term victories and then stop long enough to celebrate those victories.

Principle Twenty-seven
Measure success: We get what we inspect, not what we expect
- What is the right measurement for success?
- Metrics are for management, not just for reporting.

It is absolutely essential to set up clear metrics of success and to constantly monitor those metrics.

When we are designing a plan or assigning a project, we have to define what the metrics of success are as well as how we will measure them. This then has to be communicated to those who are leading or implementing the projects so they know what our expectations are in clear, definable terms. Finally, we have to discipline ourselves to routinely monitor and act on those metrics. As we said earlier, we get what we inspect, not what we expect. The difference between organizations that genuinely pay attention to metrics—such as FedEx and UPS—and those that don't is dramatic. Systems that closely monitor metrics and manage according to them tend to be very focused, stunningly accurate, and remarkably successful at aligning resources to achieve their goals.

Principle Twenty-eight
Find and use elevators
- Elevators take us to new levels while depleting less energy.
- Finding elevators is key to strategic thinking.

Elevators allow us to move to new levels and reach our goals with less effort and usually in less time. Even if we could get there in the same amount of time without using the elevator, we would expend energy and resources that can be used elsewhere.

Finding and leveraging elevators is a key element of strategic thinking. We have to constantly think through the key alliances, events, distribution channels, discoveries, technologies, and changes that will take us to new heights with much less effort than would otherwise be required. This is, in fact, one of the major principles that guides our work at the Center for Health Transformation, allowing us to have a level of reach and impact that far exceeds what would normally be expected for an organization our size.

Principle Twenty-nine

Cheerful persistence
- Transformational change is hard.
- Being cheerfully persistent is key to attracting allies and to succeeding.

Cheerful persistence is absolutely essential when engaged in transformational change. Transformational change will not be easy. It is likely to take a long time and require us to deal with a number of challenges, roadblocks, and, at times, failures.

> "I have not failed once. I just found 10,000 ways that didn't work."
>
> *Thomas Edison,*
> *after numerous attempts to*
> *invent the electric light*

Cheerful persistence is the only way to deal with the ongoing challenges facing us. If we give up when things get too difficult, we will never engage in the level of sustained effort needed to reach our goal. If we are persistent but not cheerful, we will be unable to attract and maintain the level of support and involvement from others needed to drive large-scale change.

Principle Thirty

Networking is key
- Successful transformation, particularly in the 21st century, requires that we create and constantly expand our networks and connections.

Building and leveraging networks has always been an important element of expanding reach and impact. But information-age technological advances, in particular the advent of electronic networks such as the Internet, have dramatically changed both our ability to connect to more people and information and the importance of doing so. One reason electronic networks are so critical is that they allow us to have a dramatic impact with a small input.

Moreover, the requirement is not to just network our team to one another (though that is vitally important) but to be connected in as many places as we can, allowing us the ability to both distribute information widely and to learn from those networks.

In addition, we want the networks to which we are connected to be as autonomous and decentralized as possible, as our reach, impact, and ability to learn will be dramatically lessened if we try to put ourselves at the center of those networks.

One book we recommend to almost every audience is Kevin Kelly's 1999 book, *New Rules for the New Economy*. While it's several years old now, it continues to serve as one of the most valuable guides we have to understanding and leveraging today's connected economy.

Principle Thirty-one
Constantly develop new insights and principles

We are just beginning to develop a sense of how transformation occurs and how different it is from the management systems of the industrial era.

The world is evolving. Technology and science are changing. New entrepreneurs from countries around the world are pioneering new and more effective ways of developing solutions, services, systems, and products.

The very nature of transformational leadership is evolving and developing. The systems available, the understanding of the habits and structures that work, and the development of new breakthroughs are going to continue evolving.

The Art of Transformation will not be the final word on transformation, but rather the beginning of a new journey of discovery, experimentation, and development. New learning and new principles, many of which will be contributed by our readers, will be shared in future editions and updates of this book.

As you develop new solutions, new systems, and new principles, we invite you to share them with us at info@healthtransformation.net.

7

Principles of Transformational Communications

Communications must be at the center of our effort to lead transformation. We can have the most brilliant ideas and amazing solutions but still fail if we have not communicated those ideas in a way that captures the minds and hearts of our audience. Furthermore, it is absolutely critical that communications must, in the end, be about education. Our ultimate goal has to be to educate people about where we're going, what our goals are, and the solutions that work.

Transformation depends on having a growing number of individuals asserting leadership, which requires us to always be mindful of what we are teaching.

Over the years we have developed a number of communication principles that we have found to be essential to successfully growing large-scale change. These principles are based on our own experiences, including the success of the Contract with America, and on lessons we learned from studying transformational leaders such as Ronald Reagan, Franklin Delano Roosevelt, Charles de Gaulle, and Margaret Thatcher.

The principles generally fall into five categories: the message, the messenger, the audience, the channel or medium, and metrics.

The Message

Assert truth
- Leaders assert truth.
- We cannot assert truth beyond the believable.
- Be prepared to win the argument or the assertion.

The first rule is to assert truth. Truth is not based on public opinion, and those who use focus groups and polls to define their truths are unlikely to ever change the world. Focus groups and polls are useful once we have defined what we believe, but they are a terrible way of getting a definition of belief because people allow, and even expect, their leaders to define truth. Focus groups should never be used to define the truth, but to help develop the right language to explain or communicate the truth.

When Ronald Reagan called the Soviet Union an "evil empire," he did not use a focus group to develop that message. No focus group would have approved the phrase. Reagan actually said it only one time because he knew it would resonate with force and decisiveness. Once he said the phrase, it was recognized as the truth and became one of the powerful assertions that defined his presidency. It helped lead to the defeat of the Soviet empire.

President Reagan followed his own instincts in one of his most famous lines: "Mr. Gorbachev, tear down this wall!" In fact, Governor Reagan had said on a trip to Berlin in 1967 "that wall ought to be torn down." Twenty-one years later, in 1988, President Reagan decided to make the line even more vivid. In fact, the State Department removed the phrase from the speech text three times. And three times President Reagan put it back in. Finally he asserted, "Tell them I am the president and it stays in." One year later the wall fell and Germany was reunited. Two years later the Soviet Union disappeared. Telling the truth had a powerful impact.

In important communications we cannot assert truth that is not believable. While we don't define our beliefs based on what a focus group would indicate, we also have to avoid making assertions that people would think are crazy. We have to have some sense of what our particular audience is able to accept.

We have to define truth at three levels:

1. The truth about the basic facts and objective reality. Are we accurately describing a world that people may have not noticed or may be hiding from?
2. The truth about our values and goals. If people agree we have accurately described reality, they then will decide if they agree with us about values and goals.
3. The truth about the specific policy or program we are advocating.

It is very important to define these truths separately and in the order listed. All too often people start defending or explaining their program or policy before they have communicated the truth about reality and values.

In defining the language, focus groups and polling can be extremely helpful because they tell us what people are hearing. What we learn can help us use the right language to assert truth. It is also very important that we avoid the language of our opponent unless we can co-opt it and use it to our advantage. One of our assertions in 1994 was that it's wrong to tax people for dying. This had been referred to as an estate tax. Through a process of focus groups and listening to what the public was hearing, we learned that most Americans viewed the estate tax as an issue that impacted only the rich. It wasn't true and it wasn't what we meant, but it's what they were hearing.

We changed the term estate tax to "death tax" and immediately changed the perception of the policy. As a result, we won the battle of public opinion. People understood instantly that it was wrong to have to visit the undertaker and an IRS bureaucrat in the same week. They understood why parents and grandparents should not be taxed on money they had already paid taxes on. The result was a decisive shift toward support for abolishing the death tax.

Communicate a sense of urgency

One of the first steps in creating change is to communicate a sense of urgency. It's difficult to move people toward adopting large-scale change without first convincing them that there is an urgent need to do so.

Once we create a sense of urgency, we not only have to provide hope for a better future but also exhibit some immediate solutions that exist today and are early examples of our ideal future. Conveying a sense of urgency without showing that there are things the audience can do is likely to create immobilizing fear or despair rather than the action we want.

Creating a Sense of Urgency: President Franklin D. Roosevelt

December 29, 1940

Tonight, in the presence of a world crisis, my mind goes back eight years ago to a night in the midst of a domestic crisis. It was a time when the wheels of American industry were grinding to a full stop, when the whole banking system of our country had ceased to function.

I well remember that while I sat in my study in the White House, preparing to talk with the people of the United States, I had before my eyes the picture of all those Americans with whom I was talking. I saw the workmen in the mills, the mines, the factories; the girl behind the counter; the small shopkeeper; the farmer doing his spring plowing; the widows and the old men wondering about their life's savings.

I tried to convey to the great mass of American people what the banking crisis meant to them in their daily lives.

Tonight, I want to do the same thing, with the same people, in this new crisis which faces America.

We met the issue of 1933 with courage and realism.

We face this new crisis—this new threat to the security of our nation—with the same courage and realism.

Draw the contrast between two futures

- Paint a picture of how your future differs from the alternative future.

Rather than describing only the ideal future we envision, it's helpful to provide a contrast between our future and the future that will otherwise exist. We want people to recognize how vastly better our future would be.

All effective communication is personal

- All effective communication is personal.
- What matters is "my life and my family's life."

"You and I have a rendezvous with destiny. We will preserve for our children this, the last best hope of man on earth, or we will sentence them to take the first step into a thousand years of darkness. If we fail, at least let our children and our children's children say of us we justified our brief moment here. We did all that could be done."

Ronald Reagan
A Time for Choosing, 1964

Creating a large-scale transformation is about starting a movement. The level of emotion, commitment, and buy-in that is necessary for transformation to happen can occur only if people understand what it means for their lives and their families. We always convey our message in terms that matter to the individual. Our general message should be one that resonates with the personal values of Americans.

When making a speech, we always start by finding the make-up of our audience. When holding a meeting, we always start by listening. Our goal is to understand what they care about. This understanding doesn't change our vision, but it does allow us to explain how our plan will relate to their values and impact them personally.

Communication is what occurs in the mind of the listener or the reader

We have to start by asking ourselves what our audience is thinking about or worrying about, what they already understand, what they believe, what their values are, what experiences are going to color their interpretation of what we're saying. If we can take our message and translate it into their world, it will make it vastly more understandable, more believable, and more important to them. Suddenly we're not talking about our project or our solution but about their project and their solution. It's a completely different model.

One reason this is so difficult, particularly in our work lives, is because we live in an age of specialization. We spend so much time and effort learning the language and the ideas of our specialty that we want to tell others about that specialty, erroneously thinking that if others understood it, they would understand our point of view.

The fact is that our audience doesn't really want to understand our specialty. It would be like taking a car into a dealership and not being able to leave until the mechanic explained in detail what he was doing to the engine. Your attitude would be, "I don't care. I don't want to learn that much about my car engine—I just want you to fix it."

We find an amazing number of very smart professionals who know a tremendous amount about their service or product and then want to tell others about it. But all their audience or their customer really wants to know is whether it will solve their problem.

Know what "yes" means
- Define what "yes" means.
- Personalize the proposition.
- Ask for "yes."
- Never mistake passivity for acceptance.

Whether we're in sales, politics, or charity work, defining in advance of a meeting or presentation what we want someone to agree to—and how to get them there—is absolutely essential. If we enter into such a situation and have failed to define what "yes" means, or to ask for it, we will leave even the most cordial meeting with a lot of warm fuzzies, but no "yes." We can do everything right in terms of communicating in their world, but if we then have not asked directly for their help or support, we have failed.

Never assume a "yes" unless you get a "yes"—and never mistake passivity for acceptance.

Knowing What "Yes" Means and How to Get to *"Yes"*

The first thing we always tell people who go to see key decision-makers is this: don't tell them your problem. Tell them what success would be. People tend to spend all of their time talking about their problem when seeking help. The person whose help they're seeking listens and says, "Let me understand: this is your problem," and the person says, "Yes, that's my problem." Once that person leaves the room, somebody else walks in saying, "Here is my problem." This typically happens before the decision-maker whose help is being sought ever has time to think about the first problem, let alone think about how to solve it.

On the other hand, if a person walks in and says, "What I need you to do is this," that is a totally different conversation. The decision-maker is relieved of the burden of solving the problem and instead is presented with a solution to consider. The chance of actually getting what we need is dramatically increased if we always share a solution rather than simply sharing a problem.

We need to understand who actually has to say "yes." It's often not the person at the top—someone three levels down may make the decision. We may not need buy-in from the top. If we do, once we get it, we need to ask them who else needs to say "yes." We've found this to be true within almost every large system we've looked at. The person at the top can say "yes" but nothing happens unless the people below him also say "yes." You have to unlock layer after layer.

If everyone says "yes," we have to be able to tell them how to implement the solution. This is critical. One of the reasons people don't do things is because they don't know how. Imagine giving a car key to someone who had never seen a car, who didn't know what a key was, or what a steering wheel was, or how to start the ignition. Even if he says he'd like to drive the car, he's not going to be able to do anything. So we have to think through the process of putting our solution into practice.

We have to understand the realities in the current and future environment that impact the people whose buy-in we need, so we can determine when they are most likely to listen to us. For example, we always know that around budget time, governors will listen to Medicaid issues because around budget time, the bad news comes in and they realize Medicaid is eating the university system.

Once we figure out when people will be compelled to listen to us, we need to think through why they will listen to us, what's in it for them, and how will they profit. We have a very simple model of how free societies work—centered on the individual. The questions everyone always asks are: How does it affect me? How does it affect my family? How does it affect my neighborhood? How does it affect my country? The "me" aspect is always there.

The final question is: what are the metrics of success? We need to define these so that, once people say yes, we know in the end whether success truly happened. Otherwise, people will change the metrics to justify whatever happens.

If we can focus on always following these five steps, the chance of getting people to "yes"—and making that "yes" actually mean something—is dramatically improved.

Getting to Yes
1. Define the solution.
2. Find out who has to say yes.
3. Describe how to implement the solution.
4. Know when they will listen and what will meet their self-interest.
5. Define the metrics of success.

Pick the right fights

- When changing the status quo, we need to fight the right fights.
- To be on offense we must represent the public good and the victim's side.
- We need to be noisy, but only on the fights we want.
- Follow the Reagan 80/20 rule—pick an issue with 80 percent public support and stand beside it smiling.

When trying to change the status quo, we are guaranteed to face opposition from those defending it. Conflict is unavoidable. It's the heart of the American model. The best approach is to stay on offense. We try to use minimum energy on defense and pivot immediately to get back on offense.

The German army rule was if you were surprised, one-third of your forces worked on defense while the other two-thirds organized the counterattack. But you never got trapped on defense. The moment something blows up, we need to immediately start thinking about how to get back on topic.

Ideally, we want to define the terms of the fight by communicating a positive message and then letting our opponents fight us. To be on offense we have to represent the public good; we have to be on the victim's side.

Leaders of large-scale change tend to be very noisy on the fights they want. When those who oppose them come in to pick a different fight, they immediately turn their energies to shifting back to the fight they want.

There's an 80/20 rule that Reagan understood perfectly. He would find an issue that had 80 percent approval, stand next to it, and smile. His opponents had two choices: they could stand next to him and smile too, in which case they would have agreed with Reagan, or they could stand with the 20 percent and frown.

The Ideal Fight

- Has 80 percent public support
- Puts us on the victim's side
- Is relevant to Baby Boomers
- Will be validated by allies
- Focuses on incentives
- Is a solution that is real
- Matters to "me and my family"
- Is something we can repeat

Be clear and consistent

- Design your message so it reaches the public with clarity, despite media biases.
- With 80/20 issues, it is possible to win despite media attacks.

This cannot be overstated—be very clear. We like 80/20 issues because if we get the language right, it is hard to clutter it to a point where it doesn't work. We first think through the argument that will work to make our point, then convert it into a clear message and straightforward, memorable slogan that makes our case.

> "We win. They lose."
>
> *Ronald Reagan, when asked early in his presidency how he envisioned the outcome of the Cold War with the Soviet Union*

For example, when making the case for the adoption of an electronic health system, we decided that patient safety was at the heart of the argument. Our slogan became "Paper Kills." This slogan resonated with both the public and the media and was quickly picked up in numerous news articles and repeated by other speakers.

A few years ago we met with several different human resources groups who were talking about the need for transparency of information about healthcare providers. The issue was getting a lot of attention from professionals and experts but was not resonating with the public or with the media. The public clearly didn't have a clue what these experts were talking about. Our advice in every meeting was to use the term "right to know."

We believed that the real issue was that people have the right to know information about the cost and the quality of health providers and services before selecting them. "Right to know" was almost always repeated in the media following our events. Interestingly, not long ago a poll was taken that showed that over 90 percent of those polled believed they had the "right to know" the cost and quality of healthcare providers.

Apply the " yes, if," not "no, because" principle

The principle of "yes, if" not "no, because" discussed in the last chapter is especially relevant when responding to difficult questions or ideas we oppose. Every time we could say "no, because," we need to train ourselves to instead say "yes, if." The psychological difference between the two is remarkable. While it is the same message, the emotional impact is quite different.

We first came up with this concept when trying to help a pharmaceutical company with an AIDS-related issue. This company was getting terrible news coverage regarding its reluctance to provide drugs to sub-Saharan Africa. Knowing the humanitarian nature of this particular company, we asked the leaders why they were exhibiting such reluctance. They explained that they couldn't give away the medicine because it would be stolen in sub-Saharan Africa and sold in Europe as contraband.

Instead of "no, because," the message should have been, "Yes, we would love to give this medicine away to help poor people if we could ensure that it would really get to them." Think about the difference. It's an example of how saying "yes, if" instead of "no, because" can dramatically increase our effectiveness even if the facts we are delivering are identical.

Use humor
Humor is able to build bridges (as well as defuse tension or anger) in

a way that can change the environment from one of resistance or nervousness to one of openness. This is true whether the audience is one person or one thousand.

Reagan was a master at this. While he never shied from delivering a strong and powerful message when necessary, he also was brilliant at using humor, often self-deprecatingly, to deal with difficult and even potentially politically damaging issues. When Reagan's age became a focus of the 1984 presidential debate between him and the much younger Walter Mondale, he quipped, "I want you to know that I will not make age an issue of this campaign. I am not going to exploit, for political purposes, my opponent's youth and inexperience."

> "At one tense situation on the University of California's Santa Cruz campus during his governorship, when Reagan's limousine was slowly proceeding through a group of hostile demonstrators, a bearded youth stuck his face up to the window, yelling, 'We are the future!' Reagan borrowed a piece of paper from an aide and scribbled a message that he held up to the window. It said, 'I'll sell my bonds.'"
>
> *From President Reagan:*
> *The Role of a Lifetime*
> *by Lou Cannon*

Aware that he was regularly accused of not working hard enough, he said during one speech, "They say hard work never hurt anybody, but I figure why take the chance." Reagan's ability to joke about himself and to get others to join in the laughter was one of his greatest assets, and his humor was one of his most successful political weapons.

Communicate vision, values, goals, and solutions
- Start by describing a better future.
- Present solutions in the context of vision.

When making a speech, giving a presentation, or writing an article, it's important to not just talk about a solution, but to first provide a framework of vision, values, and goals within which that solution matters.

First, we want the audience to be able to visualize the better future we seek to build. Next we want to relate it to the values they believe in, which leads into the goals related to those values that we are pursuing. Within that context, we then want to present our solutions. Not only does this sequence drive home the importance of the solution we are recommending, it also gets the audience thinking about the broader vision.

The Katie Couric Rule

In thinking through how to handle the media, we use what we call the "Katie Couric Rule," based on what we saw happen during the many years she served as a morning TV talk-show host. Here's the scenario. It's 7:12 on a Monday morning. We are pouring our first cup of coffee. Katie is on in the kitchen and she leans forward and says to her guest, "So let me get this straight. In order for you to make your quarterly profit, three million Africans have to die of AIDS." And we stop pouring because we want to see what kind of monster they have invited on this week.

It is the job of the guest to have an answer without attacking Katie—because remember, it's her show, it's her audience, they tune in to be with her. Attacking her is a mistake for two reasons. First, the audience is on her side. As she beats up the guest, they're all cheering her. Second, the guest is going to leave the set at the commercial break and she'll still be there. And she will keep beating up the guest into the next segment. So the smart guest will make sure not to get Katie mad but to answer the question in a way that wins the audience, such as, "You know, Katie, I am so glad you raised that because with your help, we are going to save those three million people. And this is exactly what we need to do."

Planning for an Interview: Key Questions

1. Should we do this interview? Why?
2. What is the message we want to get out? (No more than three points)
3. What do we think they will ask?
4. What is our answer? (Prepare!)
5. What is the question we don't want to answer?
6. What is our answer? (Really prepare!)
7. What is the advance material we want to send?
8. How will we immediately respond after the interview to maximize and define the resulting reverberation and echo chamber?

Measuring success is simple: Is the answer good enough? Or is the answer so bad that we are thinking, "That person is a monster. Why haven't they arrested him yet?"

The Katie Couric Rule is worth keeping in mind any time you have a difficult issue to discuss or a difficult press interview. Before the interview, always imagine the worst possible question and think through the twenty-second answer you would give Katie.

Win the moral argument
- Always address the common good.
- Make the moral case.

Margaret Thatcher had a great line: first you win the argument, then you win the vote. But don't assume you'll win the vote before you win the argument.

A key part of winning the argument is defining the argument. Change happens at many levels, but the first is changing the language. This is what Ronald Reagan understood so brilliantly. He was in a very small league of presidential and national leaders who have been able, by the sheer power of their words, to change reality.

Reagan understood that to win the argument at its most profound level, you have to have clarity, simplicity, cheerfulness, and brute repetition. Reagan didn't mind saying the same thing for twenty years. He had first said, "Tear down this wall" in 1967 as governor. He was just repeating it in 1987.

Winning the argument in America starts with making the moral case. As Alexis de Tocqueville observed in his classic, *Democracy in America*, "America is great because America is good."

Our first goal when trying to communicate the case for transformational change to the public is to win the moral argument. For example, the title of our book about health transformation is *Saving Lives and Saving Money*. We always talk about saving lives and saving money in that order, because we have to make the moral case first and the financial case second.

Communicate optimism
- Driving large-scale change requires enthusiastic allies and supporters.
- Optimism about the future is key.

When leading a transformation, one key to getting buy-in is to communicate a contagious optimism and excitement about the future.

> "What I'd really like to go down in history as is the president who made Americans believe in themselves again."
>
> *Ronald Reagan*

Ronald Reagan was called the Great Communicator largely because of his ability to make Americans feel good about America and optimistic about the future. One reason he was able to get Americans to support large-scale change was that he so brilliantly communicated optimism and hope. His ability to convey a better future, to stir excitement about changes to come, and to bring Americans together in causes as large as the defeat of the Soviet Empire created a new standard of transformational communication.

Get in front of any crisis
- Anticipate and avoid crises when possible.
- Use the opportunity to get your message out.
- Have a crisis communications plan.

Managing a Crisis

1. Get ahead of the news cycle.
2. Define the message that gets us back to the fight we want.
3. Determine who needs to know, internally and externally.
4. Develop and implement a process for contacting those who need to know immediately and getting our message to them.
5. Define and train internal spokespeople.
6. Define and train external allies who will speak for us.

When trying to overturn the status quo, be prepared for public relations crises. Some will occur as a result of things that are planned and did not go exactly as we had envisioned, which is bound to happen occasionally when we are leading a transformation. Others will be the result of defenders of the status quo throwing up roadblocks to try to prevent the change we're driving.

Of course, our first priority has to be tackling pending crises as early as possible and intervening to prevent their development. Hospitals have learned that calling the emergency response team together to intervene as soon as critical early indicators arise, rather than waiting for an emergency code, saves both lives and money. It's the kind of model that is needed as we deal with PR issues associated with transformation.

When a crisis occurs, we need to get ahead of the story as quickly as possible. Our goal is to get our message out as early as possible. We want to define the language in order to fight the fight we want to be in, not the one our opponents will try to set up.

Meanwhile, our goal should be to elevate the debate to one concerning vision, values, and goals that resonate with the American people, not focusing on solitary events or setbacks.

In order to do this, we have to have a clear and consistent message understood by our internal and external allies, as well as a plan for quickly letting them know what is happening and what message we want to convey.

Repetition is the key to ultimate success
• Repetition of the right message is the key to ultimate success.

One of our primary communication goals is to get everyone on our team and all of our allies to adopt the same language and deliver the same message. This is especially important with regard to our vision statement.

In order to create transformation, we need the maximum number of people to learn and repeat our message in order to create an echo chamber. In addition, we need to use every media interview or column as an opportunity to further distribute the message and language.

The Audience

Win the public
- Our goal is to win the public rather than the press, the elite, or the Washington crowd.

Our personal bias is that we are always in the business of winning the public; we're not in the business of winning elites. We believe, as Reagan did, that the public is smarter than the elites. FDR also believed this. There's a great line by Joseph Napolitan, a Democrat campaign consultant: we should never underestimate the intelligence of the American people, nor overestimate the amount of information they have.

While the public may not have all the information, we believe that, if we give them the right information, they collectively tend to make good judgments.

When it comes to the creation of a 21st Century Intelligent System, the ability to win the public, without needing to first change the opinion of the mainstream media and the intellectual elite, is startling when we look at the breakdown of key issues.

If we pick the right issues and use the right language, then we're going to win the public. And winning the public is what it takes to build the kind of grassroots movement that will drive transformational change.

Focus on the center of gravity
- For health, Boomers are the center of political gravity.
- Communicate in ways that vividly affect Baby Boomers' lives.

The center of gravity, when it comes to winning any type of campaign, refers to the key audience (or audiences) we must win in order to succeed. For example, the area of health and healthcare today has two centers of gravity: the Baby Boomers and AARP. If they decide that a health solution is their future, it is almost unstoppable.

Insuring that every communication resonates with our center of gravity is key. When it comes to health and healthcare, we will reach a tipping point if we can get Baby Boomers and AARP to understand

Breakdown of Key Issues

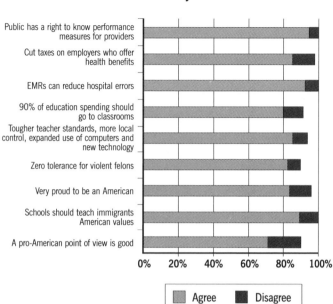

that a better future awaits them through the creation of a 21st Century Intelligent Health System.

Know the real target audience
• Know whose buy-in matters most.

One of the biggest communication mistakes people make is confusing their true audience with the medium they are using to reach that audience. Leaders often get so wrapped up in reading their own press clippings that they get into the dangerous habit of trying to appeal to the press, rather than understanding that the press is simply a conduit for communication with the American people.

As we said earlier, media is important—but only if it increases the ability to get our message out to the people we are trying to reach.

The Messenger

Select a messenger to whom the target audience relates

One of the keys to getting the message out to a variety of audiences is to have a variety of messengers. No matter how eloquent a given speaker is, when trying to get buy-in, there is no better speaker than someone with whom the audience identifies—someone who shares their concerns, their issues, and their challenges.

This is a strategy that we applied constantly in our Georgia district office. One of our approaches was to create task forces on key issues that were particularly challenging. Instead of focusing our time only on issues that had a lot of agreement and support, we wanted to address the most difficult issues and bring together citizens impacted by them to help create solutions that worked.

One of those areas was disabilities. We managed to put together a district task force of incredible people led by Carol Hughes, who had a son with cerebral palsy. Carol and her son, Jonathan, came to nearly all of our town hall meetings and when, as inevitably happened, the subject of disabilities came up, Carol always raised her hand to answer. Having someone willing to speak for us—someone who lived with the challenge of a disability day in and day out—had an impact far beyond what we could have had.

Recruit opinion leaders to maximize your reach

In 1962 Everett M. Rogers published *Diffusion of Innovations*, which has become the standard textbook on diffusion theory. The book, which grew out of Rogers' studies on farmers' adoption of a new hybrid seed corn, provides wonderful insights into why some innovations are adopted while others are ignored. The theory has been applied to fields such as economics, psychology, and politics, and is extremely helpful as we think about what type of communications will accelerate acceptance and adoption of transformational ideas and solutions.

> "Would you laugh if I told you that I think, maybe, they see themselves and that I'm one of them? I've never been able to detach myself and think that I somehow am apart from them."
>
> *Ronald Reagan,*
> *when asked what Americans*
> *saw in him*

Rogers found that a combination of mass media, such as television, radio, newspapers (and we should now add the Internet), with interpersonal interaction was helpful. However, mass media was most useful at the knowledge-gathering stage, while providing interpersonal interactions with trusted peers was most effective at the decision-making stage. Rogers was the first to categorize groups of adopters into the following categories:

- *Innovators*, who are gatekeepers in the flow of new ideas into a social system and are more likely to take risks.
- *Early adopters*, who decrease uncertainty about a new idea by adopting it and by then conveying a subjective evaluation to near-peers.
- *An early majority*, who deliberately follows, rather than takes an early lead, in adopting an innovation. They are important links for the further diffusion among the late adopters.
- *A late majority*, who often has scarce resources and hence requires that almost all uncertainty about a new idea be removed before they adopt it.
- *Laggards*, who are behind concerning awareness and knowledge and who are extremely cautious.

Early adopters are the most effective and most respected in terms of their impact via interpersonal communications. This makes it useful to define and mobilize the early adopters within a group as communicators of transformation.

Meanwhile, identifying and recruiting opinion leaders who are respected members of the audience's social system is an important communications strategy. The more time we can spend reaching opinion leaders and early adopters, the greater will be the echo chamber we create. What's important is not the size of our immediate audience, but the size of our audience's audience.

As change agents, it is our goal to maximize our audience's commitment to transformation by communicating the need for transformation and by offering transformational vision and solutions. Our success will be greatly enhanced if we can communicate with, recruit, and utilize opinion leaders as communicators within their particular social group. This is a vital strategy for building transformational momentum.

You are the message

Roger Ailes wrote a great book on communication called *You Are the Message*. Three of the key points he made that we find most helpful are:
1. All communication is a dialogue, whether it be with one person or a thousand.
2. Always believe in what you're saying.
3. Audiences gravitate toward speakers who convey optimism, concern for others, and the ability to find opportunity in the face of adversity.

The Medium

Earned media is vital
- Everything is a matter of good versus bad; there are no neutrals.
- Remember the Katie Couric Rule: what is your twenty-second answer that people will feel good about?
- "Yes, if..." beats "No, because..."
- Use conflict, scandal, and novelty to your advantage to get news coverage.

Our belief is that earned media is ten times as powerful as advertising. It is not technically true if we're in a very short time frame and can buy a lot of advertising, but in general earned media is vastly superior in terms of impact.

First, people are much more likely to trust earned media versus advertising, even in today's environment where anti-media sentiment is strong. It's why one popular approach to advertising is to confuse people into thinking that paid advertising is actually a news story.

Second, people are much more likely to remember earned media than advertising. Think about our own lives. How many billboards do we drive by on our way home from work and don't even notice?

When it comes to American media, nearly everything is either good or bad. Listen to talk radio, watch the cable news channels, read the context of news reports. For the media, there is good and there is bad. There is almost nothing in between.

Conflict, novelty, and even scandal (whether we want it or not) can get us into the limelight. The important thing is to find a way to leverage the opportunity to deliver our message.

Use and leverage e-communications

In the 21st century, the Internet is a key medium for communication. Today's e-communications go far beyond simple websites for information. Some of the most important ways to utilize this medium as a communication tool involve web-based training, creation of self-organized work groups or teams, and provision for a collaborative platform.

One of the key advantages the Internet offers is the ability to maximize our reach and impact while minimizing our time, cost, and effort.

Select the channel based on the target audience

Matching the communication channel to the target audience is vitally important. A mass media/mass message approach is one part of a two-pronged strategy. The second part is a customized or targeted media approach.

Particularly for key audiences, we have to know where, when, and through what message and messenger the audience can be reached most successfully.

For example, one of our most significant audiences in the area of healthcare is the minority population. The elimination of minority health disparities is at the top of the list of achievements that are absolute requirements for us to consider our efforts successful. There is nothing that is more directly tied to our values, our principles, and our metrics. When it comes to reaching out to African American males on health-related issues, it turns out the major way to reach them is through their barbers. Therefore, getting information to barbers in the African American community and using them as communicators is more likely to have an impact on changing the behavior of one of our key audiences than just about anything else.

Goals and Metrics

Create a template of success

When preparing for interaction with the media, we begin by defining what success would be. We have a standard template that involves thinking through the news headline, photo, quote, sound bite, and key message we would want to have appear in the next day's newspaper. Of course, we can't control what the press will report, but the likelihood of delivering the right message and getting the story we want is much greater if we've defined success in advance.

Success
General theme
Message (three key points)
Tomorrow's headline
Photo op
Key quote
Sound bite

Define and measure the results of the call to action
- Define what you want the audience to do.
- Define and measure success.

When trying to create transformation, we always think through what we want the audience to do as a result of having heard our speech or presentation.

Whether our goal is to get the audience to join an organization, buy a book, have a health screening, or call an 800 number, we need to define that goal and tailor our message with that metric in mind. Building in an immediate action capability is useful. For example, if we are talking about the importance of blood pressure screenings, having the on-site capability for such a screening lets us know if we were successful in moving the audience to action.

The goal is to monitor the metrics we defined in order to understand what impact we had, and to use that information to determine if we should change our message.

Measure communications success, not effort
- Measure success by effectiveness, not effort or time invested.
- Think through how to measure success in the media and with public spokespeople.

In communications, as in everything else we do to drive transformation, we need to measure success in terms of effectiveness, not effort. Outcomes are what matter, not time invested.

Defining metrics of success in communications requires that we consider both our goal and our center of gravity. For example, if we are trying to accelerate seniors' adoption of the new prescription drug benefit, having an article about the benefit in the AARP magazine is likely to be much more beneficial than having a general article about Medicare in the *New York Times*. However, if we haven't considered both our goal and the center of gravity for this particular effort, we would likely see a story in the *New York Times* as a more important metric.

When trying to gain control of the House in the 1994 election, we determined that it would be necessary for us to make enough noise—and enough progress in the polls—that the story about the battle for the House would be elevated to a key news story in the final weeks prior to the election. Doing so was both a strategy for expanding awareness and excitement prior to Election Day, and a measure of how well we had done up to that point.

A few of our specific key metrics were to get the story on the cover of a magazine and to get *Time, Newsweek,* and *U.S. News & World Report* to elevate the story. In the two weeks before the election, we were on the cover of both *Time* and *Newsweek*. We did this by setting a clear metric that mattered and then managing accordingly. Our metric of success wasn't how many hours we spent with *Time* reporters. Our metric was getting a cover story.

But it's important to remember that the metric of getting specific stories in the news was a near-term metric that really only mattered if it resulted in another, longer-term metric, which was getting enough voter interest and buy-in that we won the election.

Measuring effort is often easier than measuring effectiveness, but it's not as important. What's important is effectiveness.

PART THREE

Planning and Implementing Transformation

8

Planning and Leadership Model

We use a very straightforward, learnable model of planning and leadership. It is the model we used to design the Contract with America and to create the Center for Health Transformation. It grew out of a model developed and used by the Army's Training and Doctrine Command from 1979 to 1984.

Two sets of words make up our planning and leadership model: *vision, metrics, strategies, projects, tasks* and *listen, learn, help, lead.*

Planning & Leadership Model

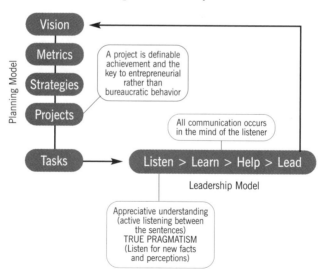

Our approach is modeled on the methods employed by General George Catlett Marshall, Army chief of staff in the Second World War, who designed the modern American military, and by Alfred Sloan who modernized General Motors in the 1920s. It also owes much to the work of Peter Drucker and W. Edwards Deming, who was the father of the quality movement. The planning model is a hierarchical system involving five levels: vision, metrics, strategies, projects, and tasks.

It should be noted that we have very recently added metrics as a distinct step in what was previously a four-step planning model. Rather than addressing metrics in the vision phase, as we did previously, we have become convinced that metrics are so vital to success that they have to be listed as a separate step.

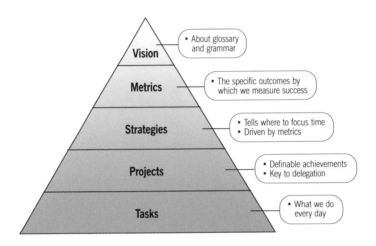

Vision
• About glossary and grammar

Metrics
• The specific outcomes by which we measure success

Strategies
• Tells where to focus time
• Driven by metrics

Projects
• Definable achievements
• Key to delegation

Tasks
• What we do every day

Vision

The first step in designing transformational change is to define our vision.

We are really defining the vision at two levels—first at the larger societal level and then back down to the level of our organization or our profession. To lead transformation, we have to define our vision of where we want our industry, the country, or the world to be ten to twenty years into the future. We then bring that vision, which we believe has to be based on improving people's lives, down to the level of what it means for our organization's vision and mission. At the organizational level, our vision should reflect that overall vision of the broader better future.

This is important for two reasons. First, no organization operates in a vacuum. It is part of a larger system and must operate within that system. Second, our overall vision has to be one of making people's lives better or we have no hope of long-term success. This means we must look out at the future landscape and define the kind of world in which people's lives will be better. Our vision will serve as our inspiration and guide to the world we want to create.

> "Good business leaders create a vision, articulate the vision, passionately own the vision, and relentlessly drive it to completion."
>
> *Jack Welch,*
> *chairman,*
> *General Electric*

A compelling vision statement should be no more than one page and ideally only a sentence or two. While there are details that will further define the statement, it is important to have an overarching vision statement that has the clarity and brevity to be remembered and repeated.

In our model we believe that our vision should also include a list of vision principles, presented in a "from-to" format. This is incredibly useful in creating a roadmap for implementing a transformational plan. Having a list of vision principles for the broader movement and our own organization, combined with a list of our values, provides a template to guide decisions as we move ahead. It helps orient new staff members and allies to what we are doing and what we believe. It defines the arguments we want to have and the arguments that aren't important. Finally, this list clarifies what we are trying to move forward, what we are trying to learn, and what is irrelevant to us. It all starts with vision, vision principles, and values.

Any new system involves learning a new glossary and grammar. The new approach has to be outlined in words that the listener or reader has to learn. Then the words are connected with a grammar that enables the new language to communicate the new vision and educate people about the new system.

Once we have outlined the vision, we have to ask a key question: If our vision is implemented, will we have achieved our goals? Will success as defined by our vision statement be enough? If yes, then we have a complete vision statement. If no, then we have to further refine our vision statement until it achieves that level of success.

Health as an Example

When it comes to health, our broader vision is of a 21st Century Intelligent Health System in which knowledge saves lives and saves money for every American. Our organizational plan at the Center for Health Transformation is that of a collaboration of leaders working and learning together to make this vision a reality.

To further define what we mean by a 21st Century Intelligent Health System, we have developed the following from-to principles. A list of vision principles, combined with a list of our values, provides a template to help guide decisions as we move forward.

Current System ➞	21st Century System
Provider-centered	Individual-centered
Price-driven	Values-driven
45 million uninsured Americans	100% coverage
Hidden price and quality information	Transparent price and quality information
Knowledge-disconnected	Knowledge-intense
Slow diffusion of innovation	Rapid diffusion of innovation
Disease-focused	Prevention and health-focused
Paper-based	Electronically based
Third party controlled market	Binary mediated market
(patient—provider—payor)	*(individual—provider)*
Limited choice	Increased choice
Punishment-driven	Incentives-pulled
Predatory trial lawyer litigation system	New system of health justice
Quantity and price measured	Quality of care and quality of life
Process-focused and administered	Metrics-led & outcomes-focused
Bureaucratic management	Collaborative leadership
Overall cost increases	Overall cost decreases

For example, one of our principles for a 21st Century Intelligent Health System is that it should be centered on the individual, as opposed to the traditional health system, which is centered on providers.

Several years ago we were engaged in a project with a number of pharmaceutical companies. We were surprised to learn how steadfastly many of them clung to the belief that they shouldn't focus on patients—that their sole focus should be on doctors because doctors prescribe the medications. We were adamant that in order to survive in the long term, they would have to change their 20th century provider-centered approach. This approach, we asserted, would profoundly damage them in the long run. The people who matter most in America are the individuals, not the doctors. In the long run, doctors will respond to the people of America, just like everybody else.

Mission

In addition to having a list of vision principles and values, we must also define our purpose. This means having a clear mission, which will help us achieve our vision. An organization that defines its own vision and mission within the broader vision and vision principles of social transformation is much more likely to change the world than one that does not.

During the Second World War, President Franklin Roosevelt and Prime Minister Winston Churchill spoke of the Four Freedoms. It was a lofty vision of a better world for people everywhere. Meanwhile, Dwight Eisenhower, as commander of the European military forces, had a mission that would help achieve that vision. It was clear and focused: we would invade the continent of Europe, defeat the German army, then occupy the German heartland. There were a lot of details, but Eisenhower got up every day knowing what he was doing.

Our mission has to be broad enough to allow us to change and grow but specific enough to define a clear purpose. It doesn't address specific products or services, but rather conveys what Drucker calls "the idea of the business." That idea becomes a part of what guides us and helps us set our course as we move toward our ideal future. Theodore Vail's idea that AT&T's business was common communications as a public service, while radical at the time, set a parameter that was broad enough to allow diverse growth but clear enough that it defined the purpose and the guidelines for that growth.

Metrics

An important part of defining where we are going is having clear metrics of how we will know when we've been successful. Metrics are the specific outcomes by which we will measure our success. They are linked to our vision and principles and help us define our strategies.

Key metrics tell us if our vision has been achieved. This is one of the important differences between metrics for reporting and metrics for leadership and management. The senior leadership's definition of the vision and of the values-defined metrics to effectively measure its achievement is an essential component of transformational leadership. Only senior leaders have the broad vision and understanding of the overall goals that enable them to define the high-level metrics that must be met for success. Below the senior leadership level, people in the organization are more focused on their specific areas and goals rather than on the broader view.

It is important, even in for-profit business ventures, that metrics address more than just financial goals. The most successful organizations have metrics related to customers, employees, and key operational indicators. Those that are truly focused on large-scale transformation also have metrics related to changes in their industry, profession, or society.

At the highest level, it's important to define the critical metrics that are most relevant to success. We have to constantly monitor them and manage according to what they tell us. There will be many other metrics at other levels throughout the organization, but at the vision level it is vital that we define the eight to ten metrics that really matter and monitor them vigilantly, making changes as needed.

The most critical metrics are related to outcomes, not inputs. Measuring how much we spend on something is not as important as measuring the return on investment. One problem with government is that it looks only at initial outlays, rather than focusing on outcomes or return on investment. Not only does this lead to the tendency to continue to fund unsuccessful programs, but it also makes it difficult to get funding for new, transformational solutions. An important rule of thumb is: measure what matters, not what is easy.

In thinking about metrics, it is vitally important to distinguish between data and useful knowledge. Most organizations collect a lot of data, but it is not analyzed and designed to be actionable or to provide effective knowledge for senior leadership. Metrics for transformational leadership are much different from the bureaucratic use of the term, which typically involves lots of data that is neither timely nor actionable.

Finally, the metrics of success that we define at the highest level should be used as a template to help set metrics at the project and individual level. Metrics at the subordinate levels must reinforce and contribute to the overall metrics.

We believe that metrics are so critical to creating change that we have devoted an entire chapter to this topic later in the book.

Focusing on Metrics That Matter: The Billy Beane Model

People often pay attention to metrics and statistics that don't really matter. On the other hand, Billy Beane, general manager of the Oakland Athletics, uses statistics to create the most cost-effective team in baseball. The Oakland As have the most wins per dollar spent of any major-league baseball team, and Beane has accomplished that by objectively focusing on the metrics statistically proven to increase the likelihood of winning. For example, on-base percentage, which includes the ability to draw walks, is more important than the things baseball scouts typically look for, like speed and power.

Beane has managed to build an effective and efficient team by using metrics to do three things: (1) select players that possess personal statistics most likely to lead to scoring, rather than players who simply look like players; (2) find players who are undervalued assets; and (3) manage the way the team plays the game, which generally means focusing on things that other teams usually don't, like drawing walks whenever possible, not trying to steal bases, and having the discipline not to go after a pitch out of the strike zone.

It's a fascinating success story told brilliantly by Michael Lewis in the book *Moneyball*. But more than that, it's a compelling model of how to define metrics that truly lead to success.

Strategies

In order to achieve our vision, we have to define the key strategies or bridges that will take us from where we are today to the ideal future we have described in our vision. The strategies, thus defined, tell us where to focus our time and are driven by metrics.

As we go through the planning process, we compare the metrics and vision principles of where we want to be to the metrics and vision principles of where we are now, then set strategies to close that gap.

Strategies should leverage internal strengths, unique capabilities, and external opportunities, while shoring up or minimizing the impact of internal weaknesses and turning external threats into opportunities. This requires us to have intelligence about both our internal status and the external environment. Our strategies will be only as good as the accuracy of our intelligence, the soundness of our principles, and the wisdom of our analysis. The objective in setting strategies is to leverage major opportunities that also fit the unique capabilities and resources that we have or plan to acquire.

Great leaders—people like Alfred Sloan of General Motors or General George Catlett Marshall in World War II—understand that big, complex systems are moved only by setting clear strategies and metrics.

There are two tests for strategies. First, if we implemented every single strategy we have listed, would we achieve our vision? If the answer is no, then we are missing some strategies and we need to add those. If the answer is yes, we must examine each strategy to see if we could achieve our vision without them. The reason for this is that people often do things out of habit. It is not unusual for people to have extra but unnecessary strategies simply because they like them. In the modern world the scale of change is so rapid and the pressures so great that it is difficult to succeed while carrying out strategies that don't make sense in terms of our overall vision.

One historic example of this occurred during the British army's attempt to solve the huge manpower crisis after Dunkirk. They had evacuated the continent in 1940 and were desperate for manpower. In analyzing the assignment of resources, they began looking at their model of having five people serve each artillery piece. Four of the people, they noticed, had specific work to do, but the fifth stood at attention at the back of the gun. They soon realized that the role of the fifth person had initially been to hold the horse that pulled the artillery and prevent it from bolting. When the army shifted to trucks and got rid of horses, no one checked the personnel assignment list, so the fifth person was never removed from the artillery team, but instead continued to stand behind the artillery, in essence holding an imaginary horse. It is amazing how many organizations today have horse-holders long after they've lost the horse.

In addition to ensuring that we have the right strategies, it's essential that we write them down, along with our vision and metrics. And it is also very important to review each of them with our team to make sure that they understand where we are going and how we plan to get there.

The Salisbury Conference:
An Example of Vision, Mission, and Strategies

In January 1994, the House Republicans gathered in Salisbury, Maryland, for a weekend retreat. Out of that gathering came a document known as the "Salisbury Statement." It became the common understanding that drew the House Republicans together and allowed us to operate as a team within the same visionary and strategic framework. A few months later, that document would lead to a project known as the Contract with America and, later that year, to the Republicans winning control of the House of Representatives for the first time in forty years—in what became known as the Republican Revolution of 1994.

Vision: To renew the American dream by promoting individual liberty, economic opportunity, and personal responsibility through limited and effective government, high standards of performance, and an America strong enough to defend all its citizens at home or abroad.

Mission: As House Republicans, we will work together to offer representative governance and to communicate our vision of America through clearly defined themes, programs, and legislative initiatives to earn us the honor of becoming the majority party in January 1995.

Strategies:
1. Propose specific legislative initiatives implementing our vision of a renewed American dream.
2. Challenge the Democratic leadership's agenda when it undermines the American dream or reinforces the welfare stare or fails to offer needed changes.
3. Successfully market a manageable number of key themes and solutions.
4. Build relationships with all potential allies supportive of our goals.
5. Create an internal culture that promotes the initiative and creativity of individual members, so entrepreneurship becomes the norm.
6. Working together as a team, House Republicans should focus our efforts on the activities that will secure a House Republican majority in the 1994 elections.

Projects

Strategies cannot be implemented by visionaries unless they can be turned into projects and turned over to managers who run decentralized operations. For example, General Marshall delegated enormous power to people like Dwight D. Eisenhower. Marshall controlled the strategy of global war-fighting but knew that individual leaders had to have command of each project—even if the project was as big as the Normandy invasion.

A project is a definable, delegatable achievement. It is a tangible assignment that has its own vision, metrics, strategies, subprojects, and tasks. Projects are key to running high-tempo large systems and the key to large-scale change. At the Center for Health Transformation, we get an amazing amount done with a very small organization, and the term "project" is part of our success.

Projects must have definable goals and clear metrics that help fulfill the overall organizational goals—if the financial metric is one million dollars, each of our projects should contribute to reaching that metric. Every project must have metrics, timelines, and monitoring. The old adage that people do what you inspect, not what you expect, is absolutely critical.

This is the heart of what Mayor Rudy Giuliani did with his crime reporting system that so dramatically decreased crime in New York. Working with police chief Bill Bratton, he built a metrics system (CompStat, for "computer statistics") that was so clear that he could get up every morning and look at the report, call various precinct stations, and say, "I noticed that 'x' happened last night, tell me about it." All of a sudden every precinct house in the city had the sense that the mayor was personally watching what was going on.

This model, which we will discuss in much more detail in Chapter Twelve, was imported by Karl Rove and Ken Mehlman to monitor and manage the 2004 Bush-Cheney re-election campaign. They created a metrics-driven model of managing what they considered critical achievements that would result in re-election. They constantly monitored metrics related to those achievements at outposts around the country to determine what was working and what was not. When the metrics were not being met, they intervened immediately to find out

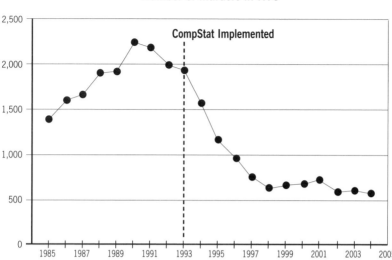

Number of Murders in NYC

why and made immediate changes.

The metrics for projects must roll into the overall metrics, so that every project is adding to the accomplishment of our overall metrics. Failure to do this will result in a series of disconnected projects that may be totally unrelated to achieving our vision.

Unfortunately, the model we're describing has not been widely adopted by government. Not long ago we met with a key government official to learn about the results of a healthcare program. She told us how many people they were serving, the size of their staff, and how many new sites they had acquired. When we clarified that we were interested in learning about the return on investment related to improved health and to the overall financial savings that should be resulting from avoiding costly health complications, she didn't have a clue. Her systems were not asking the right questions and were not designed to get answers that mattered.

This is an example of what's wrong with government and why it's so hard to implement change there. When making decisions, the tendency of the government is to focus only on the budgetary outlay. The failure to establish and monitor metrics related to health and overall financial savings prevents intelligent decision-making about what we should and should not be spending our money on. The government focuses on inputs when it should be measuring outputs, and emphasizes processes when it should be emphasizing achievements. The result is that we continue to support 20th century programs that aren't working rather than investing in 21st century solutions that can save lives and save money.

At the Center for Health Transformation, we constantly seek out new solutions that have proven results related to better health at lower cost and share those with the government and with other leaders to demonstrate that there is a better way. We are also working to transform the way that government scoring is done. In essence, our goal is to shift the government toward a project focus, in which "project" means a definable, delegatable achievement with very clear metrics of success.

One last point: in delegating projects, the less you ask people to do that is new, the more you can delegate without instruction. Delegation does not mean abdication. If it is an area where people have little expertise, we have to spend a considerable amount of time supervising them until they learn how to do it. But the long-term goal is to be surrounded by people who so thoroughly understand how we do things that when we assign a project, we seldom think about it again because that person can just get it done. It's the secret to creating a very high-tempo organization.

Tasks

The fourth level is tasks—what we do every day. We divide tasks into two categories: first, project tasks that are connected to a specific project, and second, tasks that are daily habits related to the culture, doctrine, and values of the organization.

Project Tasks

All team members should be focused on daily and weekly activities and metrics that relate to the completion of a project. This project should help implement one or more strategies, which in turn help fulfill the organization's vision and overall metrics. Breaking projects into tasks and then monitoring and rewarding the completion of those tasks is how we ensure that the projects we launch are getting done. In addition, most successful political campaigns know that constant reinforcement of the connection between what team members do each day and the broader vision is essential to engendering and sustaining passion and commitment. This creates extraordinary teams that help build a transformational movement.

The impact of this approach was seen perhaps nowhere more dramatically than in World War II under the leadership of General Marshall, who insisted on keeping his troops aware of the big picture. From experience he knew that Americans were very poor at taking orders but would fight better than anyone if they understood why they were fighting. He recruited Oscar-winning director Frank Capra to make a series of films called *Why We Fight*. The series became an award-winning model of effective communication. It brilliantly focused on the values that were at stake in defeating the Nazis, Fascists, and Imperial Japanese. The result of having the American Army aware of the big picture was that the soldiers became a much more committed and powerful force than the German army, even though the German army had been fighting for a longer time and was by training a more professional army.

Habits

There are certain routine behaviors so central to an organization's success that they need to be ingrained in what every member of the team does every day. They are not related to just one project, but rather are taught and adopted as "the way we do things." While project-related tasks are generally set at the operational level and occur as part of the implementation of a specific project, habits tend to be more universal within the organization and should be reflective of overall values and principles.

For example, a student of ballet learns a series of steps and moves related to dancing a specific ballet. These are project-related tasks. She also performs certain routine daily tasks that are part of the profession of a ballerina, such as practicing every day. These are what we mean by habits.

The Leadership Model

Defining our vision, metrics, strategies, projects, and tasks will accomplish little if we don't have people to make them real. We have to listen, learn, help, and lead.

There is a sharp difference between the five words for planning and the four words for leadership. Planning is a hierarchy: vision defines metrics and strategies, strategies define projects, projects define tasks. However, the four words that make up our leadership model are not a hierarchy. They are each equally important but must occur in a specific order.

Listen. We try to always start meetings—with those we want as allies, or with those who are seeking our advice or involvement, or even with those with whom we disagree—by listening, not talking. There are three reasons for this. First, our goal is not to sell the other person, even a prospective customer, on something that isn't what they need or want, so it is critical to first understand their reality. Second, by listening we can learn critical information that may give us new insight. We have had many meetings with prospective customers or allies that didn't result in revenue or an immediate alliance but that enriched our understanding and improved our plans so much that the meeting was every bit as valuable as one that led to immediate agreement or buy-in. Third, by placing the other person at the center of the meeting, we assume a role that, if nothing else, is transactionally helpful to someone who simply wants to be heard.

Learn. We added the word "learn" after the word "listen," because Americans do two things they confuse with listening. The first is standing at a cocktail party in boredom, eyes glazed over, while someone else babbles. This is called patience—it doesn't involve listening. In fact, if we can learn to get people to talk about things we don't know, we can change the cocktail babble into a useful conversation and resume listening.

The second thing people do is make a presentation and, as the other person starts to answer, focus their attention on how to improve their own pitch once they get the floor again. This, also, isn't listening—this is called cheating.

One way to ensure that we are listening is to keep asking the other person questions until we understand what they are saying and appreciate why it makes sense to them. This doesn't mean that we have to sympathize or agree, but it is very important to discipline ourselves to listen to them as they explain what they believe until we thoroughly understand it.

This does two things. First, it creates what consultants call appreciative understanding. We gain a better understanding of the person we're trying to deal with. We know what motivates them, we know what their problems are, we become more capable of solving their problems. If we listen long enough, we can appreciate why they feel the way they do. This does not mean we have to agree or support them. It does mean we have to have an "appreciative understanding" of what they are trying to accomplish. Second, listening helps us be in touch with facts or realities we may not have known previously. It is also important to listen comprehensively because we are trying to learn the context that gives the facts meaning. The leader who listens systematically simply has a much broader base of facts and is in closer touch with reality when designing policies and strategies.

Listening is just as important when dealing with members of our own team. Poor communication strikes at the heart of the process used to make decisions and can tear the team apart. Communication is the necessary precedent to collaboration. Lack of communication leads to inefficiency, wasted time, miscarried plans, false assumptions, and disagreement. To avoid this, the model of listening we use at the Center is based on what is known in the military as the Commander's Intent. It includes the following steps:

- Listen to the directions.
- Repeat the directions.
- Receive immediate correction of any misunderstanding.
- Recycle until absolute clarity and agreement exist.

Remember: we don't really know what the other person is saying unless we can repeat it.

Help. If we listen to people systematically and truly learn from them, we almost always help them. At the very least, having someone listen can in itself be helpful. In addition, it often happens that we have information that can help the other person, including information that can increase their understanding of a situation and correct erroneous assumptions. Best of all, we often find that there are tangible ways we can help.

Listening is particularly important as we go through large-scale change. We have to go slower at the human level so we can go faster at the technical level. It takes time to get people to understand and then decide to invest in supporting what we are doing.

Lead. If we listen to people, learn from them, and find a way to help them, they'll almost always ask us to lead. When they ask us to lead, we promptly go back to our planning model, sharing with them details of our vision, metrics, strategies, projects, and tasks. We then go right back to them and ask what they think. Note that the areas in the leadership chart at the beginning of this chapter form a cybernetic feedback loop in which the acts of listening, learning, helping, and leading lead you to describe your vision, metrics, strategies, projects, and tasks. This leads right back to listening.

By doing this, we turn every person we meet, every customer, and everyone in our organization into a consultant. We have given them permission to enrich our plans by giving us new and often better ideas.

Think about the difference. An organization that consistently—with its customers, its suppliers, and its own people—goes through this nine-word loop has an enormous capacity to gain energy and intelligence because it is constantly recruiting every single person to help improve the process. In addition, since people tend to support things they help create, having their input during the planning and creation phase helps ensure their buy-in and commitment later.

One final note. If communication is built on the listen, learn, help, lead model, the outcome is not always agreement. Effective organizations have to have someone who finally decides, and the decision has to be implemented successfully. However, the model does ensure that we achieve either "understood agreement" or "understood disagreement," rather than the "misunderstood agreement" and "misunderstood disagreement" that often characterize the old model. The result is a much more informed leadership that usually leads to much greater collaboration and support.

9

A 21st Century Implemention Model

The most difficult part of transformation is not designing a plan, but implementing it. Ninety percent of the time and energy invested in transformation will be spent on implementation.

It has been said that if we don't know where we are going, we won't know when we get there. A plan helps us know where we are going and recognize when we have arrived. However, our chances of getting there are virtually nonexistent if we don't implement our plan. It's an important corollary that is too often forgotten.

Failing to implement our plan is like planning a trip but never going, or drawing up blueprints for a house but never building it. The plan is irrelevant if it's not implemented.

In addition to managing what exists, the transformational leader is also creating the future. The implementation of that plan for the future will be much less orderly and predictable than a plan for managing and maintaining the daily activities of an existing business or organization. We would argue that every organization in the 21st century will have to do a mixture of both in order to succeed.

Our strategic plan sets our direction, but events and situations beyond our control will present opportunities and challenges that will impact its implementation. Some of these will be the result of our own activities. As we interact with the world to implement our plan, what we do will sometimes have unexpected consequences, including more rapid or more dramatic change than we had anticipated. Some of the external changes that will require us to alter our plan will result from its implementation.

There are three important things to recognize when it comes to implementing a plan for transformation:

1. The plan is a direction, not a rigid structure. Vision is certain; strategies are enduring; projects are relatively stable; tasks or tactics are fluid.

2. Change will not be predictable or linear, but will be uneven and interdependent. Small changes in one industry or area will produce complex and often disproportionate effects, including in seemingly unrelated industries or areas. One consequence is that many of our plans or projects will be rendered obsolete even as we are developing them.

3. When it comes to transformation, we are almost always simultaneously creating a movement and managing an organization. The two are very different. A movement is organic, constantly evolving. Movements involve a lot of voluntary activity, a lot of coordinated activities, and in some cases a lot of uncoordinated activities. Organizations, by contrast, are orderly, structured, accountable, and manageable. At the heart of most effective movements is an organization. The art is to recognize that both patterns have to be working within their appropriate zones to have successful large-scale transformation.

Leading Transformational Movements

Movements are not orderly activities that can be managed. As the title of this book suggests, leading a transformation is more art than science.

We can't really manage a movement; we can only encourage it. Rather than a disciplined march on a well-defined course, transformation involves a migration in a certain direction. Think of bees swarming in the same direction, with each bee engaged in its own dance.

Look again at our model of 21st century transformation:

We aren't making a sudden leap to the 21st century system. Rather, we are migrating there. Not only are we inventing new solutions, but we are also keeping and improving the existing solutions that fit into the 21st century system and letting go of those that do not.

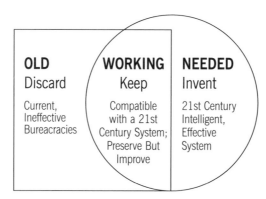

(With thanks to Senator Bob Kerrey for helping to develop this model)
©2006 Center for Health Transformation

The coherence and structure that must be present in an organization are impossible to maintain throughout the movement at large. However, at the same time, the organizations that are leading the movement and exist inside it have to be structured and coherent. Furthermore, as the movement gains momentum, additional projects, businesses, and organizations will be created that will also have a structure and coherence not found in the movement at large.

The rapidly changing environment of the Age of Transformation puts almost every 21st century leader in the role of managing an organization and leading a movement that is transforming society. This is demonstrated by the increasing use by companies of the triple-bottom line, where social responsibility is an essential ingredient of the business.

While the level and the constancy of change in the 21st century are such that transformation of society is everyone's business, the sense of social responsibility is more than just a 21st century phenomenon. It is part of the fabric of America; it is at the core of American values and at the heart of transformational leadership throughout our history.

When Thomas Edison invented the electric light and when Henry Ford invented the assembly line, each had a vision of transforming American society and improving the lives of everyday Americans. When Theodore Vail led AT&T, his central focus was the belief that every American should have a telephone, not just the very rich.

Improving the lives of ordinary people and doing well by doing good are at the heart of American entrepreneurialism.

Indeed, from the founding of Jamestown in 1607; to Benjamin Franklin's invention of bifocal glasses, the Franklin stove, and the lightning rod; to Andrew Carnegie's construction of more than 2,100 public libraries; to Bill Gates and Steve Jobs's dramatic innovations in information technology, there has been a long and continuing tradition of people being involved voluntarily and independently in trying to make America a better place for their children and grandchildren.

Migrating the society, a culture, or an industry to a dramatically different future and building alliances and coalitions to create that future requires transformational leadership skills and habits that are quite different from what would be expected of a manager overseeing the day-to-day operation of a static organization.

Today's leaders must understand and help create the transformation of society or of their industries if they are to not only fulfill the promise of America, but also lead and transform their own organizations in a way that will make them successful in the world of the future.

Four Levels of Transformation

When implementing a plan, we have to recognize that change will constantly be happening at four levels:

1. The individual
2. The organization or institution
3. The culture or society
4. Science, which dramatically changes everything

These are not sequential or separate levels. Instead, changes at the four levels happen simultaneously, and changes at one level are caused by changes at the other levels.

We have to be aware of the changes and the opportunities that surface at each level so that we can quickly move from one level to another to leverage the greatest opportunities for impact.

Transformational Change as a Migration Toward a Better Future Rather Than a Leap or an Organized March

Our goal is to migrate a constantly growing group of people and organizations in the same direction, knowing that there will be many different levels of focus and buy-in. This requires always creating a sense of urgency, communicating the vision of a better future, and accelerating people's awareness of, support for, and adoption of specific policies and solutions that move toward the future we envision. Many of our allies will not support all our strategies or officially be part of our organization or alliance, but we want them to understand and believe in where we are going and support and adopt the solutions that matter to them.

At the same time, we also need a growing number of key allies as well as internal and external leaders who are committed to the plan at a level that is beyond just moving in the same direction. This will be the group that provides leadership as the migration grows. This group has to have a much greater level of cohesiveness, integration, networking, and formal structure than the larger, more loosely connected group. Whether this group is working together on the broader movement, on changing an organization or industry, or on a shared project, their ability to use 21st century principles and habits to help lead the migration will dictate its success.

Implementation: The Plan and Principles in Action

To implement a plan, we must have an organization or alliance dedicated to it. Successful implementation must be integrated. Every leader in the organization or alliance must function as part of a system, working together for the overall objective of the whole.

Implementing a plan for transformation requires us to be aware of, responsive to, and involved in the creation of continuous change. This means that our structures have to be flexible and leadership must be decentralized. Our goal is not to create stronger centralized command and control structures but to relax them, allowing team members to react fluidly to a changing landscape.

One of our defining principles of implementation is to centralize metrics while we decentralize implementation. We want to build a team that is able to improvise in tandem toward a set of mutual goals while not requiring explicit orders to do so. In essence, this allows every member of the team to be a leader.

A 21st century team must be agile and able to maneuver within the changing landscape, but do so in a way that moves us in the right direction, reflects our overall culture, and focuses on the metrics of success we've defined. The goal is to have a team that is not guided by close management and explicit orders but by an understanding of our strategic plan and of the metrics that are being monitored and used as our primary tool of management.

We have to define values, vision, and metrics at the top but empower and liberate people to lead at their own levels. Doing it well is a real art. Some people believe only the top leadership knows what to do, and so they over-control. Others believe you have to delegate so decisively that they abdicate responsibility. Both are destructive.

It is the duty of the senior leadership to have a vision for the organization, a set of values, and a system of metrics for measuring whether the organization is meeting that vision and fulfilling those values. The senior leadership has to recruit competent people; communicate the vision, values, and metrics; and monitor the metrics to make sure the goals are being achieved.

The senior leadership should meet regularly with subordinate leaders to evaluate successes and failures, identify best practices, identify new solutions, and plan for continuous improvement. Subordinate leaders have an obligation to understand their senior leadership's intent; to understand the vision, values, and metrics; and then to lead aggressively on their own.

The key to success is remembering that in large, complex activities there have to be echelons of responsibility. The right person at each level has to have the authority and responsibility necessary to lead, be creative, solve problems, and develop opportunities at that level. The speed of the modern world means that in a well-educated and well-led organization, there will always be a bias toward sins of commission rather than sins of omission. Good leaders will encourage their subordinates to exercise their authority creatively and aggressively.

The Strategic Plan as a Guiding Framework

Even as the strategic plan evolves, it provides the framework within which a team can function in a decentralized leadership approach. There are seven elements of the plan that provide the shared understanding necessary for decentralized decision-making and leadership.

Vision. It is imperative that everyone on the team understands and buys into the vision. The vision is the primary bond uniting our team and our key allies. It is also how we are able to distinguish progress from activity. As we make decisions on a daily basis, we have to do so with our vision in mind. We have to look deep first, then mid, and then near. This approach during implementation and planning is the only way an organization can function in an integrated system toward a common goal.

Vision principles. The from-to list of vision principles helps define specifically how the future we are building is different from the current environment. It provides an important tool for us as we confront opportunities and decisions on a daily basis, giving us a template for making decisions and solving problems independently but within an understood transformational framework.

Values. The shared values that define us add a further level of cohesive clarity to our organization. Our values provide a moral compass by which, in the midst of constant change, we measure the "rightness" of our decisions. They help us determine whether, based on our core beliefs and moral values, a decision is the right one. They also help us determine whether potential team members, allies, or partners represent a good fit. While we may have partners or allies who disagree with some elements of our plan, a strong difference in values makes a close alliance nearly impossible. As many unsuccessful mergers have demonstrated, combining two organizations that have vastly different values is more likely to lead to discord and distrust than to a happy and successful union.

Metrics. It is important that members of the team understand the key metrics that define success for the entire organization or effort, as well as those metrics for which they are directly responsible. They must also receive constant and current feedback about whether the metrics are being met.

Strategies. While not all members of the team or all of our allies will be involved with every one of our strategies, we want them to be aware of what our strategies are and of the principles which led to those strategies. This is important because we want their projects to satisfy as many strategies as possible, which is likely to happen only if they know what they are. In addition, since our strategies will change and evolve, we want our team to be involved in suggesting new ones that we should add, and in letting us know when existing strategies need to be modified or re-prioritized.

Projects. Projects are the primary building blocks of change and are key to implementation success. Each member of the team should know what projects he or she owns, what specific outcomes and timelines are expected, and what are the metrics of success.

Strategies at the highest level are broken down into projects, each of which is assigned to a leader at the preceding level. That leader, after understanding the achievement expected, creates a plan for the project, which involves a vision (consistent with the overall vision), metrics (which feed into the organization's overall metrics), strategies for fulfilling the vision, and then projects and tasks that are assigned to individuals on his or her team. Those individuals in turn create a project plan and assign sub-projects to individuals within their team, and so forth, cascading down the organization.

While we want every team member to understand how his or her project fits within the vision and strategies of the overall organization, each person must have specific accountability for the projects. At every level, what is expected and when it is expected are clearly defined and monitored. Success at the higher levels becomes dependent upon the completion of projects at the levels below.

Habits. A successful 21st century team must acquire and practice habits that govern how the team operates on a daily basis. While some of these are specific to the organization, there are also habits and traits that almost any individual in the Age of Transformation should possess. This book is designed as a primer to help the reader understand the principles underlying those habits and then develop the skills that will allow them to practice those habits.

21st Century Leadership and Management During Implementation

When implementing the plan, we need to constantly monitor what's happening both internally and externally and then adapt accordingly.

Internally, the constant monitoring of metrics allows us to quickly recognize when implementation is not working. If metrics are not being met and projects are not completed according to specifications, we need to ask seven key questions:

1. Do the people responsible for the failed projects and metrics understand the expectations and metrics? If not, we need to make sure that they are clearly defined and communicated.

2. Do people have the expertise and knowledge required? If not, we need to train them.

3. Do they have the resources and tools they need, including people resources, IT tools, access to knowledge resources (including senior people who can provide guidance), and the time needed? If not, we need to provide them with those resources, or, if we can't provide the resources, we need to simplify or narrow the scope of the project.

4. Do they have the power and authority to do the project they've been given? Assigning a project to someone but not giving them the decision-making power to complete it (assuming they understand the parameters) sets up a no-win situation. If we put an ambitious timeline in place but then require an approval chain that slows the process, we need to understand that either our timeline or our approval process needs to change. (Note that a project for a new, less-experienced team member is likely to be much smaller and less complex than what we would assign to a more experienced team member who understands our doctrine and "way of doing business.")

5. Do we have the right incentives in place? If not, we need to take steps to tie incentives to the metrics people achieve. When undergoing major transformation, it is important that every team member understand not only the metrics, but that they have a personal stake in reaching those metrics.

6. Is there a systems or process problem outside their control that is interfering with their success? It's important to look at what parts of the system or what processes within the system impact their ability to succeed. For example, if we assign a certain sales quota to an on-site sales team but the supply chain has not stocked the shelves, the sales team will fail. It's an example of why systems thinking and process engineering is so important. Making sure that we get to the root cause is vital, because making changes at the point of break-down, rather than dealing with the root cause, will make the problem worse in the long run.

7. Is the project or assignment actually doable? If we keep assigning a project to new people but it continues to be a failure, we need to question whether it's possible, at least within the current parameters and scope. The options are to either break the project down into smaller projects, or, if it's not vital to our success, abandon it.

If we are sure that a project is doable and that the necessary resources, training, incentives, and authority exist but the metrics are still not being met, it's time to replace the current person with some-one who will get it done. If we lack the courage or the will to make the tough decisions, we're wasting our time. The purpose of gathering metrics is to force real change, not to simply produce reports.

Finally, if our individual projects are successful but we are not reach-ing our overall goals, we need to re-examine whether we have the right strategies and projects in place, including within the context of changes in the external environment. To manage our resources for maximum impact, we have to constantly leverage external opportu-nities and consider their fit with—and impact on—our strategic plan. Being so internally focused or so rigidly tied to a plan of action that we fail to respond to new opportunities, new crises, or new changes is as problematic as totally ignoring our plan.

While implementing the plan, we have to constantly re-evaluate our priorities within the external context. The vision, metrics, and strate-gies that are in our plan have to govern what we do. However, it's important to remember that the plan is a direction, not a rigid struc-ture. To reiterate: vision is certain; strategies are enduring; tasks or tactics are fluid.

While our strategies can change and our tasks are fluid, diverting resources away from existing strategies or key projects to new ones has to be reflected in an update of the plan. In most cases such changes will require a shift of resources away from something we are already doing and will most likely require that we abandon other projects, possibly change our metrics, or perhaps put other strategies on the back burner unless we simultaneously find resources to handle the new priorities. Failing to adjust our plan to reflect key changes renders the plan irrelevant and creates chaos and confusion that can drown an organization.

While we want operational flexibility and tactical fluidity, there has to be a guiding document or plan that defines us and brings us together through a shared vision, common priorities, and well-defined goals and metrics. When the plan changes, it has to be a conscious decision and one that is made with full understanding of the consequences and the trade-offs involved.

A Culture of Transformation

Implementing a plan does not happen in a vacuum—it happens within a culture. The shared beliefs, values, habits, and behaviors that we practice and transmit to others create an environment that will either stifle or accelerate transformation. Any plan, no matter how visionary, is irrelevant unless it is implemented. While the plan will change and evolve throughout implementation, it provides a framework and shared understanding that allows a team to function as a system working toward the same objectives. In the next chapter we will examine some of the key attributes of an organization that maximizes its ability to successfully implement the plan while also creating a culture that is able to respond to and shape the ever-changing landscape of today's world.

10

Key 21st Century Implementation
Principles and Processes

Transformation in the 21st century requires a different type of implementation than we typically saw in the 20th century. Rather than strong, centralized control, we need a culture in which all members of the team are leaders in their own right, working toward a common goal but empowered and trained to maneuver and improvise to reach that goal.

This requires that our team be able to function more as a jazz band than an orchestra. They have to understand the overall goal our organization is trying to achieve, and be able to combine the new knowledge they gain and the team doctrine they've learned with their own unique strengths to improvise in tandem in order to enrich the performance of the team.

The plan helps the team understand where our organization wants to go, what is important to us, and the way we do business. The principles and lessons covered earlier in this book can be distilled into eight key components that define the structures and the culture 21st century organizations must possess if they are to excel at implementation and execution. These attributes maximize a team's ability to effectively and successfully maneuver within an environment of constant change:

1. A metrics-driven system
2. Rapid, intelligence-based decision-making
3. Constant learning and knowledge management
4. Collaboration and coalition-building
5. Constant, effective communication
6. Continuous innovation and improvement
7. Agile, networked teams
8. A culture of shared purpose, engagement, and fun

21st Century Implementation Key Number One:
A Metrics-Driven System

Having the entire team focused on the overall metrics of success—and then on the specific metrics for which each person is responsible—is critical to creating an effective 21st century organization.

Implementation of the CompStat system (which we discussed earlier and will come back to again later in the book) resulted in New York City, once the most dangerous large city in America, becoming one of the safest. The success of that model rests on five basic principles:

1. **Specific objectives,** involving setting very specific crime reduction objectives focused on outcomes, not processes.
2. **Timely and accurate intelligence,** involving gathering and analyzing data about crime hot spots and crime patterns daily or at the very least weekly.
3. **Effective strategies and tactics,** involving members of all ranks and levels offering suggestions and solutions that help create the strategies and tactical plan.
4. **Rapid deployment of personnel and resources,** involving the rapid deployment of an array of resources to enact a tactical plan immediately after it has been developed.
5. **Relentless follow-up and assessment** on the results of tactical plans, involving semiweekly meetings with commanders to review progress, rapid replacement of failed tactics, and rapid replication of successful tactics.

The CompStat model is applicable far beyond police operations. By setting up a system with these five components, any organization can create a metrics-driven approach to leadership capable of yielding dramatically improved results.

While outcome metrics are the key metrics of success, processes cannot be totally ignored. We have to have processes in place that are tied to how we plan to change the outcome metrics. If we are successful, we want to have a record of what we did, so we can replicate it. If we are unsuccessful, the record will keep us from replicating what failed. And even with successful processes, we want the entire team focused on how we can constantly improve them.

Outcome metrics are the only way to measure success. However, we also need to know the processes that got us there if we are to repeat our success. This is particularly important as we train new members of the team who are not yet capable of the instinctive maneuvering and improvisation that often characterize the behavior of the more seasoned and expert members of the team.

The important thing is to understand that success is not measured by showing that we completed certain processes. The only way to measure success is through measuring the outcomes.

Tying incentives to metrics is a key strategy for getting our team and others we're trying to change focused on what we want to accomplish. Assigning projects with clear goals and metrics and then tying financial and other rewards to the attainment of those goals can dramatically impact success and create very high-tempo teams. The importance of metrics-led leadership is so central to the art of transformation that we devote an entire chapter later in the book (Chapter Twelve) to this subject.

21st Century Implementation Key Number Two: Exceptional Intelligence-Gathering and Rapid Decision-Making

As the CompStat model demonstrates, while implementing a plan, we must constantly monitor changes in the external environment and then respond very quickly in order to exploit the sudden opportunities—or address the sudden challenges—that arise. This is not only required of senior leadership in strategizing for the overall organization, but also must be part of the skill set possessed by teams on the front line.

We want each member of the team to be able to strategically maneuver. To understand the essence of strategic maneuvering, it is helpful to look at how the military conducts itself when engaged in maneuver warfare. Maneuver warfare is the opposite of attrition warfare, which typically involves moving massive amounts of forces and materials to enemy strongpoints. The goal is to destroy enemy forces until they can no longer fight. Attrition warfare tends to utilize centralized command structures and to require little creativity from lower-level leaders.

Maneuver warfare, on the other hand, advocates quick strategic movement to exploit enemy weaknesses or sudden opportunities. As we saw in Desert Storm, bypassing and cutting off enemy strong-points through strategic movement often causes their collapse while minimizing physical damage or the number of deaths.

Tempo and initiative are critical to the success of maneuver warfare. Therefore, the command structures tend to be more decentralized, and lower-level leaders are given more tactical freedom. This decentralized structure is one in which leaders on the front lines are empowered to exploit opportunities as they arise, always working within the commander's overall vision.

We want a maneuver-style culture within our organization, allowing our teams to be able to move quickly to leverage sudden opportunities and dramatically expand our impact with minimal expenditure of resources or effort. All team members must be trained and empowered to constantly assess the environment so that they can modify their actions to improve their performance. This is always, of course, within the context of the vision.

In addition, what those on the front lines learn should bubble up to the leadership and impact decisions made regarding overall organizational strategies. Every team member should serve in the role of scout, systematically adding to the intelligence base of the entire team.

Understanding what to look for and what really matters is critical to intelligence success. This goes back to the principle of focusing on our antelope. Knowing our strategies and key metrics provides a framework for intelligence gathering. It allows each member of the team to know what matters and to build a network of key contacts who can provide them with the information they need.

One area of intelligence gathering that every 21st century team should pursue is the emergence of new technologies and discoveries, even outside one's industry or discipline, that have the potential of decisively changing the world or impacting the assumed trajectory of change. The non-linear nature of change in the 21st century means that even small science or technology developments can have monumental consequences. Therefore, we want every member of our team reporting back on what they're seeing and learning that may impact our future plans.

At the Center for Health Transformation, as we try to drive transformation of the health and healthcare system, we are constantly scanning for and focusing on three things: first, important transformational solutions and best current practices (noting that practices will constantly be evolving); second, places of greatest need so we know where best practices and new solutions should be applied; and third, places of greatest willingness for change, so we know where we are most likely to effect the adoption of practices and solutions

Moving to the sound of the guns during implementation

Intelligence gathering adds little value if we don't use the information we gather to our advantage. As we touched on in an earlier chapter, transformational leaders must move to the sound of the guns, which means figuring out the most vital place they can make a difference and moving to that point. One aspect of this is being able to immediately recognize the presence of a crisis, since the greatest opportunity for change exists at times of crisis, and then being able to quickly move to that crisis. Moving to the sound of the guns requires that we
- are externally rather than internally oriented, so we can hear the guns;
- understand our antelope so we know if the guns are worth hearing;
- think through our deep-mid-near goals so we know which guns to respond to and what to do within the context of our strategic priorities.

Moving to the sound of the guns is an important implementation principle because leaders can have maximum impact by bringing their knowledge, power, and moral force to bear at the decisive moment. The CompStat model is a stunning example of this. Through constantly defining hot spots of crime, the police department can immediately deploy resources to the most critical areas, allowing them to apply their force when and where criminal activity is most intense.

While we need to have our vision and overall objectives firmly in place, it's important to possess the tactical flexibility, agility, and rapid OODA loop capability that lets us take advantage of unexpected opportunities.

While engaging in rapid decision-making provides a valuable competitive advantage, the quality of the decision-making is also a factor—making bad decisions fast is not the goal. The art lies in being able to make the right decisions efficiently and implementing them quickly. A key factor in doing this is being able to determine the minimum amount of information needed to make a good decision, since all time beyond that is wasted. Our level of certainty increases up to a point, as we take more time to gather and analyze the information (though that is probably becoming less true in a world of constant change). However, determining the earliest point at which we have enough information to make a sound decision and acting on it is vital.

One reason that training and clear doctrine are so important is that it increases our team's level of implicit knowledge, allowing us to act much more quickly and giving us a time advantage. We want our team to have enough training, implicit knowledge, and internalized doctrine that, in many situations, the response is almost automatic. This requires having the ability to determine when something is generic and can be solved based on existing policies or doctrine and when it is unique and requires a unique solution. In unique situations, we want team members to be able to rapidly access the information they need and combine it with their implicit knowledge and judgment, so that they can decide and respond intelligently and as rapidly as possible.

Within each phase of the OODA loop cycle, there are critical considerations that can increase the quality of our decision-making, although there can never be total certainty when making a decision, particularly in rapidly changing environments such as today's Age of Transformation.

• **Observe.** First we gather data, including outside data and observations of what is unfolding. In the 21st century, having an intelligent system with real-time information, connectivity to others, and quick access to key data is one way to speed up this phase. In particular, a screening and search mechanism that allows us to rapidly obtain the data we need can help prevent information overload or mistakes due to inaccurate information.

• **Orient.** Next we turn data into information. Our orientation is impacted by culture, heritage, new information, previous experiences, and our analytical and synthesizing skills. Our orientation also impacts how we observe, decide, and act. This is the most important phase of the cycle, as this is where we are most likely to accelerate the process through a high level of implicit knowledge—sometimes allowing us to go directly to action without a prolonged decision phase. Here we can also enter a competitor's cycle and create confusion or novelty that makes it difficult for them to quickly orient to what is happening.

• **Decide.** At this phase, we consider our various options and select the option we think is best.

• **Act.** Finally, we implement the option we decided upon. We then loop back to the Observe phase and repeat the cycle again and again.

OODA loops occur at every level of the organization. At the senior leadership level, they are used to make higher-level strategy decisions, while on the front lines they are used for tactical decision-making. The loops at various levels feed into one another; feedback from decisions at tactical loops guide decisions at higher loops and vice versa.

While the OODA loop model was created as a military tool, it provides a vitally important model for any 21st century team because it allows us to rapidly assess and adapt to—or help shape—a complex and constantly changing environment.

**21st Century Implementation Key Number Three:
Constant Learning and 21st Century Knowledge Management—
Why Constant Learning Will Replace Bureaucratic Education as
a Model**

In the 21st century, change is happening so rapidly that we have to be involved in constant learning. As Peter Drucker first observed, the center of gravity in the post–Industrial Age is the knowledge worker, not the manual worker. Moreover, knowledge is the primary product or service.

The ability to constantly create, acquire, and transfer knowledge, ensuring that knowledge is easily accessible to allow our allies and our team to benefit, is critical to implementation success. However, in the dramatically changing 21st century environment, knowledge management must shift from the 20th century model of predicting and reacting based on pre-programmed information to a faster cycle of learning, creating new knowledge, and acting based on that new knowledge.

There are six key principles related to learning and knowledge management that should be part of a 21st century organization's culture.

1. Import Knowledge, Export Work

The 21st century and the process of transformation will create too many opportunities for us to manage most of them internally. To have maximum impact, we have to be able to import knowledge that already exists and export projects that are not absolutely vital and that can be done better or more easily by someone else.

We must constantly, when confronted with new opportunities or needs, ask if we have the necessary knowledge internally; if not, we need to determine who has it and how we can import that knowledge from them.

If a new opportunity requires the launch of a new project, we must decide if this is a project where there is a good strategic fit and where we have the necessary expertise and resources. If so, we should assign it internally. If not, we need to either ignore it, or, if we think it is important to reaching our vision, we need to export it to someone who is better prepared to manage it and who has a self-interest in doing so.

2. Use After-Action Reviews and Lessons Learned

One of the best times to learn is immediately after we have engaged in a key activity or project.

The after-action review process developed by the U.S. Army helps teams learn quickly from their successes and failures and share their learning with others on the team. It involves reviewing what should have happened, what actually happened, and why it happened. It allows participants to learn how to sustain strengths and improve on weaknesses in subsequent tasks or projects.

One secret to continual improvement and to being a learning organization is to constantly review, as honestly and objectively as possible, the results of an undertaking immediately after it happens. A team that fails to do this is destined to repeat mistakes and is unlikely to exhibit substantial growth or improvement from one trial to the next.

3. Engage in Continuous Quality Improvement

Continuous quality improvement is one of the hallmarks of a learning organization. It involves understanding what matters to the customer, then defining the critical metrics of success that are tied to customer satisfaction. This is followed by monitoring the metrics and implementing changes to the process in order to improve the results.

Every person in the organization has to know the critical metrics that really matter, understand which ones he or she is personally responsible for, and be involved in helping define and implement the changes that will improve the process in order to reach the metrics. In addition, we believe that each person's incentives and bonuses have to be tied to the metrics if we are to truly change behavior.

The "plan" stage includes gathering data on the current situation and past history. The "do" stage is where possible improvements are tested as pilots on a small scale. The results of those experiments are studied during the "study" stage. The "act" stage is when we change the solution, if unsuccessful, or disseminate it more broadly if it were successful. We then go through the cycle all over again. An important

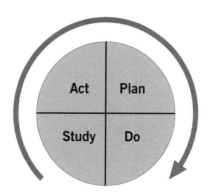

point to note, as we seek continual improvement, is that making changes related to normal variation inherent in the work process is where we can trigger explosive improvement. Concentrating on improving responses to the generic or most common events leads to 94 percent of all improvement. Only 6 percent of improvement is from focusing on special causes. Yet managers tend to emphasize the unique or the one-time event that arises from circumstances that are not part of the normal work process. They take for granted common causes. But it is by improving the common causes that we can dramatically improve performance.

Finally, in keeping with our transformational model, it is vital that we look at solutions outside our industry and that we consider new technologies and breakthroughs as we work to improve processes. Today is an age of constant, dramatic breakthroughs. Being bold enough to implement those new solutions on a small scale during the quality improvement cycle can result in dramatic improvement and even, ultimately, a transformation of our way of life.

4. Imitation Is Cheaper Than Invention
Corollary: Creative Imitation = Opportunity

Finding solutions that are proven to work, or people who have solved the same problems we face, is far better than taking the time to invent something new. Drucker spoke of "creative imitation," by which he meant taking something that someone else has done and improving it or adapting it to fit a new need or situation. It's an approach that is at the heart of successful transformation.

> **Creative Imitation x Cheerful Persistence**
>
> "I was 52 years old. I had diabetes and incipient arthritis. I had lost my gall bladder and most of my thyroid gland in earlier campaigns, but I was convinced that the best was ahead of me."
>
> *Ray Croc,*
> *describing his life right before*
> *founding McDonald's*

The creation of McDonald's is a great example. Fast-food chains already existed when Ray Kroc first became interested in a restaurant in California owned by the McDonald brothers. Kroc, who was a milkshake machine salesman at the time, realized that the McDonald brothers' model of having a limited, consistent menu provided at low cost in an efficient setting fit perfectly with the American psyche of the 1960s.

He subsequently bought out the two brothers and launched the McDonald's chain, which became a national (and eventually an international) franchise built around efficiency, cleanliness, low cost, and consistency in everything from its menu to its recognizable golden arches. Within two years of his purchase Kroc had opened 500 McDonald's restaurants and had sold a billion hamburgers. He accomplished all this not by inventing something totally new but by brilliantly engaging in Drucker's concept of "creative imitation."

5. Collaborate, Don't Dictate
Building a collaborative environment and providing electronic tools to make collaboration effective and efficient will dramatically expand the team's ability to learn, to create, to innovate, and to succeed.

Collaboration is important for two reasons: (1) having the best ideas from all the members of our team, partners, and allies will enrich the quality of what we create; (2) since people are more likely to support what they help create, it heightens the level of investment and commitment from others, thus creating greater momentum and adding more weight to our efforts.

6. Create a 21st Century Intelligent System
Knowledge management in the 21st century is by nature dynamic. It requires not a storage-and-retrieval system, where information is simply kept and re-used, but a constantly evolving and adapting system. What is required is not simply a repository of information that provides us with a set of rules for playing the game, but a system that allows us to realize when the rules are changing, or even when the game itself is changing. Not only must the system be aware of such changes, but it also must be designed so that it can adapt to such changes.

Added to the complexity is the human element. While IT is an important tool for collecting, sharing, and accessing information, the human aspect will determine both how, what, and when knowledge is created and used. In the age of the knowledge worker, much of the knowledge is in the head of the worker, which makes it impossible to ignore the human variable and makes our challenge of retrieving, storing, and managing key knowledge even greater.

The Plan-Do-Study-Act (PDSA) cycle, also known as the Deming cycle, is a model for continuous improvement and for testing a change in the real work setting by planning it, trying it, observing the results, and acting on what is learned. In essence, it's a scientific method used for action-oriented learning.

Knowing = Information x IT x Human Capital

In addition, a major trend of the 21st century is to increasingly make relevant information available to our external allies and customers and to involve them in creating new knowledge as we move toward a future of greater transparency and collaboration.

Successful 21st century organizations employ processes and IT that allow workers and customers to create and access the specific information or knowledge they need when they need it and where they need it. The cycle of constantly and collaboratively creating new knowledge, embedding that ever-changing knowledge into new processes and products, and making that knowledge available in an easily accessible, searchable, intuitive, and real-time manner will be one of the biggest challenges and most defining opportunities of the 21st century.

While volumes could be written about knowledge management, we believe there are ten critical elements that make a 21st Century Intelligent System of knowledge management much different from the last century. And, while the system is much more than IT, it's clear that IT must have a central role in a world where speed, geographic reach, and networking are vital.

1. A 21st century system must be agile and flexible. The system and the knowledge it houses have to evolve in order to adapt to a changing business model, ever-evolving knowledge, new innovations and technologies, and the changing needs of the organization, workers, customers, and allies.

2. The system has to be embedded within the decision-making cycle, which means that it must be able to provide just the knowledge that is needed at the time and place that decisions are being made. This means providing access to relevant knowl-

edge and to experts not only in the board room but also to networked teams on the front lines. In addition, the system must be able to "learn" and change, based on the information coming out of the OODA loops at all levels.

3. In order to get busy teams to help create and actually use the system, it has to add value within the context of the business model, the future vision, the defined metrics, and customer service. It has to allow the worker to perform his job more efficiently and effectively. It also must be part of the usual workflow process, making it as easy as possible to gather and use information, rather than adding another level of complexity into the work experience.

4. The system has to consciously convert tacit knowledge into explicit knowledge, including human aspects like principles, ideals, and values. As many of the Baby Boomers retire over the next few decades, it will be important that we convert the unique knowledge they possess into storable, retrievable knowledge.

Two Critical Knowledge Creation Opportunities

Decision-Making: When engaged in making key decisions, it is vital that leaders record the process that led to the decision, rather than just the decision. Making such knowledge explicit by putting it into documents will become a valuable resource to help others understand the patterns and variables that should be considered when making decisions.

Lessons Learned: Doctrine should require documentation, storing, and sharing of "lessons learned" during after-action reviews held immediately after critical actions or projects. The goal is for the organization and team members to be able to learn and change based on past experiences that teach us, in particular situations, what works, what doesn't, what processes we should change, and what unexpected consequences or variables may impact success.

---

5. Our human capital assets have to be managed as part of the knowledge management process. The people who have the highest degree of knowledge or understanding about our business have to be involved in knowledge creation and should be available to other members of the team, both in real-time and in

stored, accessible documents, including video and audio. Understanding the rhythm, culture, and language of the organization involves a level of exposure to those who best understand the organization that goes beyond simple documents.

6. The system has to be capable of being integrated within the entire enterprise and across enterprises, with the capacity to constantly expand and to become integrated with a perpetually changing and growing network of allies and customers. This means that interoperability is key. Twenty-first century organizations will have to provide a high level of interoperability and transparency while maintaining privacy and security for confidential information.

7. People must be at the center of the system, and the system must respond to the needs of the individual, including providing a customized approach that allows people to control what knowledge they receive or create and how and when they receive or create it. This includes allowing people to learn and to receive e-training wherever, whenever, and however they choose.

8. The ability for technology to discern patterns and make predictions based on constantly changing knowledge has to be a key element of knowledge management in the 21st century. The most successful systems will require not only constant real-time data, but also the ability to rapidly integrate new human intelligence and data that has typically been tacit, rather than explicit, into the process.

9. Collaborative tools that are easy to use and that automatically add to the knowledge base are essential in the 21st century. Not only does this increase creativity, but it also provides the ability for novice-level workers to observe interactions that help them learn how to shape decisions and how to engage in innovation.

10. Perhaps most important, the system has to be focused on the overall organization and future vision, not just on the accomplishment of daily tasks and tactics. Its purpose is not one of simply providing information that allows us to do things right but on managing knowledge that helps us determine if we are doing the right things.

21st Century Implementation Key Number Four: Creating Coalitions and a Team of Leaders

One person cannot create or lead a transformation. A primary focus has to be on constantly recruiting and training new leaders and leveraging their strengths to expand our reach and impact.

The leaders we recruit are both internal leaders who become part of our organization and external leaders who can also help us reach our goals.

Leaders who are part of our organization must be taught about specific doctrines and habits of effectiveness. They also have to be focused on the goals, projects, and metrics of the overall organization. Our goal is to ensure that they have the training and structure necessary to become trusted agents who will use their strengths in a way that is consistent with our vision, values, goals, and metrics.

However, organizations can't look only internally for allies and partners, any more than they can measure their success by looking internally. They have to be externally oriented. The organization is part of a system. The existence of the organization, like an organ in a biological system, is impacted and sustained by the external system in which it resides. As an organ, it is dependent upon the viability of the system in which it exists, and it cannot survive if it is part of a dying system.

The organization must, therefore, create external alliances and coalitions that will sustain not just the organization but also the external environment. Those relationships will be vital to drive change, whether it's creating a market, working together to develop a new application or solution, providing or implementing another's solution, or transforming the industry or society that represents the larger system of which the organization is a part.

While we need to have long-lasting, formal partnerships with allies committed to our vision, the real key to success in the 21st century is the creation of coalitions by bringing together temporary allies who will work with us toward a specific achievement, even if there is little else on which we agree.

Building a network and team of leaders requires attention to four key transformational principles:

1. Constantly Acquire and Sustain Allies

During implementation we have to continue to broaden and strengthen the network of leaders we began building during the planning and design phase. While every transformation starts out with a small group of dedicated leaders, that group must constantly grow and dramatically expand to accomplish anything. Sustaining and growing a critical mass of allies involves:

- Communicating with them to provide a sense of relevance, and giving them the information, tools, and training they need to help create and drive the transformation.

- Constantly practicing listen, learn, help, lead to recruit new allies and to learn from and retain the commitment of existing allies.

- Using the "import knowledge/export work" principle to involve external allies in creating the transformation by implementing projects and serving as validators and/or distribution channels for the message.

- Networking allies to one another in order to create partnerships that will allow for the creation of new solutions or more rapid transformation than either could achieve alone.

- Ensuring that allies are receiving what they expected from the giving-and-getting coalition-building contract.

- Constantly identifying and reaching out to new allies including unexpected allies who will become part of a coalition to achieve something specific, even if they are not committed to our entire agenda.

- Taking time to celebrate victories and reward contributions in order to keep our team and external allies energized and enthusiastic.

2. Focus on Strengths

We can't build on weaknesses. Rather, we need to use the strength of each member of our team to build joint success. Our greatest impact will be leveraging the strengths of our team and allies, not improving their weaknesses. Successful implementation is more likely to occur in an organization that figures out how to use and hone every worker's strengths, rather than one that spends time and energy on the 20th century's preoccupation with trying to strengthen weaknesses.

3. Connect Islands of Excellence with Invisible Bridges

General Edward "Shy" Meyer, while chief of staff of the U.S. Army, taught us this lesson in 1979. He asserted that a key to organizational effectiveness was to quietly and deliberately build networks among competent people without regard to the organizational chart or the official hierarchies. He described it as building invisible bridges between islands of excellence.

All large organizations are lakes of mediocrity with islands of excellence. If we can identify the islands and build invisible bridges between the islands (both within an organization and between organizations), it is amazing what we can get done. But if the bridge is visible, it is likely to be covered up or washed away as the organization, with its structures and rules, climbs aboard. In order to build bridges between islands of excellence, we need to do the following: first, determine who represents an island of excellence; next, determine with whom they need to be networked; and last, connect them as quietly and informally as possible.

We have found that this kind of informal implementation structure can greatly accelerate the tempo of the system and the speed of transformation.

As we engage in connecting people or organizations, a key principle to remember is that we want most networking to take place without our direct mediation. If we insist on putting ourselves at the center of all networking interactions, the speed and frequency of networking will be limited by our availability. The result will be a deceleration rather than acceleration of the very activities that are necessary for system-wide transformation to occur.

When we first built the model of networking for the Center for Health Transformation, the design featured ourselves at the center. It soon became obvious that such a model dramatically slowed down the networking that was necessary, which led us to develop a new model with our role not at the center but to the side, providing a platform for convening opportunities where interactions occur.

Old Networking Model

New Networking Model

In reality, the networking model is much more complex than the illustration conveys, as each of the areas we've listed as primary network partners have networks of their own, which have networks of their own, etc. It's the viral effect of our network, our networks' networks, the networks of our networks' networks and so forth that accelerates our impact and creates system-wide transformation.

4. Build E-Communities

Building e-communities and providing electronic collaboration tools are absolutely essential if we want to create a 21st century transformational movement. Electronic communities and online collaboration are the most economical way to communicate with large groups of people. To create real transformation, the amount of involvement needed is tremendous. The only way to sustain a system that big is through electronics.

21st Century Implementation Key Number Five: Effective and Constant Communication

Throughout implementation, constant communication is necessary both to keep our team informed and energized and to attract new allies. While collaboration is central to success, we have to communicate before we can collaborate.

Our communication reach can be greatly expanded if we consider every member of the team and every ally to be a potential spokesperson and a listen, learn, help, lead agent. Whether their communications and interactions will be with large audiences, small civic groups, or the people they talk to at work, at home, via e-mail, or at social gatherings, they must be able to communicate our vision of the future.

In addition, think about the organic growth of ideas and public sentiment that happens via the Internet, which in many ways is the water cooler of the 21st century. Whether we're seeking buy-in and involvement from our internal workforce or the broader society, fostering that type of organic growth during implementation can have a dramatic impact on winning allies and winning the public.

The communication principles detailed in the previous chapter are key principles to remember during implementation. As we operate on a daily basis, timely and effective communication is absolutely central to the success of any major change effort, which means we must constantly pay attention to the following ten rules.

1. Keep Our Team and Allies Informed and Equipped
We want our team to know what is going on and we want key leaders and spokespeople to understand and be able to deliver the same message. This includes making sure that they understand and can articulate our vision, values, and goals. They must also know and use the right language and the key messages we've developed both for general communications and for responding in a more targeted way to immediate situations or specific issues.

2. Repetition, Repetition, Repetition
Repetition has been proven to increase retention of facts or ideas. Therefore we want to focus on repeating both individually and as a group the same message over and over.

Repetition Increases Understanding
1st time = 10% retention
2nd time = 25% retention
3rd time = 40-50% retention
4th time = 75% retention

Source: Haines, Stephen. *The Systems Thinking Approach to Strategic Planning and Management*, CRC Press, 2000.

3. Corollary: Meaning x Repetition = Memory
Meaning or personal relevance combined with repetition will dramatically impact our audience's attention to and memory of our message. This takes us back to the principle of contextualizing our message and tailoring it to our audience. What we believe in doesn't change based on the audience, but we have to talk about it in the context of their lives and in language they understand. Our goal is to trigger a responsive chord in our audience's mind.

4. Speed Is Critical
When communicating critical information, speed is of the essence. Sending an e-mail that is less than perfect is more important than laboring for days to write a detailed and perfect report that will arrive

long after the critical time to act has passed. This is particularly important when dealing with the press, where responding rapidly (but with sound judgment) to breaking news that matters to us is key to making the news cycle and getting our message in the story.

5. Move to the Sound of the Guns as a Principle of Communication
When it comes to communication, the principle of moving to the sound of the guns is vital. The greatest opportunity for delivering our message and impacting awareness of the need for change often occurs when an external event or breaking news story has the attention of the public or of a key audience. This means that we must be alert to such opportunities and flexible enough to shift our resources in order to take advantage of them.

The devastation of Hurricane Katrina was a terrible tragedy, but we quickly realized that it provided an opportunity to communicate with America about the importance of electronic health records. The countless victims who were left without any medical history or information about their treatment regimen or medications provided a real-life example of the dangers of a paper-based system, and we were able to use the situation to make substantial progress in driving the demand for electronic records.

6. Constantly Expand Our Network of Spokespeople
As we implement a plan, one of our goals is to constantly grow our list of spokespeople to expand our reach and broaden our expertise. In particular, we should routinely add:
  • Experts who can educate us, help develop our ideas, and validate what we are saying
  • Opinion leaders who can influence specific audiences that matter
  • Members of key constituencies who can relate on a personal basis and communicate in the language of that constituency
  • People who support us despite being members of groups or constituencies that generally oppose us

7. Leverage Distribution Channels
Most people seldom leverage the channels of communication that are available to them. When trying to drive transformation, we have to systematically use the distribution channels of our allies, our partners, and our team as well as Internet channels. Utilizing every pos-

sible channel is key to getting the message out to a broad audience. In addition, it creates an echo chamber that maximizes the reach and impact of what we do, making us both more effective and efficient.

8. Focus on Our Center of Gravity

With each issue, we have to define the audience we need to win in order to be successful and then focus our communication efforts on that audience. This means thinking about what they care about, where they get their information, and when they will listen.

Know Your Audience

Who will they listen to?
What do they care about?
Where do they get their information?
How do they learn and understand?
When will they listen?
Why will they listen?

---

9. Use E-Communications to Maximize Electronic Connectivity

Using e-communications is absolutely essential in today's world. Not only does it meet the important goal of speed, it also provides a level of efficiency that is critical. Additionally, the nature of the Internet allows a type of organic growth of our network that can broaden our reach without dramatically increasing our effort.

10. Have Clear Communications Metrics

As we discussed in the previous chapter, it is essential that we have metrics of success built in for our overall communications and that the communications activities we undertake be related to those metrics. We have to have the discipline to avoid getting distracted by communication activities that may lend visibility but that have nothing to do with the vision, strategies, or metrics that we have adopted.

21st Century Implementation Key Number Six: Continuous Innovation

Constantly creating or acquiring information and quickly turning it into new tools or solutions for rapid distribution is central to the innovative excellence that is at the heart of transformation. It is through this continuous process of innovation that we create new solutions, new projects, new processes, and new products and services. Transformational teams have to look outside the plan they've created to constantly monitor changes occurring in the external environment that may mean a change in what they are doing.

Innovation has to be practiced by every member of the team. The need for innovation is most likely to be discovered by those on the front lines, and successful organizations don't wait until the need is so obvious that it has reached top-level management.

Sources of Innovation Opportunity

In his book *Innovation and Entrepreneurship*, Peter Drucker describes seven sources of innovation opportunity. The first four occur within an industry or area of service and the last three occur outside the specific industry. Each of these areas should be on our radar screen throughout both planning and implementation.

> "Innovation opportunities do not come with the tempest but with the rustling of the breeze."
>
> *Peter Drucker*

1. The unexpected success, unexpected failure, or unexpected outside event
2. The incongruity between reality and assumed reality
3. Innovation based on process need
4. Unexpected changes in industry or market structure
5. Demographics
6. Changes in perception, mood, and meaning
7. New knowledge, both scientific and non-scientific

Discover, Develop, Disseminate, Deliver

Just as a rapid OODA loop cycle speeds up decision-making, a rapid discover, develop, disseminate, deliver cycle can speed up the innovation process.

> "The truly important events on the outside are not the trends. They are changes in the trends."
>
> *Peter Drucker*

Dr. Andrew von Eschenbach, former head of the National Cancer Institute, first came to us with the discover, develop, deliver model, which we have since expanded. Dr. von Eschenbach believes that we can eliminate cancer as a cause of death by 2015, but we will have to engage in a rapid, seamless cycle of discover, develop, deliver.

- Discovery is the process of generating new information.

- Development is the process of creating and evaluating new tools and solutions related to that information.

- Delivery involves promoting and facilitating the adoption of the tools and solutions.

In studying the model and observing the failure of widespread adoption of best practices, Robert Egge, who heads up our cancer project at the Center, determined that a key part of the process was missing. He noted that there is often a breakdown between the develop phase and the deliver phase. This led us to add a fourth part, between development and delivery, which we call disseminate. In our model, dissemination focuses on how the breakthrough "travels" to the point of care, while delivery refers to how the breakthrough is applied at the point of care (involving issues such as access, disparities, quality, etc.).

The most successful 21st century organizations and industries will be those that can rapidly create or acquire new information, quickly translate that into new products or services, and then rapidly market and distribute them. One of the things that can speed up the process is for transitions to be seamless. This includes identifying and creating key partnerships that can accelerate the process. For example, as Dr. von Eschenbach points out, having the FDA more involved as a partner in the entire process of drug development, rather than coming in only at the approval phase, would potentially dramatically decrease the time between discovery and approval.

The "seamless four-D" strategy, specific to the area of cancer, can speed translation of investigator-initiated discovery into the development of new interventions and then accelerate the rate at which proven interventions are put into widespread practice. Beyond reducing the time from bench to bedside, investing in initiatives that create greater seamlessness is important because it will yield new tools and new platforms for collaboration, enabling members of the research community to test their ideas quickly and move worthy science forward faster than ever before.

The model, though initially designed for the National Cancer Institute and modified by us as part of our cancer project, can be applied to various organizations and industries to accelerate the creation and distribution of innovations that can get us to a better future faster.

Accelerating Adoption of Innovations

During implementation, a major focus is on the successful adoption by a wide audience of transformational ideas and projects that help fulfill our strategies. There are five perceived traits defined in Rogers' *Diffusion of Innovations* that dramatically enhance the likelihood of an idea's adoption:

- **Relative advantage**. The degree to which an innovation is perceived as better than the idea it supersedes.
- **Compatibility**. The degree to which an innovation is perceived as being consistent with the existing values, past experiences, and needs of potential adopters.
- **Complexity**. The degree to which an innovation is perceived as difficult to understand and use.
- **Trialability**. The degree to which an innovation may be experimented with on a limited basis.
- **Observability**. The degree to which the results of an innovation are visible to others.

According to research, an innovation that is perceived as having high compatibility, relative advantage, trialability, and observability while having low complexity is more likely to be adopted. The five elements should be remembered both as we design solutions and as we try to persuade others to adopt them.

In particular, in a world that is changing rapidly and constantly, the complexity of change is a major factor. People want technologies that make their lives easier, not more difficult. Thomas Edison was brilliant because he invented technologies that were easy to use—we don't have to know how electricity works to turn on a light. For groups that may be overwhelmed by the scale of change, finding a way to simplify and embed technology into their environment and routine activities is essential to moving them toward a 21st century system.

21st Century Implementation Key Number Seven: Agile, Networked, Resilient Teams

Teams that are networked and agile are critical to successfully implementing transformation in the 21st century. The most effective teams will possess:

- Interoperable information technology that allows them to have immediate access to real-time information, as-needed training, and efficient remote communications with team members and leaders in other locations.
- Training in doctrine and habits that allow them to know how to respond without having on-site management or extrinsic orders.
- Tools, training, and culture that allow them to quickly observe, orient, decide, and act.
- A culture that encourages and provides the knowledge and training that allows intelligent risk-taking.
- Shared vision, metrics, habits, and team training that make it possible for the team to improvise in tandem toward a shared goal.

Being able to handle unexpected challenges and setbacks is a key element of success during times of great change. We believe that such resilience is not innate but rather is made up of a number of learned habits.

While a number of books have been written on the subject, we have found five habits to be particularly prevalent in resilient teams:

1. Quickly pivoting to new solutions and opportunities rather than being discouraged by failures.

2. Seeing things in the context of our vision and strategies rather than as discrete activities, allowing us to find new paths when old paths are blocked.

3. Understanding the underlying patterns and relationships between tasks and projects so that handling multiple activities as is required during large-scale change becomes more coordinated and less daunting.

4. Possessing the rapid, competent, informed decision-making ability discussed earlier, allowing us to quickly adapt to a changing landscape.

5. Building into our plans a level of flexibility that allows us to adjust to sudden changes or setbacks without toppling the entire project or venture.

As we engage in the difficult process of implementing and leading during change, we will find that there is no substitute for a team that is well-networked, agile, and exhibits the five habits of resilience.

21st Century Implementation Key Number Eight: A Culture of Shared Purpose, Engagement, and Fun

One of the most critical aspects of growing and sustaining a critical mass of internal or external allies is the creation of an environment where the individuals are very engaged and share a sense of significance, purpose, and fun. In that regard, a transformational movement is more like a well-run political campaign, with enthusiastic volunteers, than like the approach typically taken by businesses or government.

Gallup has conducted surveys that show that only 29 percent of employees are engaged, by which they mean consistently performing at high levels, using their strengths and working with passion. Fifty-five percent are not engaged and 16 percent are actively disengaged, meaning that they actively undermine the organization. Gallup tells us there is evidence that the level of disengagement is even worse in the area of healthcare, where disengaged workers actually represent a key factor in medical errors.

As in a well-run political campaign, we need to involve the right people and then work to get them engaged. We must give them:

• A sense of moral purpose and meaning, which is created by constantly communicating our vision;

- An understanding of why the future we are creating is better not only for our country and for society but for them and their family;

- An understanding of (and the necessary tools to fufill) their specific roles and projects, which utilize and develop their specific strengths and interests and which contribute to the overall success of our endeavor;

- The opportunity to help create, give input and lead the migration to our idealized future, including serving as advisors, scouts, and leaders;

- A sense of team belonging, including the creation of a work environment that is fun and meaningful and where there is an attitude of "we're all in this together";

- Recognition and celebration for successful completion of their projects and tasks, as well as for attainment of broader metrics to which everyone contributed.

PART FOUR

21st Century Transformational Leadership

11

Quality and Systems Thinking

The combination of quality and systems thinking is one of the most powerful tools available for transformational leaders. When combined with metrics, which we will cover in more detail in the next chapter, this combination begins to create a revolution in leadership capability.

W. Edwards Deming defined a system as "a network of interdependent components that work together to try to accomplish the aim of the system." As noted earlier, systems thinking is a way of understanding change by understanding the relationships among parts of the system or various sub-systems and how changes in one impact the others as well as impact the system at large.

The interacting, interrelated, and interdependent components of a system form a complex and unified whole, and, by unraveling the patterns and the processes within the system, we are able to determine where making a change will impact the cycle that created an event. If the event was positive, we can act to accelerate or strengthen its occurrence; if negative, we can act to prevent or lessen its future occurrence.

Systems thinking focuses on the long-term versus the tactical, concentrating on the interactions between various parts of the system that can move us more quickly toward the desired outcome. By looking at the ripple effects that are likely to occur as a result of an event or action, we can understand and begin to anticipate those consequences and define the key leverage points where a small act can have a profound impact. Systems thinking is important because it allows us to design enduring solutions to problems, rather than temporary fixes to small symptoms.

The evidence that systems thinking is powerful is all around us. Only two hundred years ago the vast majority of the world was poor and lacked food, clothing, and housing. Transportation was primitive. Quality of life was harsh and lives were short. In just two hundred years, the length and quality of our lives and range of physical possessions have improved dramatically.

One of the keys to the dramatic increases in effectiveness and productivity in the industrial era was the emergence of systems thinking. Systems thinking was largely engineered by specialists in process engineering and then imposed on workers who did what they were told.

That original explosion in productivity and effectiveness was greatly expanded by the rise of quality as a model of continuous improvement, in which every worker worked to improve his effectiveness. The combination of systems thinking and quality are the foundation of much of the modern world's extraordinary capacity to produce goods and services.

Any transformation effort has to include a strong foundation in systems and quality thinking. Since quality as a pattern grew out of systems thinking, it is useful to first outline the rise of systems and then develop the process of quality and continuous improvement.

A History of Systems Thinking

As leaders and managers learned to think of activities as part of systems, they increased their effectiveness and their production of goods and services.

Systems thinking is not new. The Roman and Chinese civilizations were very good at engineering and at systematic thinking. There are a number of examples throughout the Middle Ages of systems thinking; one is the Venetian Arsenal and its ability to mass-produce galleys for the Venetian navy. In the late 18th and early 19th centuries, systems thinking began to spread and became the standard for modern organizations.

Adam Smith described the merging world of extraordinary productivity increases in *The Wealth of Nations* (1776). He noted that individuals in a specialized needle factory could produce much more when they focused on individual tasks than in the traditional system, in which each worker produced an entire needle. In his remarkable book, Smith outlined the first great revolution in modern wealth and productivity.

A few years later, Eli Whitney became one of the first great systems innovators in America. In 1798 he developed a system for manufacturing guns using standardized parts and an assembly line. That process made him a wealthy man. Yet Whitney's fame is based on an earlier invention—which landed him in court and did not make him much money. In 1793 (when the American government was only four years old and Whitney was twenty-eight) he invented the cotton gin. The Patent Act of 1793 had some loopholes exploited by his competitors, and Whitney could not validate his claim until 1807. For fourteen years his greatest invention was tied up by lawyers. Some things never change. However, during that period, Whitney made his fortune by manufacturing guns through a very efficient systematized manufacturing process.

The concept of production as a system took a big leap forward when railroads were developed. Railroads are inherently a system. There has to be an engine, cars for people or products, fuel, tracks, places to stop, schedules, personnel to maintain the various components, managers to keep everything running, salesmen and publicists to get people to use the railroad, etc.

The sheer mechanics of building and running a railroad required the growth of modern corporate management. Many business historians believe virtually all industrial-era American systems of management can be traced back to the rise of the railroad and its requirements for sophisticated systems of personnel and activities.

One of the North's greatest advantages over the South in the Civil War was the scale of the Northern railroad system. The North could simply move more men and materiel faster, cheaper, and for longer distances, and as a result had an enormous advantage in producing and applying power. This remained an American competitive advantage from 1861 through the entire 20th century, enabling America to drown the Axis powers in World War Two and the Soviet Union during the Cold War.

Near the turn of the century, Frederick Taylor developed a model to improve productivity by focusing on the elementary parts of a task. This allowed workers to increase productivity without working harder and longer. His associate Henry Gantt, an expert in the order of operations, began focusing on Navy ship construction during World War One. He developed the Gantt chart, which is still used today to outline the sequence and duration of all tasks in a process.

At about this same time, Henry Ford built on the Whitney model of standardized parts and the assembly line, and in 1905 began to mass-produce automobiles on a scale most people thought impossible. Within a few years Ford had mastered the engineering of standardized parts and had integrated production to such a degree that he was able to reduce the price of the Model T every single year it was in production. With Ford's genius at production dedicated to lowering prices, average Americans were in cars three generations before their European counterparts.

This concept of thinking about systems led to the rise of operations research in the Second World War. The American and British ability to analyze entire economies, think through production systems, and identify vulnerable key components gave the Allies an enormous advantage over the Japanese and Germans. Systems analysis became a key component in identifying where to apply British and American combat power to achieve the greatest results.

Systems thinking enabled operations researchers to identify key nodes for scientific development, for the acceleration of production, and for crippling the enemy with the most effective application of power. It was this ability to think through systems of development, production, and application that enabled the British and American forces to overwhelm the German submarine threat with new science, new production, and new tactics (see Meigs's *Slide Rules and Submarines* for a clear introduction to this process and to the cultural and bureaucratic resistance traditional systems used to oppose or minimize the role of scientists in solving military problems).

Henry Kaiser applied standardized parts and an assembly line approach to building transport ships—called Liberty ships—for the American war effort. On one occasion the Kaiser shipyards produced an entire ship in one day, just to prove it could be done. The German and Japanese navies were defeated by courageous, dedicated, and well-trained men and women using a combination of sound intelligence focused on systematic analysis, massive production capabilities based on systems thinking, and identifying and developing the scientific and engineering breakthroughs needed to win the war.

After the Second World War, this ability to think and plan systematically was further refined by Admiral Hyman Rickover in the development of the nuclear submarine's capability to contain the Soviet Union. Rickover needed to simultaneously develop a submarine-launched missile, the missile warhead, and the submarine that would carry the missile while also developing the principles for operating the submarine-missile system and the training system for the entire complex.

To plan and implement this very detailed process in the shortest possible time, the Navy developed the PERT (project evaluation and review technique) system. It is a very disciplined model of thinking through every step of developing and implementing a complex project. It enables senior management to know what the "critical path" is for the task that will take the longest and on which the project depends. The PERT system was popularized as the "critical path" method.

Every large, complex project should have this kind of thinking built into its planning and management.

The Rise of Quality and Continuous Improvement

Mass production had become the standard when Western Electric, the manufacturing arm of AT&T, began to think systematically about how to improve the quality of production. In a series of landmark experiments at the Western Electric Hawthorne plant in the late 1920s, it was realized that people played a big role in productivity. A system that involved human talent in thinking through production was even more productive than an engineered approach that viewed workers as unthinking implementers who had to meet quotas without regard to their own ideas and creativity.

One of the participants in studying what became known as the Hawthorne effect was a young statistician named W. Edwards

Deming. He became convinced that involving people in thinking through their own jobs and systematically developing better approaches, better processes, and better solutions would dramatically increase their productivity.

Deming also came to realize that there was never a complete solution. There was always the potential for further improvement. With that realization he began to develop the concept of continuous improvement, in which every person had the opportunity—and even the obligation—to work every day to find small breakthroughs that would improve a company's productivity and lower its costs.

Five Core Principles of Deming

1. The customer defines value
2. To improve results, you must improve the processes that generate them
3. People want to do a good job and are key to improving the system
4. Every person, process, and job is part of a larger system
5. Continual learning is the basis for continual improvement

After the American system of production defeated the Japanese in World War Two, Japan's industrial leaders were convinced they had to learn from the Americans. While it is hard for younger Americans to believe, in that period Japanese manufacturing was considered a joke. People associated Japanese production with plastic goods, flimsy products, and inexpensive, inferior production. Japanese workers were paid dramatically less than American workers and no one would have expected a Japanese company to be a leading example of quality production.

Japanese industrial leaders set about to change this condition by learning from the very Americans who had defeated them. In 1950 they invited Deming to come to Japan and teach a four-day course on quality and continuous improvement. This course was so powerful that Deming was still teaching a version of it forty years later when we worked with him in the early 1990s.

Japanese industrialists brought together an estimated 70 percent of the industrial capital in Japan for that first Deming workshop. They decided collectively that they had to undertake a dramatic modernization of their systems and master the concepts of quality and continuous improvement. One result of this was that the annual prize for the best-run company in Japan is called the Deming Prize.

This initial Japanese investment in learning quality and continuous improvement found its most famous codification in the Toyota Production System. Toyota is now recognized as the most consistently quality-oriented automobile company in the world. Its ability to produce at a stunning quality level with very little waste is regarded as a model for virtually all processes. The principle of doing the right thing right the first time (as it was popularized by an American writer) has become the benchmark of quality production systems. Its emphasis on the constant search for *muda* (Japanese for waste) has involved every worker in the worldwide Toyota system in helping the company run profitably.

The story of the Toyota model of lean production is told brilliantly in the book *The Machine That Changed the World* by James Womack, Daniel Jones, and Daniel Roos, which was based on the MIT study of the auto industry. The power of Toyota's focus on productivity to enable the company to produce the right car with the right quality the first time was contrasted vividly with the then best European mass-production system, Mercedes.

The authors noted that Mercedes achieved its quality through very intense inspections that sent one-third of their cars back for modification. By contrast, Toyota was focusing on doing things right the first time rather than focusing on inspection and rework. The result was that Toyota was reworking only 3 percent of its cars. They suggested that a system that reworked 33 percent of its production simply could not compete with the system that redid only 3 percent. Over the following decade this insight gave Toyota an enormous advantage.

None of these systems approaches are magic. All require hard work. All can be learned by any company, team, or individual who wants to acquire the advantages of systems and quality. As American companies realized they had to go through the same transformation in productivity, many of them turned to Deming and his work. The former president of Ford, Don Petersen, wrote a terrific book, *A Better Idea*, in which he outlined Ford's process of learning systems and quality from Deming and applying it in a unionized environment.

We were able to see firsthand the impact this had at the Hapeville, Georgia, Ford plant, when union members found themselves involved in advising management for the first time. There was a palpable excitement as blue-collar workers in Georgia traveled to Detroit to meet with designers and engineers to work out better and more effective ways of getting things done.

The Big Three auto companies (GM, Ford, and DaimlerChrysler) still have a lot of challenges with their inherited cost structure, their unionized work rules, and the slower, more bureaucratic decision cycle they bring to understanding the customer and competing with foreign companies. Nonetheless, they have made great strides in narrowing the gap in productivity and applying systems and quality thinking at all levels. In fact, if they had not made those changes over the last twenty years they would not be in business today.

Quality in the Service Industry

Many readers will shrug off the concepts of quality and systems thinking as useful for manufacturing but of little help to service industries. In fact, all of us have almost certainly experienced the power of systems and quality in services.

Visit any "normal" hotel. Now visit a Ritz-Carlton, Four Seasons, or Mandarin hotel. The difference is not simply money. These four- and five-star hotels cost more, but they earn the difference. They typically not only have nicer lobbies and better rooms, but their biggest advantage is the quality of service and the attitude and competence of their employees. These hotels have institutionalized service for the customer into a system so clear and so well-trained that you experience similar attentiveness and quality all over the world. This is not a personality-dependent system of hiring the right manager (although that does matter). This is a process of recruiting and educating people so that they perform far above the standard.

Ritz-Carlton

Ritz-Carlton is a stunning example of an organization focused on quality. This is reflected in the company motto and credo, which are expected to be "known, owned, and energized" by all employees.

The Credo

The Ritz-Carlton Hotel is a place where the genuine care and comfort of our guests is our highest mission.

We pledge to provide the finest personal service and facilities for our guests, who will always enjoy a warm, relaxed, yet refined ambience.

The Ritz-Carlton experience enlivens the senses, instills well-being, and fulfills even the unexpressed wishes and needs of our guests.

Motto

At The Ritz-Carlton Hotel Company, L.L.C., "We are ladies and gentlemen serving ladies and gentlemen." This motto exemplifies the anticipatory service provided by all staff members.

Source: www.ritz-carlton.com

Every Ritz-Carlton employee receives more than one hundred hours of customer service training annually. Employees are expected to know and live the three cornerstones of customer service:

1. A warm and sincere greeting. Use the guest's name.
2. Anticipation and fulfillment of each guest's needs.
3. Fond farewell. Give a warm goodbye and use the guest's name.

The Ritz-Carlton commitment to quality customer service is captured in the service values that every employee learns and is required to practice on a daily basis. The list is an example of a very clear, very systematic approach to customer service that ensures that both Ritz-Carlton and its employees know what is meant by customer service and quality. In addition, the values are designed not only to create exceptional customer service but also to instill pride in the workers.

The list of twelve service values, titled "I am proud to be Ritz-Carlton," include the following:

1. I build strong relationships and create Ritz-Carlton guests for life.

2. I am always responsive to the expressed and unexpressed wishes and needs of our guests.

3. I am empowered to create unique, memorable, and personal experiences for our guests.

4. I understand my role in achieving the Key Success Factors and creating The Ritz-Carlton Mystique.

5. I continuously seek opportunities to innovate and improve the Ritz-Carlton experience.

6. I own and immediately resolve guest problems.

7. I create a work environment of teamwork and lateral service so that the needs of our guests and each other are met.

8. I have the opportunity to continuously learn and grow.

9. I am involved in the planning of the work that affects me.

10. I am proud of my professional appearance, language, and behavior.

11. I protect the privacy and security of our guests, my fellow employees, and the company's confidential information and assets.

12. I am responsible for uncompromising levels of cleanliness and creating a safe and accident-free environment.

Source: Ritz-Carlton.com

Every Ritz-Carlton hotel has a daily SQI (Service Quality Indicator) displayed throughout the hotel and on flat screen monitors in the corporate office to enable all departments to monitor the key production and guest service processes in order to address challenges and areas of need immediately. Using tools ranging from quality improvement teams to guest surveys, Ritz-Carlton employees examine every process in the hotel to ensure the most efficient, customer service–driven approach.

Ritz-Carlton, like other successful service systems of quality, succeeds by focusing a great deal of time and resources on:

- defining the mission
- defining who needs to be recruited in order to achieve that mission
- training employees into a very high standard of service and of positive attitude
- empowering employees to solve problems and design solutions to improve performance and ensure customer satisfaction

What does all this mean for customers? Consider the following:

A front desk project team at The Ritz-Carlton in Osaka reduced check-in time by 50 percent.

A cross-functional team from the two Atlanta hotels and corporate headquarters developed a company-wide guest recognition database used to meet and anticipate repeat customers' preferences and requirements.

Hotel engineers from resorts and city hotels developed a system called CARE (Clean And Repair Everything) to create the most defect-free guest rooms in the industry.

At Hotel Arts Barcelona a cross-functional team of hourly employees and managers tackled the problem of guest room readiness. By staggering the lunch hours of the housekeeping staff and streamlining the guest room inspection process, they created a process to ensure that every guest's room is ready when he or she wants to check in.

Disney

Anyone who visits Disneyland or Disney World has experienced the systematic thinking, planning, recruiting, training, and leadership that go into making an enjoyable and memorable visit—and, from Disney's standpoint, creating an incentive for their customers to return again and again.

Disney puts a premium on the people it hires. The company is careful to get the "right fit," which includes optimism, a positive attitude, and the right skill set. Every employee—no matter what his or her title or organizational level—is trained into the Disney culture of customer service and quality.

> "I have blind faith in the policy that quality, tempered with good judgment and showmanship, will win out against all odds."
>
> *Walt Disney*

Language is an important part of the Disney culture: customers are Guests, employees are Cast Members, and the employment process is Casting. No matter what their job, Disney employees learn that they are in the entertainment business and that there is nothing more important than the interactions that happen between the Cast Members and the Guests.

Disney concentrates on providing Cast Members with a clear-cut understanding of company expectations and giving them the training and information they need to do a good job. Cast Members are empowered to make sound decisions and to do what it takes to create magic moments to surprise and delight Disney's Guests. They are rewarded and recognized for their success, both individually and as part of a team.

At Disney the Cast Members feel special, and their number-one job is to make the Guests feel special as well.

The Disney people have perfected the art of recruiting and training on a grand scale, so much so that today Disney has its own training institute to teach people from a multitude of industries and disciplines how to apply the Disney "magic" to their business.

Disney offers two courses. One teaches how to take care of customers. The second teaches how to take care of the people who take care of customers.

A friend of ours from Boston took the two courses and reports that in a year's time, largely due to what he learned, he doubled the gross sales of his business.

Singapore Airlines

Virtually everyone who has flown Singapore Airlines agrees that it has a unique standard of quality. The airline has been one of the consistently most profitable in the world, largely based on its commitment to customer service and quality.

Singapore Airlines offers hot meals, free alcoholic beverages, free headsets, hot towels with a unique and patented scent, personal entertainment systems, and video-on-demand in all cabins. Even at a time when other airlines are reacting to financial pressures by cutting customer service and benefits, Singapore Airlines succeeds by continuing to concentrate on customer service, reasserting its focus on employee commitment to customer satisfaction, and on the constant addition of new innovative services, including being the first airline, in 2005, to introduce high-speed in-flight Internet service and live international television broadcasts.

Consistent with many of the same standards employed by Ritz-Carlton and Disney, when people discuss what makes Singapore Airlines special, we frequently hear about:

- A mission and core values that focus on quality and customer service

- Constant training of employees

- Constant internal communications to ensure that everyone is learning from each other

- A commitment to continuous improvement, including constantly finding new ways to improve customer satisfaction through learning from best practices both within and outside the airline industry

- Employee incentives tied to superior service

- An overall culture of customer satisfaction and continuous improvement. Singapore Airlines defines its profits as "the applause we receive for providing consistent quality and service to our customers."

Disney, Ritz-Carlton, and Singapore Airlines are just three of many examples of how quality results can be achieved in a service setting. They serve as proof that quality and systems thinking can transform the service industry (including government) as much as they have manufacturing. The challenge is to master them and then successfully apply them to how we do business.

Applying Systems and Quality to Our Efforts

If we want our efforts to be as productive and effective as possible, we will have to master the art of systems and quality thinking. It is a topic we will not be able to avoid if we want to create a 21st century system of effectiveness and productivity.

As we learn to think in systems and to constantly seek quality (and to involve everyone in our organization in doing so), we must also embrace another element that dramatically increases our leadership capability—the capacity to use metrics to define and lead our organization.

12

The Emerging Revolution in Metrics-Driven Leadership

The principles and examples presented throughout this book give you some flavor of how different leadership must be in the Age of Transformation. In addition, they offer a glimpse of how dramatically that kind of leadership can change the world.

We have, in this book, come back again and again to the importance of metrics and a metrics-led system, which we believe is absolutely essential to the art of transformation.

Consider CompStat, the New York City crime-fighting system discussed earlier. CompStat reduced crime by 70 percent. It made New York City the safest city per thousand people in America (four times safer than Houston). It is so easy to learn that it has been carried to Los Angeles—now the second safest city in America.

A system this powerful is worth studying and its underlying principles are worth learning and applying. Metrics-led leadership is the heart of that system.

CompStat reflects an emerging revolution in the use of metrics, which has enormous potential for dramatically improving the effectiveness of large institutions, including government.

Mayor Rudy Giuliani and his first police commissioner, Bill Bratton, deserve a lot of credit for developing CompStat and having the courage and discipline to implement it.

When CompStat began, it required reporting on crime every night from every precinct. It brought real-time information to the senior leadership, and they used it to force real change in the system. In the first year of the Giuliani-Bratton metrics system, they replaced three out of every four precinct captains in the city. When 75 percent of the key leadership of an institution changes in one year, something decisive is happening.

There is no question about the impact of the CompStat system. When Mayor Giuliani took office, crime was a major factor undermining the quality of life in New York City. Prior to Giuliani, America's largest city felt that it was losing the struggle for public safety. Many people felt that Mayor David Dinkins simply was not doing enough to keep them safe. Crime became the defining issue that helped Giuliani win the race for mayor in 1993.

At the time, most criminologists and other social science experts generally believed that police could not control crime. They thought police could repress it, but not control it. However, Giuliani subscribed to a theory put forth by James Q. Wilson and George E. Kelling in a 1982 essay titled "Broken Windows." Their theory asserted that allowing graffiti, broken windows, street derelicts, and other symptoms of disarray created an environment in which crime became easier to implement. In effect, if you lived in a disrupted neighborhood, the barrier to thinking about crime had been lowered. On the other hand, if you erased or painted over the graffiti, repaired the windows, and kept the neighborhood tidy, it would raise the barrier against thinking about crime.

The broken windows theory led Mayor Giuliani to hire Boston police chief Bill Bratton. When he interviewed Bratton, Giuliani asked one simple question: "Can you reduce crime?" Bratton replied, "At least 10 percent the first year." The actual result was a 14 percent decline in crime the first year. New York City residents began to feel safer under Giuliani's leadership because they were in fact safer. For the first time in a generation, crime was on the run.

Mayor Giuliani described his commitment to a metrics-based system in his book *Leadership*, a wonderful and inspirational book that outlines principles of leadership we think will help anyone charged with leading an organization, whether public or private.

A more detailed explanation of the development of CompStat can be found in Bill Bratton's *Turnaround*. Bratton is a career policeman who loves policing and loves the men and women who dedicate their lives to policework. He brings enthusiasm and commitment to his desire to protect the public. In *Turnaround* he outlines the lessons he learned in a lifetime of policing and the way he applied them to develop the CompStat system in New York City.

We have watched Chief Bratton and his team implement CompStat in Los Angeles and it is an amazingly powerful tool for senior leadership, greatly enhancing their ability to communicate with, train, focus, and measure the entire force. It is a system every American should be aware of, because it contains the core ideas that can be used to create a revolution in the effectiveness of senior leadership.

The CompStat Approach

The key first step in developing effective metrics is thinking deeply about what we are trying to achieve and how we can measure that achievement. Chief Bratton's experience in developing CompStat is particularly helpful as a model of asking the right questions.

Historically, police had measured activities such as number of arrests or speed of answering 911 calls. These were measures of activity, but, as Bratton understood, they were not measures of effectiveness.

Citizens ultimately did not care about how many arrests were made or how fast the police responded. Being told you lived in the precinct with the greatest number of arrests would not make you feel better. Indeed, it would probably make you feel worse.

Bratton began focusing on the actual incidence of crime. How many serious felonies were there last night? Where did they occur? What patterns seemed to be involved? Was there something that could be done to make an area have less crime and therefore be safer?

Precinct captains began to focus on the patterns and sources of crime in their precincts. They knew that analysts were tracking every crime by neighborhood, by time of day, by day of the week. There was an operations research element of CompStat that began to make crime dramatically more understandable and more preventable.

By focusing on the right outcomes—less crime and more safety— Bratton began to build an entirely new dialogue inside the New York and now the Los Angeles police departments. His precinct leaders began to communicate the same messages to their subordinates.

Every week four or five precincts would come down to One Police Plaza in New York City and the Parker Building in Los Angeles and present a review of their precinct's current public safety status, what they had achieved, and what plans they had in the works to improve the situation. Sitting through a CompStat planning session is a remarkable experience of a Deming-style focus on continuous improvement and leadership at every level from empowered people who believe they can make a genuine contribution to the team's goals.

On one occasion we watched as a twenty-eight-year-old police sergeant in Los Angeles reported on a six-month-long project involving the most crime-ridden shopping mall in the city. As he walked through the data, the analysis, and the proposed solutions, he was bringing data to life and turning it into a tool for solving problems. At the end, he pointed out that a lot of the tools he had used were from courses he had been taking to get a master's degree online from the University of Phoenix.

Bratton's great achievement has been his ability to convince an entire department that there is a better system, and that they can better serve the public by learning and implementing that system.

Moneyball: Metrics and Baseball

There is another, remarkably different book we can study to see the effect of metrics in creating a revolution in outcomes—Michael Lewis's *Moneyball. Moneyball* is the story of Billy Beane and the Oakland Athletics and their use of metrics to dramatically improve their baseball team.

Baseball is a good place to draw the contrast between data and statistics on one hand and the systematic use of the right metrics by senior leadership on the other. In baseball there are historically a lot of statistics and data. Many people memorize batting averages, home run records, number of errors per year, and a host of other facts. However, no one had thought to find the best and most powerful systems of defining what data mattered. In other words, they had data but not metrics.

Baseball offers a vivid example of cultural rejection of metrics by people who would have claimed they were immersed in statistics. *Moneyball* is must-reading for every student of effective leadership, and Billy Beane is a leader who deserves to be heard widely. We had him brief the members of the Center for Health Transformation and they found him to be very helpful in thinking through transformational models.

As Lewis reports in *Moneyball*, baseball scouts had a strong cultural bias toward believing that they could identify high school students who would grow into future stars. In a very real sense, their prestige, their incomes, and their place in the organization were based on a theory of intuitive analysis that precluded a data-driven system.

The first great breakthrough in applying metrics to baseball was the recognition that there simply is not enough data about high school students to make an informed judgment. Only when a player had been in college or in professional baseball could statistics begin to emerge that were valid enough to be used for metrics. At the high school level the competition was too uneven for numbers to prove anything.

Since scouts had made their careers out of looking for high school students, this was a direct threat to their legitimacy and their cultural status. They resented it deeply.

The next great breakthrough was analyzing what actually helped a team win. While this may seem an obvious question to ask, in fact it had never been asked before the late 1990s. This was partly because modern computing made it possible to gather and analyze a lot more data. It was also because the new analytical tools of arbitraging value were being developed in the financial world and were then gradually being utilized by a handful of baseball enthusiasts.

In any event, by the mid-1990s Billy Beane and the Oakland Athletics were prepared to use metrics to look for the best available baseball players and to measure their value against their cost. The result was a systematic, disciplined process of finding better players for less by looking at new data in new ways.

This metrics-led revolution had two great results. First, it led to more wins for a lot less money. The Oakland Athletics win their games for one-third of the price per victory of the New York Yankees. Second, success did not lead people whose cultural values were pre-metric to applaud the new system. In fact, they resented and deeply disliked it.

The experience of baseball at gathering statistics but not thinking through metrics is in fact the norm in the modern world.

When we describe metrics to a lot of people they say "yeah, yeah, we are already doing that" and then they produce a lot of reports with a lot of statistics and data. In fact their easy assumption that they understand metrics is a major hurdle to getting them to study and learn about the real thing.

There are many government agencies and many big corporations that think they have metrics because they have data. They think they have a leadership-led system because they provide lots of reports to their leadership.

There are some simple tests by which we can determine whether we are in a leadership-led metrics system or simply a bureaucratic data and statistics reporting system:

- Who defines the data to be gathered? Has the senior leadership invested the time to understand what it is trying to accomplish and to determine what data will give it the information it needs for vital decisions in a timely way?

- How rapidly is the data being reported? Metrics need to be reported every day to be effective. Bratton insisted that every precinct report every night. It was clearly a revolution in responsiveness and required Bratton to raise the money to get every precinct a computer so they could do it. Computers were not in the budget and he was not prepared to wait years to start the change. A private foundation came up with the money. Wal-Mart starts every morning with flash reporting from its worldwide stores designed to inform senior management about key patterns. McDonald's gathers data worldwide on 37,000 stores every night so senior leaders will know what is happening. When the Baghdad command reports once a month in a thick book, that is an act of data and statistics. That is not creating metrics. When a school system reports once a year on test scores, that is data and statistics. Real metrics are evaluated in virtually real time.

- Does a change in data lead senior leadership to change strategies or resources? The great failure of public bureaucracies and even many large private corporate bureaucracies is their inability to turn knowledge into action. Even if they get the right data, they simply cannot bring themselves to act on it. We knew every month we were failing to generate enough electricity in Iraq yet we could not change the systems fast enough to get things done. We know which inner-city schools have been ruining children every year by failing to educate them, yet we cannot bring ourselves to value the children enough to change the schools. If things aren't changed in response to the flow of information, then we do not have a metrics system, we have a data system.

- Do all the subordinate leaders understand the metrics and understand why they have been used to define the organization's experience? Are they educated into leading at their level and getting the job done so the metrics they are focused on are the right ones? A key difference between leadership-led metrics and traditional reporting systems is that this approach to metrics is designed to liberate subordinates so they can focus on solving problems at their level. It is precisely because senior leaders can be comfortable that they have focused their team on the right goals that they can then release the team to use their own creativity to achieve those goals.

- When there is a substantial gap in metrics between the high-performing and low-performing components, does the senior leadership intervene to retrain or replace the failing systems in a decisive manner? Do results have consequences, or are they simply embarrassing data to be explained away and avoided?

Cultures that have comfortably lived with statistics and data are deeply threatened by a metrics-led system. Unionized credentialed bureaucracies in public schools that fail reject the data and protect the failure even at the expense of the children who are being cheated.

Large government bureaucracies that are failing to deliver simply hide the bad outcomes or promise studies to eventually fix things but nothing really changes. Look at most civilian American institutions in Iraq–the failure to control the southern border, and the intelligence community are examples of this bureaucratic behavior.

Any effort to develop a metrics-led system must be approached with the understanding that it will probably yield both outcomes. If we persevere like Mayor Giuliani, Chief Bratton, and Billy Beane, we will create a substantially more effective system. On the other hand, the people whose lives, status, and values have been invested in the less-effective, less-productive, and less-systematic patterns of the past will deeply resent the changes and try to stop them even if they are succeeding.

Metrics-based leadership may well be the most powerful tool in effective leadership for large systems since the rise of the modern general staff system in the 1850s. By focusing the entire team on key values and creating a common discourse with a common measure of achievement, it is an amazingly effective, extraordinarily empowering and liberating system. Combined with clarity of vision and a dedication to continuous improvement through systems thinking and quality, it can dramatically transform our careers, our businesses, and our government, ultimately leading to a healthier, safer, more prosperous future for all Americans.

13

Bringing It All Together

The principles and models we've described throughout the book form the foundational basis of what we call the art of transformation. But what does it mean as we lead organizations and institutions? What roles must we assume? What questions should we be asking? And where should we focus our energies?

There are ten areas where the top leadership of organizations have to be directly involved and where they alone can provide the necessary leadership:

1. Vision

The question that must be asked first is: what is our vision of what we are trying to achieve? Until we can write down a vision statement (of one page or less), we really cannot begin to think through where we are going and how we will get there. A vision statement helps us both organize our activities and communicate their purpose and goal to others. Since achieving almost any vision will require the effort of more than one person, it is important to be able to explain it in terms others can understand.

Vision statements often carry moral purpose and a sense of fulfillment, and cannot necessarily be measured in purely market or financial success terms. They are at the heart of an individual's plan for himself, his company, his profession, or his country. It is the foundation on which everything is built.

2. Values and measures

How will our efforts be valued and measured? This is not a simple question. In fact, three other questions follow it:

- First, how will we measure success so that over time we can tell whether we are succeeding?

- How will the market measure success? If in business, will it be by our profit margin? If in academia, will it be by achieving tenure? If in the scientific community, will it be the number of our publications and awards? It is very important to be honest and accurate in setting down the values and measurements that will be important in measuring the achievement of our vision.

- How will others whose judgment and opinion we value measure success? Will we be succeeding according to their standards? If we pick a path that is lonely and rarely traveled, that's fine. But we then should understand that we may have little external reinforcement. It is important to be clear about these kinds of judgments at the beginning of the journey, not the end.

3. Key metrics of success

It's absolutely critical that we establish the specific metrics that matter to the senior leadership (which in a small company may be only the founder and in a big system may be many people).

Metrics are vital because they center the entire system on achieving the key goals the senior leadership has decided really matter. They give the entire team clarity of vision and mission that allows us to decentralize implementation, so everyone is involved in developing better solutions at each level.

The very clarity and centrality of a few key metrics then enable us to decentralize leadership both to local leaders and, equally important, to every person working in the organization.

On a routine basis (ideally weekly or daily) the key implementation leaders should be communicating with the senior leaders about metrics as a reflection of reality. At least weekly, the senior leadership ought to be systematically reviewing metrics and shifting resources (including their own time and energy) to solve problems and strengthen important but underperforming areas. These leaders should also be recognizing and rewarding those who are excelling at achieving the defined metrics. Whenever possible the experiences, habits, and systems of the most effective achievers should be benchmarked to provide models for others to learn from, so new standards of performance continuously help the organization migrate to greater productivity and more effectiveness at achieving the defined goals.

4. Strategies, goals, and projects

If we are clear about our written vision statement and the various methods by which we intend to measure success, then it is time to think through the strategies that will be necessary to achieve our vision. We should then reduce each strategy to a series of measurable goals and definable, delegatable projects. Goals and projects are important tools for distinguishing between activity and achievement. Without them we can be merrily busy and energetic and yet not really be achieving our strategies.

5. A system, set of habits, and culture that can achieve the defined goals and metrics

Humans achieve their greatest potential over time when they have a system, a set of habits, and a culture to sustain their efforts.

Great institutions like the American military are inherently characterized by strong institutional frameworks with deep historic memories that shape and define a culture that is then translated into a set of habits.

The Marine Corps has been an extraordinarily effective shaper of young people into honorable men and women. Their exemplary behavior is sustained by a memory beginning at basic training to long after retirement. Consider the importance of the annual Marine Corps birthday party, celebrated worldwide wherever there are Marines.

Institutions of celebrated quality like the Four Seasons and Ritz-Carlton chains, Tiffany, the Federal Bureau of Investigation, the Centers for Disease Control, the Massachusetts Institute of Technology, and the Georgia Institute of Technology have turned their values and goals into a systematic, repetitive set of patterns, which become daily habits that lead to the desired achievements.

We need to translate our vision, values, and goals into an institutional setting in which the culture will sustain the habits needed to achieve the metrics we have defined.

6. Distinguishing between requirements for maintenance, reform, and transformation

Once we have a clear picture of where we are trying to go, how we will measure getting there, and the kinds of human institutions we will need for success, it is important to review our existing institutions and decide whether they need to be maintained, reformed, or transformed. Each of these activities is very different and makes very different demands on the leadership.

Maintenance

Whenever possible, maintain the existing system. Change is hard and risky. It takes time away from achieving already defined goals and serving existing customers. It will be much easier if our existing system is acceptable and simply needs energetic and enthusiastic leadership to keep up the morale and energy level of the team.

Maintenance does not mean coasting. Excellent institutions work every day at sustaining excellence. The best Four Seasons hotel in the world has a management team that works very hard every day to sustain that excellence. The best Army, Navy, Air Force, or Marine Corps unit in the world has a leadership team that works long and intense hours every week to sustain that quality of excellence.

The key difference for leadership is that, in a maintenance setting, its efforts are focused on maintaining momentum and solving challenges within the framework of an accepted and powerful system.

Reform

When the existing system is not getting the job done but the required changes are definable within the existing framework and terms of reference, then the senior leadership should focus on reform.

Reform is preferable to transformation because it requires less change, will meet with less resistance internally, and involves less risk. Reform starts with an assumption that most of the existing systems and culture are productive and only marginal improvements are needed to achieve the goals and metrics as defined by the senior leadership.

In a reform environment, people are being asked to change specific things, but the core nature of the institution, the patterns of the culture, and the habits they practice primarily remain intact.

Reform leads to some resistance because people inherently dislike changing things they are used to, but that resistance is usually minor compared to the trauma involved in transformation.

Transformation

When an institution is clearly incapable of achieving its goals and metrics, then transformation has to occur. Sometimes transformation can be done inside the existing institution. Sometimes the required changes are so great that a new institution has to be invented.

Transformation should never be undertaken lightly. The scale of the change will maximize resistance from the existing interest groups, who will see their identity and interests with the old order. Transformation often requires learning new habits, creating new cultures, and establishing new institutions. The very cost of so much change can be a threat to the existing institution. The challenges may prove too great and the diversion of resources and leadership from sustaining the old system to try to launch the new system may collapse the organization before it can cross the bridge to a new model of behavior.

Despite these factors, there are circumstances when only transformation will enable the achievement of the vision, goals, and metrics that are the organization's reason for being.

The rise of the Internet and the personal computer clearly require transformation for any system that still relies on paper (health, education, and most governments). It is simply impossible for the best paper-based system to keep up with the speed, accuracy, efficiency, and complexity of a modern information system–based organization.

The rise of a global market requires transformation in self-measurement and analysis for any company that has been focused on meeting local, regional, or national competition. If the people who may put us out of business are 4,000 miles away, it does us little good to be better than our old competitor forty miles away. Measuring ourselves against the real competition can be a transformational moment.

Changing customer demands can be transformational. A great five-star hotel benchmarked itself against customer demand and discovered to its shock that its closets were too big and its bathrooms were too small. It had been built in an era when people traveled by train and stayed for three weeks. Now they flew in for two nights. They wanted big, luxurious bathrooms and relatively small closets. The hotel was still rated at five stars but it spent $100 million just to meet the new customer expectations before they became a problem.

Letting the requirement define the amount and type of effort

If we can simply lead an ongoing organization, we should relax and focus on those skills. We won't get many changes, but we won't need them. Sustaining excellence is its own reward.

If we have to lead a reform effort, we should be prepared to spend more time and energy but expect bigger changes as a result.

If we conclude we are facing a transformational challenge, then we must be prepared to invest the scale of time and energy needed to carry people through a level of change that will inevitably lead to considerable confusion and resistance. Transformation can be very powerful but it inherently requires a substantial effort and is a last resort, not a first step.

7. Communicating our vision, values, metrics, strategies, and goals to the entire team

In the information age, every member of the team matters. If they don't matter, why are we paying for them to be on the team? Even if they are volunteers and we are leading a volunteer organization, they still take up time and energy, which means we are actually paying for them even if money does not change hands.

Since every member of the team matters, each one has to know what the overall objective is and how it will be measured. This requires a systematic effort to communicate.

Chief Bratton, in *Turnaround*, provides an insightful explanation of his use of a weekly video for police officers whom he knew would not read a letter or pay attention to a memo from downtown. By having a video every Friday for the lineup in every precinct, he could talk directly to the force and in effect have a face-to-face chat with every cop.

Today we have a wide range of tools, including iPods, phone calls, videoconferences, webcasts, meetings, and written materials. The key is to measure effect rather than effort. Does our team understand where we are going, and do they understand what their jobs are in helping us get there?

8. Educating the team

Communication helps the team understand where and why. Education helps them understand how.

If we are charting a new direction with new strategies, goals, and metrics, why would we expect the existing team to know how to do the new jobs and achieve the new goals? Sound communication can get our team to nod yes and applaud at the right places, but it will not help them implement and achieve the goals and metrics we have outlined. The larger the change, the more education required for the team to be effective.

Maintenance of existing success requires a lot of communication and relatively little education.

Implementation of reform requires targeted education within a pattern of communication.

Transformation requires a major investment in education that will far outweigh the energy and time put into communication. The more profound the transformation, the more time and energy have to be put into education. We have to build in an education budget (time and resources) as well as a communication budget. It is cheating the current team to assume that people can implement goals in a transformed setting without the right education into the new metrics, systems, habits, culture, and rewards.

9. Designing our communication and our structure of rewards so the team understands the new direction and accepts ownership for its achievement

We do not merely want people to understand where the top leadership is going. We want people to understand where they themselves are going and accept ownership and responsibility for helping to get there. We want everyone on the team to understand that this is about their lives, their careers, and their achievements.

If the center of responsibility is with only a few leaders, then those leaders are carrying the burden of the entire organization. If everyone has a sense of responsibility, the entire team is carrying the weight of the organization.

One of the great limitations of the CEO-centric model of recent American business mythology is that it overstates the value of the CEO and understates the value of everyone else in the organization. In the long run, a team-centered system will defeat an individual star-centered system because it can simply bring more human talent, energy, and creativity to bear. This is the heart of Deming's model of continuous improvement through the team pursuit of quality.

Our team will know whether we are prepared to listen to their ideas and reward their achievements. In the long run there has to be a substance of team ownership for people to genuinely commit themselves to helping implement new strategies and build new systems and habits.

10. Continuous improvement and transformational change that is multi-directional, rather than top-down or bottom-up

We have to create a culture of team leadership and team collaboration. The great opportunity of the information age is to enable everyone to offer new ideas and new solutions. This is far more than shifting from a top-down model of leadership to a bottom-up model of information and advice. In the information age, virtually anyone can have a good idea.

The cost of shifting information from one person to another is dropping so dramatically that ideas and solutions can come from anywhere and go anywhere. No one has yet developed the open source models of innovation, improvement, and transformation that are inherently possible in the information age. The MySpace, Craig's List, eBay types of self-organizing systems are early examples of how information systems will enable the flow of ideas and concepts from anywhere in the extended organization (including customers and suppliers) to any point of implementation in the organization (including senior management).

We are entering a new age of continuous evolution, which will require the widest possible participation to meet the challenges and standards of the 21st century.

14

Leadership and Citizenship

In the 21st century, every American will have to become a leader. Leadership is the key to getting anything done. Leadership is the art of knowing something needs to be done; taking responsibility for getting it done; having the energy to work at it; the discipline to stay focused; the persistence to continue despite frustration, failures, and the opinions of others; and, finally, the sense of moral responsibility to believe that you have to get it done.

> "Management is doing things right; leadership is doing the right things."
>
> *Peter Drucker*

Ten years ago this chapter would probably not have existed; we would have focused only on the role of the senior leader. Ten years ago there would have been an emphasis on the central importance of that key leader in bringing about transformation.

Today we feel very differently about leadership. We think leadership has to come from every level. Every person has to be thought of as a potential leader, and every person has to think of him or herself as a leader. Leadership is rapidly becoming synonymous with citizenship.

This is a profound transformation in the nature of organizations and leadership; we are shifting from a hierarchical CEO-centered and bureaucracy-(public or private) centered system to an individually empowered system.

This will prove to be the most profound reassertion of historic American patterns since big corporations, the assembly line, and large bureaucracies began to emerge a hundred years ago.

For the last century, the dominant organizing model has had a key leader at the top, strong bureaucracies defining choices and actions, and relatively passive and narrowly defined employees at the bottom. This pyramid of authority and achievement was the dominant organizational model. It is now increasingly obsolete as the world evolves toward an information age in which every individual has leadership potential.

As Peter Drucker asserted in *The Effective Executive*, it is the nature of a knowledge-based society that every worker inherently becomes a leader. Unlike the sweat labor of the agricultural-era peasant or the monitored and inspected laborer in the industrial-era factory, knowledge workers cannot be coerced and inspected, but rather have to be led to productivity. Their productivity comes largely from within.

Drucker noted that in an information age almost every worker will become a knowledge worker, and therefore will have to be inwardly motivated and have an inner sense of responsibility and accountability. No one else will know if they are reaching their potential, making their best contribution, or truly trying to help their co-workers and their neighbors. The information age is one of self-accountability.

Fortunately, as Daniel Pink observes in *Free Agent Nation* and Glenn Reynolds describes in *An Army of Davids*, most people like to be creative, engaged, and productive. They may do it in ways no factory manager ever dreamed of. They may do it on a schedule that does not fit the 9-to-5 world of the past. They may do it with unique characteristics that would not fit the country club image of leadership in the last generation. They are today's pioneers, creators, inventors, contributors, and leaders.

A Nation of Citizen Leaders: An Historical Perspective

America is uniquely positioned for this world of universal leadership because it was founded on the premise that "all men are created equal and they are endowed by their Creator with inalienable rights among which are life, liberty and the pursuit of happiness." Note that our Founding Fathers believed these rights came from God and were absolutely inalienable (meaning bureaucrats, lawyers, and the government could not take them away), and they involved the pursuit of happiness.

Pursuit is a very important word. It is an active verb, not a passive one. To pursue happiness requires a definition of happiness and a willingness to work and learn. The pursuit of happiness requires an active citizenship that takes on the moral responsibility to understand what happiness is and then be prepared to spend time and energy pursuing it.

Jefferson originally wrote the term as the pursuit of *property*. The Founding Fathers believed that private property rights were essential to freedom. They had seen tyranny during the English Civil War of the 17th century and they had endured what they saw as a tyrannical British government in the 18th century. They wanted to protect Americans from any future government taking away their liberty, and they saw the protection of their property rights as a major barrier against tyranny.

However, as the drafting committee thought about the language, they were convinced they wanted the rights to be broader than property. During the 18th-century Scottish Enlightenment, the term "pursuit of happiness" had come to mean the pursuit of knowledge and wisdom. It was seen by the Founding Fathers as the sum of good civic responsibility and of being a mature adult (and therefore a mature citizen).

Thus America's very founding document, the Declaration of Independence, asserted a unique right and responsibility to every citizen. This was not just a political document. It was a reflection of the powerful culture of individual responsibility and individual opportunity that America had grown into during the previous hundred years.

This sense of every individual as a potential leader was what motivated the silversmith Paul Revere to take his midnight ride warning that the British were marching on Concord and Lexington. It was this sense of civic responsibility that led Benjamin Franklin to invent the bifocal glasses, the lightning rod, the Franklin stove, the American philosophical society, the public library, an insurance company, and the first continental post office. Franklin may rank with Thomas Edison as one of the two most important inventors in American history, and Franklin's contributions were far wider in type (though not as powerful in technology) as Edison's. In both cases inventing was a form of citizenship designed to solve problems and improve people's lives.

The British military could never come to grips with the self-organizing, individually responsible, constantly evolving energy and courage of the Americans—who were determined to be independent. As David Hackett Fischer makes brilliantly clear in *Washington's Crossing* (a study of the crossing of the Delaware and the defeat of the Hessians and British on Christmas Day 1776, and at Princeton in early January 1777), it was the extraordinary, continuous arrival of militia and civilian helpers that ultimately made it impossible for the British army to safely occupy New Jersey or defeat the American army.

Throughout the 19th century and up to the Great Depression (1929–1939) the dominant cultural image of Americans was self-reliant, self-organizing, energetic, responsible, creative, and determined to make their lives and their children's lives better. In books, movies, and common culture, this was the archetype of the American.

The Girl Scout manual of 1913 is entitled *What Every Girl Can Do for Her Country*. At one point it urges every girl to learn two skills so she can earn a living at the second if the first one disappears. This was a message for young women of self-reliance, preparation, and energy.

Alexis de Tocqueville had observed these same attitudes and traits a century before, during his travels in America. The French aristocrat wrote back home of the constant energy, inventiveness, adaptability, and creativity of the average American.

This model of America was overshadowed when the assembly line produced enormous gains in productivity by dividing people into a small number of leaders and a vast number of followers. This was reinforced by the rise of Ludendorff's "war economy" in Germany during World War I. Suddenly power could be centralized in a handful of key "brilliant" people, who decided prices, rationing, and bureaucratic organization.

The German development of a command and control system for the industrial age was rapidly copied in Great Britain and the United

States. For a short period of two or three years, it was a very powerful method for focusing energy and resources.

The academic class loved the new model of bureaucratically controlled "scientific economics." It was a huge shift in power from the economic and scientific entrepreneurs to the college professors. It was a further shift of power from the individual randomly pursuing happiness and seeking achievement to an omniscient group of paper-pushers who would define your life, determine your income, and prescribe what you could and could not do.

Adam Smith (the most influential member of the Scottish Enlightenment) had argued in his first great book *The Theory of Moral Sentiments* that people inherently had consciences and innate desires to do the right thing and to help their neighbors. Within that moral context, in his second and more famous work, *The Wealth of Nations*, Smith argued that a market in which people freely set the price for their goods and labor and other people freely decided what they wanted to pay would create an invisible hand that would improve the wealth and happiness of the individual far more than any government in history.

The literati had hated this free market when tied to industrialism because it gave power and success to non-intellectual people who invented machines and created businesses. The resentment of the intellectual class led to most of the left-wing critiques of the 19th century.

The concept of a government-run economy and government-defined set of rules enabled the academic and literary class to assert control over the inventors and job creators, but also over the individual. It was this sense of bureaucratic power that attracted John Kenneth Galbraith as a young economist during World War II, when he found himself as a government bureaucrat setting prices and deciding on rationing. His knowledge and academic degrees had given him power over others, and he liked it.

It was this transfer of power from the individual to the bureaucrat and the lawyer (who defined the rules for the bureaucrat) that created much of the American system that had evolved by 1980. You were too dumb to educate your child, but a professional you had never met, credentialed by a system you had never seen, operating within a curriculum over which you had no input, and organized by a union that would consistently protect its members against both you and your child was somehow a more effective system—even if it were clearly failing to educate your child.

The welfare system taught passivity and dependence and transferred power to bureaucrats and lawyers.

Even in corporations, the spirit of individual incompetence and bureaucratic competence ran rampant. You could not think through your own health needs. A "professional" in the human resources department of your company would do it for you.

The age of the mainframe computer, with massive power mediated by a professional guild of information systems experts, was in some ways the high-water mark of this kind of paternalistic, restrictive, and controlling model. You could not run your own computer. You had to have a mediating group of information high priests who would decide where you were on the priority list and would stand between you and the machine.

Four things began to simultaneously break down this model of centralized power and individual impotence:

1. It very often simply did not work and was not achieving its results. Welfare was not helping the poor; it was hurting them. A government- or company-defined health plan was not satisfying the needs of unique individuals. The 9-to-5 job of passively obeying other people was not proving very satisfying personally, even if it were lucrative financially.

2. New technologies and new capabilities were dramatically empowering individuals and eliminating the need for layers of bureaucracy and "professionals" who knew things you did not. The rise of Travelocity and Expedia allowed us to become our own travel agents. The rise of self-organizing sales co-ops are beginning to change the real estate world. The rise of ATMs allowed us to become our own bank tellers. The creation of laptops and modern software liberated us from the computer high priests and enabled us to undertake an amazing range of things

we could never have done before. Glenn Reynolds in *An Army of Davids* and Alvin and Heidi Toffler in *Revolutionary Wealth* capture this explosion of new empowerment. It turns out that when people can be independent, many of them like it.

3. The rise of the Internet, the laptop, and the cell phone empowered people to create rapidly shifting and very fluid patterns that no cumbersome bureaucracy could keep up with. The gap between the productivity and effectiveness of the information age individual and the industrial age corporation began to shift decisively in favor of the individual.

4. The world is changing so rapidly that no single leader can be current. You may know a lot about the center of today's production, and therefore you should lead. Tomorrow there may be a new topic someone else knows a lot about, and then they should lead. This ability to have a flexible, floating style of leadership is very threatening to industrial and bureaucratic hierarchies, but it is almost certainly the future.

W. Edwards Deming preached the need for every individual to be seen as a problem solver, and therefore as a leader during the problem-solving period. Deming deeply disliked the Taylorism approach to managing and organizing people with stopwatches and carefully controlled assembly lines. He believed Henry Ford and Taylor had created a dehumanizing system that limited the growth of people and their ability to lead.

Deming wanted every worker to participate in a process of continuous improvement. He wanted everyone to understand the vision of what the company was trying to achieve and then to be encouraged to participate in offering ideas and solutions to constantly improve.

The American Military as a Model of Decentralization

The American military has been a forerunner in developing new opportunities for flattening the hierarchy and empowering every person to be effective and creative.

While there is still a lot of industrial era hierarchy in the Pentagon, there is also an amazing amount of participatory planning and decentralized implementation.

The Special Forces in Afghanistan implemented a constantly evolving campaign plan in which privates, corporals, and sergeants wielded levels of power and made decisions that in World War II would have required higher commands to be deeply involved. Admiral Ed Giambastiani, the vice chairman of the Joint Chiefs, personifies the concept of a "yes, if," decentralized, constantly imitating system. He instructs people in his command that only three people can say no—himself and his two top subordinates. Everyone else is empowered to try to figure out how they can say yes to a request or an idea. His goal is to maximize everyone's ability to move forward. It is a system that values errors of commission over errors of omission. We may have to improve or fix something, but at least everyone is trying to progress.

If we were to analyze how many people can make innovative and independent contributions in an American force (100 percent) with how many could make a decision in the Iraqi military under Saddam (three—Saddam and his two sons), we can see why the Iraqi forces simply could not move at the decision speed of the Americans. Ironically, the anti-Iraqi terrorists are surviving because they are much more decentralized and have many more independent leaders than any traditional army. If they were as slow and hierarchical as a traditional army, they would have been decisively defeated in weeks.

Seven Leadership Characteristics

If everyone is going to be a leader, and if leadership and citizenship have many overlapping and common characteristics, then what does it take at a personal level to be an effective leader? We think there are seven major characteristics that define most leaders. They are:

1. Moral responsibility
2. A vision of success and achievement
3. Energy
4. Learning ability
5. Ability to listen to and rely on others
6. Resilience and persistence
7. Awareness of strengths and limitations

No one has all these characteristics. No one is "the perfect leader."

Note that looks, popularity, special knowledge, unique authority, or position are not included on this list. As Peter Drucker noted forty years ago in *The Effective Executive*, effectiveness is a set of learnable habits. People with a wide range of personalities, looks, and relationships can learn the habits. In many ways, Drucker's book could have been called *The Effective Leader*, and in America, it could also be called *The Effective Citizen*.

Briefly consider the seven characteristics.

1. Moral responsibility

The effective leader has to be prepared to bear the moral responsibility of undertaking something others may not have undertaken or may not even believe needs to be undertaken. This assumption of the risk of doing something and the acceptance of the responsibility for getting it done is essentially a moral act. If we can't accept the moral burden of stepping forward and having others look to us for achievement, then we can never lead. That is why it comes first.

> "There are many qualities that make a great leader. But having strong beliefs, being able to stick with them through popular and unpopular times, is the most important characteristic of a great leader."
>
> *Rudy Giuliani*

2. A vision of success and achievement

Leading is a forward motion. Where are we going? How will we know when we get there? These questions require that we have a vision of where we are going and what we are trying to achieve. The journey to our vision may have many twists and turns and unexpected obstacles. If we haven't defined where we are going or what we are trying to achieve, the journey becomes pointless. There is a huge difference between activity and progress, and leaders avoid the former and focus on the latter. Only a clear vision enables us to distinguish between the two.

> "Where there is no vision, the people perish."
>
> *Proverbs 24:18*

3. Energy

Leading takes a lot of energy. Whether it is the energy of a good politician going to a lot of meetings and shaking a lot of hands or the energy of Ray Kroc persevering to solve all the problems involved in launching

McDonald's, or the energy of the scientist who undertakes hundreds and sometimes thousands of experiments seeking new knowledge, leadership requires energy. The Founding Fathers all knew this, and they expected American citizens to be energetic.

The couch potato will be a passing phase during the shift from an industrial to an information age. Success in the information age will require a level of energy incompatible with the couch potato model. And every citizen will have to have the energy to be a leader, because citizenship and leadership will be synonymous. This does not mean leadership is reserved only for those with huge amounts of energy. It does mean the first responsibility of every citizen is to take some of the energy he or she has and invest it in leading.

> "Energy and persistence conquer all things."
>
> *Benjamin Franklin*

4. Learning ability

Leaders must learn constantly. The world is bigger than any one of us. Whatever we knew yesterday has changed some (and sometimes a lot) while we were sleeping. Whatever we were good at yesterday may or may not be what we need to be good at tomorrow. Learning is not the same as IQ or academic degrees. A lot of very, very smart people are so arrogant that they do not know how to learn. A lot of academically credentialed people are so trapped by whatever they learned to get a degree that they find it very hard to learn new things.

> "The significant problems we face cannot be solved at the same level of thinking we were at when we created them."
>
> *Albert Einstein*

Pragmatism is the one uniquely American contribution to philosophy. It is a philosophy based on facts and reality. It is a reflection of the four-hundred-year-long American tradition of carving a civilization out of the wilderness by learning new things, adapting that civilization to technological change, and integrating millions of people into one society by learning new things.

Learning is a natural American trait that one hundred years of increasingly bureaucratized, unionized, credentialed, industrial era education bureaucracies have failed to drive from our culture. As people learn more and more outside of a school setting and as the

Internet and self-motivated learning increasingly replace the coercive and often boring model of teaching, the ability of all Americans to learn will increase dramatically. It is one reason we are so optimistic about the future of American leaders.

Learning is especially important for leaders (and since in America citizen and leader should be synonymous, it becomes important for all Americans) because the very skills and insights of leadership are complicated and take time to learn. Furthermore, wisdom requires time, thought, and learning. In the end we want wise people rather than smart people, and people willing to learn rather than people with advanced degrees.

5. Ability to listen to and rely on others

Leaders have to listen to others and rely on them to achieve their goals. David Hackett Fischer brilliantly draws the contrast between the councils of war chaired by General George Washington and those chaired by the British general Charles Cornwallis. Washington had large meetings and anyone with useful information could participate. He would frame the issues but then listen as people talked their way to a consensus. By contrast, Cornwallis chaired perfunctory meetings of very few people, and he had usually made up his mind before the meeting began. The result was that Washington increasingly operated with better information, more creative ideas, and more enthusiastic implementation than Cornwallis could generate in his hierarchical structure.

> "The best executive is the one who has sense enough to pick good men to do what he wants done, and self-restraint enough to keep from meddling with them while they do it."
>
> *Theodore Roosevelt*

Effective leaders in America understand that others know a lot (after all, they are listening to other Americans who are also potentially leaders) and that listening is often a first step toward getting. Since they know they will have to rely on others for implementation, they find that listening first increases the chances of success. In addition, they understand the strengths of their team and focus on those strengths, knowing that success depends on maximizing the strengths of each team member, not focusing on individual weaknesses.

6. Resilience and persistence

> "When one door of happiness closes, another opens, but often we look so long at the closed door that we do not see the one that has been opened for us."
>
> *Helen Keller*

Leaders are invariably going to encounter failure and frustration. They are invariably going to run into resistance, ignorance, and refusal to cooperate. Leaders are guaranteed that things will not work the first and sometimes even the second and third time. For example, it, took us seven failures (1980, 1982, 1984, 1986, 1988, 1990, 1992) to finally develop a Contract with America and win the first House Republican majority in forty years. We made a lot of mistakes and had a lot to learn.

If a leader does not have resilience, he or she will not be able to recover from a failure or an argument. If the leader does not have persistence, he or she will not be able to keep moving forward after recovery. These two characteristics are at the heart of success for most would-be leaders and achievers.

7. Awareness of strengths and limitations

Leaders have to know their own limitations and how to focus and pace themselves. But, more important, they have to understand what their strengths are—just as they understand the strengths of the people surrounding them—and they have to use those strengths to achieve their goals and bring value to their organization or undertakings. Effective leaders focus on strengths and opportunities, not on weaknesses and problems.

> "I seldom think about my limitations, and they never make me sad. Perhaps there is just a touch of yearning at times; but it is vague, like a breeze among flowers."
>
> *Helen Keller*

By using strengths rather than focusing on limitations, leaders can overcome the most extreme limitations and challenges. President Franklin Delano Roosevelt had lost the use of his legs to polio. In an age when people in wheelchairs simply did not work in public, he succeeded in communicating such a sense of optimism and fitness that most people did not know he was in a wheelchair. He thought through his situation and adjusted as necessary.

Helen Keller became deaf and blind at nineteen months of age, but with enormous support from her parents and her teacher, she became the first blind and deaf person to graduate from college and went on to become an inspiring national leader.

Some people need very little sleep and have a lot of energy. Other people have frail bodies but very strong wills. Every citizen has to understand his or her own strengths and weaknesses. We can't accomplish more than God gave each of us the ability to do, but if we study ourselves, we will be surprised how much God has enabled us to do.

> "One cannot build on weakness. To achieve results one has to use all the available strengths—the strengths of associates the strengths of the superior and one's own strengths. These strengths are the true opportunities."
>
> *Peter Drucker*

Conclusion

The seven characteristics of leadership are personal. They are the kind of things each potential individual leader/citizen needs to take into account. They are at the heart of the human ability to help create and achieve.

The specific tools and techniques for leadership can be found throughout this book and in many other books. At its heart though, leadership and creativity are about the person—not about the knowledge. Leadership and citizenship, in the end, are about each of us and what we as individuals are willing to do.

PART FIVE

Applying Transformation to Two Key Areas

15

Applying Transformation to Government

21st Century Entrepreneurial Public Management as a Replacement for Bureaucratic Public Administration

It is simply impossible for the American government to meet the challenges of the 21st century with the bureaucracy, regulations, and systems of the 1880s. The challenges of the 21st century are stunningly complex, so much so that April 1861 may be the most meaningful comparison for where Americans find themselves today.

In April 1861, Abraham Lincoln responded to the firing on Fort Sumter by calling for 75,000 volunteers for ninety days. Even so, the 1861 crisis ultimately led to four years of civil war and cost the lives of 660,000 Americans. America is not confronted with a civil war, but we are confronted with profound challenges that we must face as a nation: dramatic scientific and technological change; the economic rise of China and India; the success of more people living longer and posing stresses on our Social Security and Medicare systems; the breakdown of will on the part of America's leaders to control our borders and ensure that new immigrants learn to be American; a disaster response system that failed dramatically after Hurricane Katrina; the long war against the Irreconcilable Wing of Islam; and the potential for rogue dictatorships to acquire and use nuclear or biological weapons.

Together, these and other challenges rival the scale and complexity of the problems that Abraham Lincoln faced. And yet Americans are frustrated with a government that can't adequately do what it is supposed to do: protect our lives, our property, and our way of life.

In government, implementing policy effectively is ultimately as important as making the right policy. In national security we have an absolute crisis of ineffective and inefficient implementation that undermines even the best policies and risks the security of the country. In health, education, and other areas we have cumbersome, inefficient, and ineffective bureaucracies that make our tax dollars less effective and the decision of representative government less capable. People expect results, not excuses. Getting those results in the 21st century will require a profound transformation from a model of bureaucratic public administration to a model of 21st century Entrepreneurial Public Management.

There is a practical reason government cannot currently function at the speed of the 21st century. Modern government as we know it is an intellectual product of the civil service reform movement of the 1880s.

Think about the implications of this fact.

A movement that matured more than 120 years ago developed in a period when male clerks used quill pens and dipped them into ink bottles. The processes, checklists, and speed appropriate to a pre-telephone, pre-typewriter era of government bureaucracy are clearly hopelessly obsolete.

Imagine walking into a government office today and seeing a gas light, a quill pen, a bottle of ink, a tall clerk's desk, and a stool. The very image of the office would communicate how obsolete it was. If you saw someone actually trying to run a government program in that office you would know instantly it was a hopeless task.

Yet the unseen mental assumptions of modern bureaucracy are as obsolete and as ill-equipped for keeping up with the modern world as that office would be.

Today we have a combination of information-age and industrial-age equipment in a government office run in an agricultural-age system. It is made even slower and more risk-averse by the attitudes of the inspectors general, the Congress, and the news media. These three groups are mutually reinforcing in limiting energy, entrepreneurship, and creativity.

The inspectors general are products of a scandal- and misdeed-oriented mindset that would bankrupt any corporation. The inspectors general communicate what government employees cannot do and what they cannot avoid. They emphasis a petty dotting the i's and crossing the t's mentality that leads to good bookkeeping but slow, unimaginative, and expensive implementation.

There are no inspectors general seeking to reward imagination, daring risks, or aggressive leadership over achievement.

Similarly, the members of Congress and their staffs are quick to hold hearings and issue press releases about mistakes in public administration but there are remarkably few efforts to identify what works and what should be streamlined and modernized.

Every hearing about a scandal reminds the civil service to keep its head down.

Similarly, the news media will uncover, exaggerate, and put the spotlight on any potential scandal but it will do remarkably little to highlight, praise, or recognize outstanding breakthroughs in getting more done, more quickly, with fewer resources.

Finally, the very nature of the personnel system leads to timidity. No amount of extra effort can be rewarded and no amount of incompetent inaction seems punishable. The failure of the system to reinforce success and punish failure leads to a steady drift toward mediocrity and risk avoidance.

The difference in orientation between what we are currently focused on and where we should be going can be illustrated vividly.

Building a 21st Century Intelligent, Effective, Limited Government Versus Marginally Reforming Current Ineffective Bureaucracies

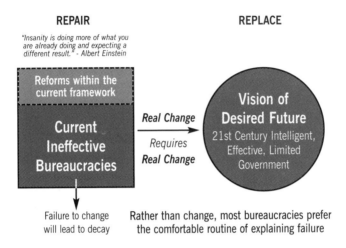

Of course, it is not possible to reach the desired future in one step. It will involve a series of transitions, which can also be illustrated.

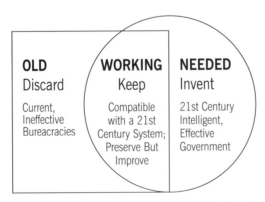

(With thanks to Senator Bob Kerrey for helping to develop this model)
©2006 Center for Health Transformation

Without fundamental change, we will continue to have an unimaginative, red tape–ridden, process-dominated system that moves more slowly than it did in the industrial era and has no hope of matching the speed, accuracy, and agility of the information age.

The Wal-Mart model is that "everyday low prices are a function of everyday low cost." The Wal-Mart people know that they cannot charge overtime less than it costs them. Therefore if they can have the lowest cost structure in retail, they can sustain the lowest price structure.

This same principle applies to government. The better you use your resources, the more things you can do. The faster you can respond to reality and develop an effective implementation of the right policy, the more you can achieve.

An information-age government that operated with the speed and efficiency of modern supply chain logistics could do a better job of providing public goods and services for less money. Moving government into the information age is a key component of America's ability to operate in the real-time worldwide information system of the modern world.

Moving government into the information age is absolutely vital if the military and intelligence communities are to be capable of buying and using new technologies as rapidly as the information age is going to produce them. It is unavoidable if police and drug enforcement agencies are to be able to move at the speed of their unencumbered private sector opponents in organized crime, slave trading, and drug dealing. It will be a key component of America's ability to meet its educational goals and save those who have been left out of the successful parts of our society. It will be vital for developing new energy sources and creating a cleaner environment with greater biodiversity. It will be critical in America's ability to transform the health system into a 21st Century Intelligent Health System.

Developing an information-age government system is going to be one of the greatest challenges of the next decade. What is needed is much more than almost acceptable government created by marginal change. What is needed is the profound transformation of the current system. This new model can be thought of as 21st Century Entrepreneurial Public Management.

21st Century Entrepreneurial Public Management

We chose the term 21st Century Entrepreneurial Public Management to deliberately distinguish it from bureaucratic public administration. We need two terms to distinguish between the new information-age system of entrepreneurial management and the inherited agricultural-age system of bureaucratic administration.

The only constant is the word *public*. It is important to recognize that there are legitimate requirements of public activity and public responsibility that will be just as true in this new model as they were in the older model. Simply throwing the doors open to market-oriented entrepreneurial incentives with information-age systems will not get the job done. The system we are developing has to meet the higher standards of accountability, prudence, and honesty inherent in a public activity.

We have to start with a distinguishing set of terms because we are describing a fundamental shift in thinking, in goals, in measurements, and in organization. Change this profound always begins with language. People learn new ideas first by learning a language and then by learning a glossary of how to use that new language. That is the heart of developing new models of thought and behavior.

Shifting the way we conceptualize, organize, and run public institutions will require new models for education and recruitment as well as for day-to-day behavior.

We must shift from professional public bureaucrats to professional public entrepreneurs. We must shift from administrators to managers. The metrics, rules, and expectations will be profoundly different.

A first step would be for schools of public administration to change their titles to schools of entrepreneurial public management. This is not a gimmicky word trick. Changing the name of the institutions that attract and educate those who would engage in public service will require those schools to ask themselves what the differences in curriculum and faculty should be.

The president, governors, mayors, and county commissioners should appoint advisory committees from the business community and from schools of business to help think through and develop principles of 21st Century Entrepreneurial Public Management.

The Federal Legislative Role in 21st Century Entrepreneurial Public Management

Congress as it is currently organized and operated cannot possibly meet its constitutional responsibilities. It is a failing institution, and as the challenges grow greater, so will congressional failures. Congress today resembles failing airline and auto industry management much more than the rising leadership of successful entrepreneurial information-age companies.

Congressional transformation is vital because the legislative branch is the keystone of the Constitution. While the news media emphasizes the president and commander in chief, especially in wartime, the Founding Fathers centered freedom on the legislative branch.

The legislative branch comes first in the Constitution. It was described in the *Federalist Papers* as the branch closest to the people, and the one that should normally have the most power.

Yet the many challenges facing America threaten to overwhelm the legislative branch's capacity to fulfill its central role in our democracy. The United States must meet four radically different national security threats: the long war with the Irreconcilable Wing of Islam; the danger of an aggressive dictator acquiring biological and nuclear weapons that could destroy our country; the rise of China as a long-term scientific, technological, and economic competitor; and the precariousness of relying on potentially hostile regimes for our energy supplies.

The United States has to create secure borders while eliminating the inherent danger from foreigners who are already illegally in the United States. To achieve this will require a new system for controlling—but not closing—the border, combined with an effective legal system of guest workers and a new standard for citizenship that requires passing an American history test in English and giving up any allegiance to other countries.

Competing with China and India will require the United States to transform its litigation, regulation, education, taxation, and health policies simply to be effective enough as a country to sustain its high standard of living and military strength while competing with countries with four times its population.

American competitiveness in the world and security at home will require a new strategy that combines energy, the environment, and national security into a program for developing new technologies. This will simultaneously create an affordable American system of energy, minimize damage to the environment, maximize biodiversity, and minimize our dependence on unreliable sources of energy.

Education in particular will require dramatic transformation. It is impossible for the United States to remain the leading country in the world when its children fail to learn math and science. In the period from 2006 to 2031 there will be four to seven times as much new scientific knowledge gained as in the last twenty-five years. This will require dramatic changes in our learning systems for the United States to remain the world leader.

Beyond educational transformation, the United States needs bold new approaches to help those trapped in a culture of self-destruction (prisoners, drug-infested neighborhoods, communities of poverty) and to help the least productive and least prosperous in America achieve middle-class incomes and productivity. America cannot compete with China and India if the least productive and least prosperous third of Americans are not fully engaged.

The Baby Boomers' longevity is a good thing, but it will have consequences. No society in history has attempted to have so many people live into their eighties, nineties, and beyond. This will require transformation in pensions, in the very concept of retirement, in the nature of assisted living and long-term care, in the structure of the Social Security system, and in the structure of Medicare and Medicaid.

All these challenges require a strong, effective legislative branch capable of moving at the speed and with the intelligence of the 21st century information age.

That 21st century intelligent, effective legislative branch does not exist today. Yet under our Constitution it is extraordinarily difficult to create an executive branch more capable and more competent than the legislative branch.

The legislative branch sets an agenda for the executive branch by the way it engages in oversight. It defines the structures and activities of the executive branch by the way it writes laws. The legislative branch determines what the executive branch can spend and how it can spend it by the appropriations bills it passes.

Without a transformed legislative branch engaged in 21st century oversight, writing 21st century legislation, and passing 21st century appropriations, it is virtually impossible to have a truly transformed executive branch or an effectively balanced judicial branch.

The scale of change will make congressional transformation unavoidable. The only question is how long and how painful the process will be. We are on the edge of a dramatic transformation in government. The gap between the system of government we have inherited and the requirements and capabilities of the 21st century is simply becoming too big to defend government as is.

Our system of inherited government has enormous power. It defines the careers and intellectual investments of millions of civil servants in local, state, and federal government. It defines the intellectual capital of most lawyers, public managers, academics of public administration (including public health, the Foreign Service, the military, and congressional staffs) and the news media that cover government and politics.

We cannot successfully marginally improve this obsolete system.

It is already visibly failing.

In Katrina the city of New Orleans failed. The state of Louisiana failed. The government of the United States failed. It is important to use the word *failed* because we have to understand that we are not faced with marginally improving a relatively healthy system. We are facing a system that is failing and has to be transformed rather than reformed.

The scale of change in our daily life has been extraordinary. The lack of change in government is striking. One first step toward creating a 21st century intelligent, effective, limited government is to create a new model of oversight.

21st Century Oversight

Oversight is the easiest area in which to begin transforming government, because it is a low-risk place where members of Congress and their staffs can learn about the future and the present without having to write a new law or spend more money.

It is possible to design a new model of 21st century oversight that would transform how Congress learns and the questions it asks. In the process Congress would begin to shift the executive branch, the news media, and activists toward new ideas, new questions, and new approaches.

This new model will require members and staff to do some fundamental learning before they launch the oversight. There will be substantial resistance in Congress because this is very new.

Many members and staff will yearn for the old model of congressional scapegoating and blaming, allowing members and staff to get good media coverage while doing limited learning or work.

That model is destructive for the executive branch and for America. It is an adversarial model that teaches the executive branch timidity and focuses congressional time and attention on trivia. It demeans both the leaders of the executive branch and the members of Congress. It diminishes the American government's ability to get things done for the American people.

A model 21st century oversight process should:

• Define the positive aims of the oversight process openly and publicly so people could hold the committee or subcommittee accountable for meeting its own stated goals. Establish that this will be a collaborative process and the executive branch will be involved from the very beginning in thinking through and improving oversight. Establish from the very beginning that the goal is not to play "gotcha" but to say "together we can do better for the American people."

• Establish from the beginning with the cooperating members of the executive branch that the approach will be "yes, if," rather than "no, because." Experts have a habit of explaining what can't be done. Lawyers have a habit of hiding behind "no" or "that is not permitted." Bureaucrats are made more comfortable by simply saying "no, because." The productivity of creative and entrepreneurial teams is enhanced by insisting that new ideas and new suggestions be met with a positive "yes, if" attitude that seeks to find out how something could happen rather than comfortably shrugging it off as undoable. This attitude change is fundamental to the scale of transformation needed in government and society over the next two decades.

• Define the positive goals and values the American people want achieved in a particular area. This requires studying the way in which Mayor Giuliani and Police Chief Bratton developed CompStat as a model of asking the right questions to reduce crime in New York City. Crime declined by 5,000 felonies a week (260,000 felonies a year) in the eight years Giuliani was mayor. Since then, under Mayor Michael Bloomberg and Police Chief Raymond Kelly, the system has reduced crime further. Today there is 70 percent less crime than in 1991 and New York City is the safest city in the United States per thousand people. Chief Bratton has used the same system to make Los Angeles a model to be studied by every member of Congress and congressional staff.

• Once the goals and values are clear, the committee or subcommittee, with its executive branch colleagues and outside experts, should establish the processes likely to achieve those goals.

• The entire world should be scanned to benchmark companies, institutions, and systems that have the best track record of achieving those goals.

• Hearings should be held on what works outside government and how it could relate to government. This initial phase is simply transformational learning and brainstorming. The goal is to have a wide range of people with successful experience outside government educate those who are seeking new and better solutions inside government. In some cases, the New York City and Los Angeles use of metrics would be an example, and the benchmarking would include outstanding government leadership.

- Once the committee or subcommittee and its executive branch colleagues had learned enough about various dramatically better ways of getting things done, the next stage would be to brainstorm how those insights could be applied to a particular aspect of government. There should be a major focus on establishing the right metrics to enable people to focus on achieving the right goals and to establish a clear public record of how activities will be measured in the future.

- Draft legislation (whether of a bill or an amendment) should then be widely disseminated so people from many backgrounds (including the witnesses at the earlier hearings) could comment and offer improvements.

- Congress should establish its own "Lessons Learned" system modeled after the Joint Forces Command to develop and continue a critical, self-aware approach to reviewing congressional behavior, developing better systems and doctrines, and educating members and staff. The 21st century information age is going to require continuous learning from everyone, and that includes the Congress.

This is a boldly different model from the current Congress.

With C-SPAN and the THOMAS system for public information, the Congress has already started to make some steps in the right direction. It will be the nature of the 21st century to require more transparency and more accountability from every person and every institution. Congress needs the equivalent of Sarbanes-Oxley applied to its own institutional behavior, structure, and culture. Over time the American people will demand it.

Creating a new model of transformational 21st century oversight is the least risky and lowest-cost first step toward a 21st century intelligent effective Congress. It should be initiated at once.

Additional Changes Required to Develop a Government Based on the Information-Age Principles of Entrepreneurial Public Management

In the legislative branch, we will need to:

- Replace the current civil service personnel laws with a new model of hiring and leading people, including part-time and temporary employees. Moreover, these people should have the ability to shift to other jobs across the government and the ability to train and educate themselves on an individualized Internet-based system

- Radically simplify the disclosure requirements that have become a major hindrance to successful people coming to work for the federal government

- Write new management laws that enable entrepreneurial public leaders to set metrics for performance and reward and punish according to the achievement level of the employees

- Within appropriate safeguards, create the opportunity for leaders to suspend and when necessary fire people who fail to do their jobs and fail to meet the standards and the metrics

- Work with the major departments to reshape their education and training programs and their systems of assessment so they can begin retraining their existing work force into this new framework

- Transform the Congressional Management Institute so it plays a leading role in developing the new legislative version of entrepreneurial public management (some states have similar institutions)

- Develop a new set of goals and definitions for the inspectors generals' jobs and refocusing those professionals into being pro-active partners in implementing the new entrepreneurial public management approach

- Design a new salary structure that reflects the remarkable diversity of capabilities, hours worked, level of knowledge, independent contracting, part-time engagement, etc., that is evident in the information-age private sector

- Pass a new system of procurement laws that encourage the supply-chain thinking that is sweeping the private sector

- Develop a new model of congressional and state legislative staffing to ensure that enough experts and practitioners are advising legislators at the federal and state level, so they can understand the complex new systems that are evolving and transforming capabilities in the private sector

- Transform the General Accounting Office, the Congressional Research Service, and the Congressional Budget Office into institutions that understand and implement the principles of Entrepreneurial Public Management

- Develop a system for educating new members of Congress and new congressional staff members about these new principles

- Create an expectation that within two years, every current congressional staff member will have taken a course in the new method of entrepreneurial government management

- Rethink the kind of hearings that ought to be held, their focus, and the kind of questions government officials ought to be answering

- Design a much more flexible budget and appropriations process to permit the kind of latitude effective entrepreneurial leaders need

- Establish for confirmation hearings the kind of questioning that elicits from potential officeholders how they would work in an entrepreneurial public management style, and apply these

questions with special intensity to people who come from a
long background in traditional bureaucracy

With this set of changes, the legislative branches will have prepared
for a cooperative leadership role in helping the executive branch
transform itself from a system dedicated to bureaucratic public
administration into one working every day to invent and implement
21st Century Entrepreneurial Public Management.

16

A 21st Century Intelligent Health System

In most areas of life, Americans enjoy the ease and convenience offered by advances in technology, communications, and transportation. Every day we experience the 21st century model of America, which is one of effectiveness, accuracy, speed, flexibility, efficiency, lower cost, more choices, and greater achievement. We can shop online, compare prices for goods and services, and when decisions need to be made, we have access to a wide array of information sources to assist in making those decisions. In short, Americans enjoy great latitude in our power to determine what is best for us.

This is not, however, the case when it comes to health and healthcare. In our current healthcare system, individuals are dependent on a structure that has resisted the natural progress and modernization achieved by market-oriented, 21st century industries.

The information age has been leaving health behind.

While it is the nature of a science- and technology-based entrepreneurial free market to provide more choices of higher quality at lower cost, in the healthcare sector, prices continue to rise, quality is inconsistent, and individuals lack the information, incentives, and power to make choices.

The Urgency of Health Transformation: Not a Choice, but a Necessity

The area of health and healthcare is one where transformation is not a choice, but a necessity. That reality has been driven home by a number of recent events and ever-growing challenges:

Health and Homeland Security

The very nature of our times gives us no choice but to transform or decay. With the looming threat of a potential avian flu pandemic or other natural or engineered biological disasters, it is imperative that we reinvent our health system.

Hurricane Katrina served as a wake-up call. By homeland security standards, it was not an unexpected or exceptionally large event. Yet we witnessed a collapse of the healthcare system in the Gulf in its aftermath. Millions of paper records were lost at the very time they were most needed. Hurricane victims in need of emergency medical care faced additional difficulty and risk because caregivers were unable to access patient histories. And while floodwaters rose, needy patients and caregivers were trapped in hospitals where power had been lost with little or no hope of receiving help, since there was no centralized communication system in place by which to triage an emergency response.

Hurricane Katrina was a stunning reminder of the fragility of our healthcare system; it exposed the weaknesses of a system in which demand has far exceeded capacity. The American health system is rooted in a 1950s model of paper records stored in filing cabinets, hospital basements, and warehouses.

If we were incapable of responding to a disaster on the scale of Katrina, imagine what would happen if we were required to withstand multiple crises simultaneously—something that we have to accept as a very real possibility in today's world.

Transformation of our healthcare system, therefore, has become a matter of the highest national security. If the leaders and key decision makers in healthcare and government neglect to confront the serious failings of the current system, they place themselves in the position of having ignored their most basic duty: to protect the lives of Americans.

Demographic Changes: The Aging of America

In 1965, the average life expectancy was 70.2 years. Today it is over 77 and is expected to increase to 78.5 years by 2010.

It is a testament to American innovation and values that we are living longer. Our ability to extend life is a great success but presents some enormous challenges. We must face the reality that seventy-six million Baby Boomers are nearing retirement and consider how their retirement will affect the future of our health and healthcare system. When confronted with such emerging demographic realities in the past, we have historically set up command and control structures to limit access and to restrict choice in an attempt to control costs. These methods have routinely failed us, and there is no reason to believe that they can succeed in the future. Indeed, Baby Boomers are the least likely group to accept being trapped into a bureaucratic, red tape–ridden, regulatory, third party–payer system with fewer choices, lower quality, and increasing costs.

Baby Boomers will spend more years in retirement than any other generation, so in thinking about longevity for them and their children, we should recognize that Boomers have a very different idea about retirement than their parents. They will want to make their lives in retirement even more interesting, productive, and active. And they will want to be in control—they will not sit by passively while others make decisions about their lives. Baby Boomers are the most market-oriented and savvy generation to reach retirement in American history. They understand investing, modern technology, and communications.

> Baby Boomers want a second start, not a retirement.
>
> *Bill Novelli*
> *President, AARP*

Boomers also understand that the natural pattern of the 21st century is to have more choices and greater quality at lower cost, because these choices have been their experience over their lifetimes. Thanks to modern technology and science, in an entrepreneurial market-oriented system, they have come to expect better products and services at the lowest possible price. In fact, they know that as quality improves, prices often decrease. This is true for many of the products and services they use daily: mobile phones, computers, online travel services, and home entertainment systems.

As they age, Boomers will begin to use the healthcare system more and more. What they will expect is what they have always received: high quality at low costs. It is impossible to talk to Baby Boomers about rationing, about scarcity, about limited choices, or ask them to accept skyrocketing costs. However, if we continue on the current path, government spending on healthcare is predicted to rise from 6.6 percent in 2002 to almost one-third of the GDP by 2050. Three-quarters of that increase is related to the aging of our population.

The attitude and expectations of the Boomers, along with their financial impact on the system, will force us to rethink and replace our current system with a 21st century system of better healthcare and more choices at lower cost.

Medical Errors and Unnecessary Deaths

A 1999 report by the Institute of Medicine revealed that as many as 98,000 people die in our hospitals annually due to medical error. That's the equivalent of a jet crashing and killing 250 Americans every day.

We are 2,000 times more likely to die in a hospital from a medical error than in a civilian air crash. But this only tells part of the story. Medical errors often lead to illness or disability but not death. Studies reveal that five or six out of every 100 patients will be victims of a medical error. In addition, 5 to 10 percent of those who are hospitalized acquire a hospital-induced infection, leading to an estimated 88,000 deaths per year in addition to those categorized as deaths from medical errors.

In America, statistics like these are simply unsustainable. And, with public awareness increasing, there is a growing demand that our leaders do something to fix our ailing system.

Disparities in Outcomes

The increasing evidence of disparities in outcomes is a critical factor that makes a compelling and tragic case for why a new system of health and healthcare is not just a choice but an absolute necessity.

At the top of the list are racial disparities. Recent studies have shown that, relative to whites, infant mortality rates are 2.5 times higher for blacks, life expectancy is ten years less, and blacks have significantly higher mortality rates from heart disease, stroke, and cancer. The racial divide when it comes to health and healthcare is a moral issue that simply cannot be dismissed, and a tragic reality that is at the heart of the need for change in our current system.

Equally disturbing are various studies indicating that there are significant disparities in outcomes related to sex, geography, hospital, and even individual doctors. Furthermore, evidence shows that individual genetic makeup can determine both how likely we are to develop certain conditions and how successful certain treatments might be. The tragedy is that our current 20th century paper-based system does not allow us—as a country or as individuals—to use such data to determine what treatment, what provider, or what behaviors might improve the quality and the length of our lives.

As Americans hear more and more about the discrepancies that exist, there will be a growing public outcry demanding a new system, one that improves quality of care for every American, regardless of race, sex, genetics, or geography.

The Epidemic of Diabetes and Obesity

The number of Type 2 diabetes cases in the United States has doubled in the past two decades to an estimated 20 million (when undiagnosed cases are included). This makes diabetes the country's fastest-growing public health problem. Furthermore, the CDC predicts that one in three American children born in 2000 will join the ranks of those afflicted with Type 2 diabetes. Diabetes is the only major disease with a death rate that is still rising—up 22 percent since 1990—and it is the leading cause of kidney failure, blindness, and non-traumatic amputation.

The American Diabetes Association estimates that, when we include both treatment and lost productivity, diabetes costs the United States economy about $132 billion per year.

Obesity, primarily a result of Americans' eating and exercise habits, is a major contributor to the increase in diabetes. The most recent figures from the Centers for Disease Control and Prevention show that 65 percent of U.S. adults—or about 130 million people—are either overweight or obese. And obesity is on the rise. Over the past twenty years, obesity among adults has risen significantly in the United

States. This increase is not limited to adults. The percentage of over-weight young people has more than tripled since 1980. Among children and teens aged six to nineteen, 16 percent (more than nine million young people) are considered overweight.

These increasing rates raise concern because of their implications for Americans' health. Being overweight or obese increases the risk of many diseases and health conditions, including the following:

- Hypertension
- Dyslipidemia (for example, high total cholesterol or high levels of triglycerides)
- Type 2 diabetes
- Coronary heart disease
- Stroke
- Gallbladder disease
- Osteoarthritis
- Sleep apnea and respiratory problems
- Some cancers (endometrial, breast, and colon)

In addition to decreasing quality of life and increasing risk of premature death, obesity costs the nation an estimated $117 billion per year, including both direct medical costs and costs related to lost productivity. Combined with the quality of life issues, the financial impact of our growing diabetes and obesity epidemic will make it almost impossible for us to avoid overhauling the system. And it is clear that government will have to be involved in the transformation, when we consider how much of the cost is absorbed by Medicare and Medicaid. (Note that the table below includes only medical costs and data from two separate studies: one by National Health Accounts (NHA) that includes nursing home costs and one by Medical Expenditure Panel Survey (MEPS) that does not. The numbers are in *billions* of dollars.)

Insurance Category	Overweight and Obesity		Obesity	
	MEPS (1998)	**NHA (1998)**	**MEPS (1998)**	**NHA (1998)**
Out-of-pocket	$7.1	$12.8	$3.8	$6.9
Private	$19.8	$28.1	$9.5	$16.1
Medicaid	$3.7	$14.1	$2.7	$10.7
Medicare	$20.9	$23.5	$10.8	$13.8
Total	**$51.5**	**$78.5**	**$26.8**	**$47.5**

Note: Calculations based on data from the 1998 Medical Expenditure Panel Survey merged with the 1996 and 1997 National Health Interview Surveys, and healthcare expenditures data from National Health Accounts (NHA). MEPS estimates do not include spending for institutionalized populations, including nursing home residents.
Source: Finkelstein, Fiebelkorn, and Wang, 2003

The inclusion of nursing home expenditures in the NHA estimates causes most of the difference between the MEPS and NHA results.

Shortage of Healthcare Workers

Our 20th century system of healthcare has created an environment that has led to a growing and critical shortage of healthcare professionals. The nursing shortage is perhaps the most obvious, with a shortage of 126,000 in 2001, expected to rise to 400,000 by 2020.

Critical physician shortages exist on a regional and specialty basis. Furthermore, Stephen Foreman, assistant vice president of research at the Pennsylvania Medical Society, recently released a study indicating that there will be a substantial shortage of physicians by 2020 that cuts across most specialties, predicting a 25 percent shortage nationwide.

Key factors leading to the shortages include a frustrating work environment—largely a function of a managed care approach that has taken decision-making power away from the provider and patient and given it to a third-party payer; cuts in reimbursement, which have led to cutbacks that make the job more difficult and less financially rewarding; the aging of the Baby Boomers, which is putting a new strain on the system; and our litigious society, which is driving up the cost of medical litigation-protection insurance and forcing many doctors out of practice.

The Uninsured

To put it simply, insuring all Americans is a moral imperative. Eighteen thousand people die every year because they are uninsured. According to the Institute of Medicine, uninsured adults under sixty-five have a 25 percent higher death rate than their insured counterparts. Uninsured trauma victims are less likely to be admitted to the hospital or receive the full range of needed services. They are 37 percent more likely to die of their injuries. A recent *Health Affairs* report projected that by 2013 the number of uninsured will rise from the current 45 million to 56 million. This means that without change, excess deaths for those without insurance will increase to over 24,000 lives each year.

Uninsured children are 70 percent more likely to go without care for common childhood conditions such as asthma, ear infections, and sore throats. They are five times more likely to have an unmet need for medical care each year.

The uninsured are 33 percent less likely to get a routine physical exam and 25 percent less likely to visit a doctor for an illness. Uninsured women are 36 percent less likely to get a Pap smear and 60 percent less likely to get a mammogram. Uninsured men are 40 percent less likely to get a prostate examination.

The ripple effects of being uninsured and having poor health are felt throughout society. Uninsured children have impaired development and poor school performance. Uninsured adults have more absences from work, more unscheduled sick days, and greater rates of disability. The cost of treating the uninsured is listed as one of the major challenges facing hospitals today.

A 2004 Kaiser Family Foundation study found the societal costs of the uninsured to be $125 billion. Regardless of how one views the issue, the cost to society is high. Without insurance, the health, lives, and financial security of families are at extreme risk.

Unsustainable Increase in Costs

The cost of healthcare is going to force us to rethink the entire system. Government healthcare spending alone is currently 6.6 percent of the GDP, but at the current trend it is predicted to climb to over 32 percent by 2050!

Meanwhile, employers are seeing healthcare spending become a major corporate issue. What used to be a topic confined to human resources departments is now discussed in corporate boardrooms, as healthcare costs threaten the financial stability and the very survival of many corporations. According to GM, $1,500 of the cost of every car is a result of the cost of providing healthcare to their employees.

Small businesses are increasingly making the decision not to insure their workers because the costs of doing so have become unsustainable. And, with more and more of the costs of insurance passed on to individuals from their employers, Americans are becoming increasingly aware of just how expensive the system is. Premiums for family coverage in employer-sponsored health insurance plans have increased by 73 percent since 2000.

The Bureau of Labor Statistics calculates that America's healthcare costs have risen at twice the rate of inflation since 1970. Total costs amount to about $2 trillion annually, and almost half of that is government spending. Here are the biggest components:

- Hospital care: $571 billion
- Doctors' services: $400 billion
- Prescription drugs: $189 billion
- Nursing-home care: $115 billion
- Private insurance: $96 billion
- Dental services: $82 billion
- Home healthcare: $43 billion

Insurance premiums have risen even faster than healthcare costs overall, with a 9 percent increase in 2005 alone.

The difference between the downward price pressures in the rest of society and the price increases of health and healthcare will increasingly fuel the demand for dramatic change in the system.

Growing Public Awareness and Demand

The notion that healthcare in the U.S. should be safe and affordable resonates with Americans who are beginning to sense that our expensive health system is obsolete. The public is eager to experience the same conveniences in healthcare as they enjoy in the rest of their lives. The momentum of demand for health transformation continues to be compounded by people's negative encounters with the health system, such as overcrowded emergency rooms, months-long waiting lists for physician appointments, confusing health pricing mechanisms, and exposure to media coverage of waste, fraud, abuse, and neglect in the health system.

A March 2006 Gallup poll showed that "availability and affordability of healthcare" topped a list of twelve issues of most concern to Americans. A full 68 percent of respondents said they worried about this a "great deal," compared to 51 percent who were worried a great deal about Social Security, the next highest issue area.

A recent *Reader's Digest* poll found that two-thirds of adults twenty-one and older said they feel they "can't afford to be sick." Among those identified as middle class and "underinsured," one in three said that healthcare is "completely" or "mostly" unaffordable. About half say they've put off or refused medical treatment for a serious condition, or delayed taking or renewing prescription drugs, while 46 percent have postponed routine annual physicals and 27 percent have avoided surgery of some sort.

As the public becomes more and more aware of and concerned about our healthcare system, those who cling to the status quo will find it more and more difficult to turn back the tides of change.

Four Key Drivers

There are four major drivers of change to create a 21st Century Intelligent Health System:

1. Focusing on patient safety, which will provide the moral authority for transforming the system

2. Building an IT system characterized by increased accuracy, speed, efficiency, and ability to focus on outcomes, with genuine privacy and security

3. Developing a culture and system of quality

4. Insisting that the individual take personal responsibility for his or her own health

Measuring Success

A solution's transformational value in any of these four areas should be measured by its ability to achieve one of the following results:

- Better health or healthcare outcomes at lower cost
- The same health or healthcare outcomes at lower cost
- Better health or healthcare outcomes at the same cost
- Lifesaving measures at any cost as an American value

The Solution: Replacing the Current Healthcare System with a 21st Century Intelligent Health System

Health Transformation

Where we are currently going

*Where we **should** be going*

Reforms within the current framework

Current Healthcare System

Real Change

Requires

Real Change

21st Century Intelligent Health System

Failure to change will lead to decay

Rather than change, most bureaucracies prefer the comfortable routine of explaining failure

If our health system is to sustain the challenges of the 21st century, we have to replace it with a whole new system, starting by defining our vision of that new system.

The Vision

A 21st Century Intelligent Health System in which knowledge saves lives and saves money for every American.

Vision Details

In an intelligent health system, the individual is the center of knowledge, decision making, and responsibility for his own health. Knowledge of health and finances are available in the most accurate, least expensive, and most convenient manner possible.

In a 21st Century Intelligent Health System, individuals have accurate, timely, personalized knowledge about their health and treatment options, including information about cost and quality. They have the assurance that their treatment is based on the most up-to-date evidence-based medicine, and the focus is on preventive care and early intervention. The system encourages and rewards wise healthcare purchasing decisions and offers more choices of higher quality at lower cost.

A key test for any new system is its ability to provide affordable access to quality care for the poorest and sickest among us. The elimination of health disparities must be a critical goal: no one can be left behind. A 21st Century Intelligent Health System must provide access to affordable insurance coverage for those currently uninsured.

By creating a 21st Century Intelligent Health System, we can transform the current problem of inadequate health outcomes combined with steadily rising costs into two great opportunities:

1. The system will improve health outcomes, quality of life, lead to longer lives at lower cost, and save individuals, companies, and governments billions of dollars.
2. It will be the greatest single 21st century source of high-paying jobs and foreign exchange earnings as people across the world discover they want the quality of life, the level of health, and the effectiveness of healthcare that an American intelligent health system will make possible.

Vision Principles

As we move from today's 20th century system to our new vision of a 21st Century Intelligent Health System, the following principles must guide the transition and serve as a template as we decide what policies and solutions to adopt:

Current System ⟶	21st Century System
Provider-centered	Individual-centered
Price-driven	Values-driven
45 million uninsured Americans	100% coverage
Hidden price and quality information	Transparent price and quality information
Knowledge-disconnected	Knowledge-intense
Slow diffusion of innovation	Rapid diffusion of innovation
Disease-focused	Prevention and health-focused
Paper-based	Electronically based
Third party controlled market	Binary mediated market
(patient—provider—payor)	*(individual—provider)*
Limited choice	Increased choice
Punishment-driven	Incentives-pulled
Predatory trial lawyer litigation system	New system of health justice
Quantity and price measured	Quality of care and quality of life
Process-focused and administered	Metrics-led & outcomes-focused
Bureaucratic management	Collaborative leadership
Overall cost increases	Overall cost decreases

21st Century Model of Health

A 21st Century Intelligent Health System and its principles can be distilled into three essential components, reflected in the following model:

Triangle Model of Health and Healthcare Transformation

Individual-Centered
Incentive
Psychology
Empowerment

The Right to Know Information about
Price, Quality, Providers,
and Personal Health Status

Prevention
Early Detection
Self Management
Best Practices

IT
Quality
Expert
Systems

Component One: Centered on the Individual

Putting individuals at the center of the system requires that they be given the incentives, the information, and the power to make wise choices. However, the 20th century system we inherited is one in which individuals seldom have information about cost or quality, have no financial incentives for wise consumption, and generally have decisions made for them rather than choosing for themselves.

Starting with the decision in 1943 to go to a third-party system, we've turned healthcare into a rental car. The problem is, almost no one washes a rental car.

We see two startlingly different patterns when we compare most areas of healthcare today with the few areas where individuals have direct control. Consider the difference in price trends for cosmetic surgery and Lasik eye surgery—areas where the individual has financial incentives, information, and the power to choose—to other areas of healthcare where this is not the case:

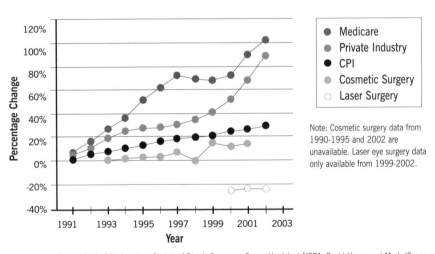

Source: CMS, CPI, American Society of Plastic Surgeons, Devon Herrick at NCPA, David Harmon at MarketScope.

Clearly, individuals making decisions and being directly financially impacted by them dramatically influences the price.

We see similar outcomes when we apply a consumer approach—giving the individual both information and incentives—to health benefits design. The financial savings for employers who have implemented such a design have thus far been extraordinary, as illustrated by the chart below.

Better Health Is Leading to Lower Costs

Consumer-driven healthcare, early success examples

#	Company	CCHC Plan/Tools	Budgeted Health Inflation Trend for first year of CCHC Plan	Actual Health Inflation Trend First Year After CCHC Plan Introduced	# of Participation Emplyees	Notes
1.	Technology Company (CA)	Lumenos	+14%	-9%	2,294	2004 Results
2.	Manufacturing Company (MN)	Lumenos	+14%	-27%	1,704	2004 Results
3.	Healthcare Company (TX)	Lumenos	+18%	-12%	4,000	Avg. 2003 and 2004 Results
4.	Hospital System	Humana	+15%	-31%	7,300	2003 Results
5.	Trover Health Solutions (KY)	Humana	+19%	-26%	750	2003 Results
6.	Logan Aluminum (KY)*	Aetna	-	-18.7%	1,000	2003 Results
7.	Mercy Health Plan (MO)	HealthTrio	+16%	-9%	300	2003 Results
8.	Wise Business Forms (PA, GA, IN)	Definity	+10%	-13.3%	500	2002 Results

Note: *The above are early results and are not necessarily representative of the experience of each company utilizing consumer choice health plans. Year-to-year claim activity will vary; annual results will show more volatility if the population is small. For small employers with slightly higher or lower numbers, large claims will have a significant impact.*

In even the most conservative cases, once a consumer approach was implemented, the difference between the anticipated trend and the actual trend in spending resulted in savings of over 20 percent.

Right to Know

Allowing individuals to choose will work only if we also provide them with the information needed to make informed choices. Yet the current healthcare system is absurdly secretive. When it comes to healthcare, Americans typically have no way of comparing the cost and the quality of the various health services, products, or providers they are considering. This situation is tantamount to asking someone to shop for a car when the dealer hides the prices, rolls back the odometers, and does not disclose that his lot is filled with a fleet of rental cars.

Yet, fueled by the health consumer's growing demand for information, we are beginning to see some progress, even in government. As of this writing, Medicare will soon post the prices it pays for common medical procedures. Our hope is that in the near future, Medicare beneficiaries—and all other healthcare consumers—will have the right to know not only the cost but also the quality of the physicians and hospitals they depend on.

While the vast majority of states keep secret the cost and quality data they collect, we turn to Governor Jeb Bush and Florida's former Agency for Health Care Administration secretary Alan Levine, who made Florida the first state in the country to openly report a wide range of cost and quality measures for its hospitals and outpatient facilities.

Florida CompareCare.gov has a wealth of information on everything from hospital infection and mortality rates to the cost and frequency of surgical procedures performed. Knowing which hospitals have the highest and lowest death rates—and the highest and lowest prices— allows the consumer to choose the best-performing, highest-value hospital. What surprises many is that high quality and low price often go hand-in-hand. By shining a light on the poorest performing hospitals and outpatient facilities, Governor Bush and his team are saving lives and saving money for all Floridians.

A second Florida site, MyFloridaRx.com, further promotes the consumer's right to know by providing retail pricing information for the fifty most commonly used prescription drugs in Florida. This site helps consumers get the most for their money. A quick search of one ZIP code in Miami shows that, in the case of one drug, the cost of thirty pills ranges from $91 in one location to $220 in another.

Demonstrating a commitment to consumer-driven healthcare, Florida has taken a monumental step toward genuinely empowering its citizens to be better healthcare consumers.

Personal Responsibility

In a 21st Century Intelligent Health System individuals have certain rights, including the right to know cost and quality information and the right to be assured that their providers are practicing the best standards of care. But they also have responsibilities.

First, individuals are expected to be informed and to use that information to make wise decisions. It will be futile for us to provide information about cost and quality if people don't use it to make intelligent decisions.

Second, individuals are expected to engage in (and encourage their children or family to engage in) healthy behaviors, related to both nutrition and exercise, that are proven to prevent illnesses and complications. If they develop a chronic illness, they are expected to learn and follow best standards of care to avoid costly complications. Prevention, early detection, and good self-management are part of the 21st century focus on health, as opposed to healthcare. While others can develop the tools and provide the lessons, individuals must apply them to their own lives.

Third, individuals are expected to help pay for their care. Everyone should be required to participate in the insurance system. Those whose incomes are too low should receive vouchers or tax credits to help them buy insurance. Those who oppose the concept of insurance should be required to post a bond to cover costs. Allowing individuals to pass their health costs on to others reinforces the attitude that it's not their problem and adds to the irresponsible, unhealthy behaviors that are bankrupting the current system.

Personalized Health

The 21st century individual-centered system will be a personalized system of health, resulting in dramatically better health for everyone. Imagine a future where tests will allow us to know exactly what combination of medicines will protect us from the specific diseases or conditions to which we are most susceptible, based on our genetics. Consider a world where we know that health and treatment regimens are designed specifically for each individual.

We are already seeing glimmers of how the future of medicine is likely to change as we move toward a more personalized system. Not long ago, the newspapers ran a story about a drug that scientists learned, in reviewing years of data, had a stunning impact on preventing heart attacks in African American males. This was not the original purpose of the drug. Moreover, the drug had no such impact on white males. In a 21st century, IT-rich, intelligent system, we will be able to recognize these patterns much more quickly and to share them more widely in order to prevent illnesses, thereby saving lives and money.

Today, we are already able to send a saliva or blood sample through the mail and have it analyzed to determine our likelihood of developing specific diseases, and as a result we can change our diets and habits and receive early screenings for specific diseases. Drug companies are already planning for an era of personalized medicine, when drugs are likely to be designed specifically for the individual.

All of this is just a preview of a 21st century system of personalized medicine that will dramatically change the future for us, our children, and our grandchildren.

Component Two: Information Technology and Quality

The personalized system of health we just described cannot be possible without a system that is IT-rich. The system must allow easy but secure sharing, analysis, and usage of information about health and health history and about the cost, quality, and outcomes of treatments we are considering.

We not only have to transform for the future, but we also have to transform to catch up with the last thirty years. Consider ATMs, self-service gas stations with credit card–enabled pumps, Travelocity, e-tickets, and cell phones—and compare those to the paper-based, non-connected nature of our healthcare system. A friend of ours from UPS tells us that when a UPS driver enters the average physician's office with his handheld tracking and recording device, the computing power of that office doubles.

The difference between health and healthcare and other sectors of society when it comes to information technology is dramatic. And it has had a dramatic impact on the lives—and deaths—of the American people.

Paper Kills

Paper kills. It is that simple. Instead of saving lives, our current paper system is often taking them. With as many as 98,000 Americans still dying as a result of medical errors every year, ridding the system of paper-based records and quickly adopting health information technology will save lives and money.

But getting physicians and other clinicians to adopt IT has proven to be a Herculean task. A 2005 study by the Centers for Disease Control and Prevention concluded that only 31 percent of hospital emergency departments and 17 percent of doctors' offices have electronic health records to support patient care.

Each day that we refuse to move from a paper-based to an electronic system, people are dying needlessly. This is not just conjecture—health information technology's tremendous potential to saves lives and money is real and is happening in some of the most forward-looking practices and transformational institutions in our country.

- It has been proven in places like the Indiana Heart Hospital in Indianapolis, where medication errors were reduced by 85 percent with the completion of a new paperless facility. At the same time, implementation of health information technology helped reduce physician administrative time by 30 percent, allowing doctors to spend more time with patients rather than on paperwork.

- The Central Utah Multi-Specialty Clinic, the largest multispecialty group in the state, implemented an electronic medical record system provided by Allscripts Healthcare Solutions. During a one-year study, the clinic experienced spending reductions/revenue increases amounting to more than $952,000 over the previous year, and it anticipates savings of about $14 million over the next five years.

- The Agency for Healthcare Research and Quality believes that thousands of lives and billions of dollars could be saved if we were to implement health IT nationwide.

Today: $100 billion a year wasted, tens of thousands of lives lost unnecessarily

Submitted by Agency for Healthcare Research and Quality (April 28, 2003)

Solution	Result	Savings
Computerized Physician Order Entry (inpatient)	↓ rate of serious med error by 55%; ↓ rate of potential adverse drug events by 84%	Total annual savings range from $7 to $14 billion (nationally)
Clinical Decision Support Technologies	↓ ordering of drugs that pt. is allergic to; ↓ in orders for wrong (ineffective) meds;	↓ antibiotic cost by ~$200 per hospitalization; lower cost of hospital care ($26,315 v $35,283) and shorter hospital stays (10 v 12.9 days)
Automated Medication Dispensing Systems (inpatient)	Significantly fewer missed doses of drugs (↓16.9%)	One hospital realized savings of $1.28 million over 5 years.
Bar Coding Technologies	75% decease in errors caused by administration of wrong meds; 93% reduction in errors from wrong med to wrong pt.	Annual national savings of $15.3 billion
E-Prescribing in Physician Practices	Decreased medication errors; Improved physician efficiency	One study demonstrated ↓ pharmacy costs of $1.15 PMPM; 30% decrease in physician to pharmacy phone calls;
Computerized Physician Order Entry (outpatient)	Eliminate 2 million adverse drug events; Avoid 1.3 million office visits and 190,000 hospitalizations	$27 bilion savings in medication expenses (nationally)
Electronic Medical Records (Primary Care Settings)	34% reduction in adverse drug events; 15% decrease in drug utilization; 9% decrease in unnecessary lab utilization	↓ Spending by $44 billion per year; Savings of $86,400 per provider over a five year peiod.

Note: *The above are early results and are not necessarily representative of the experience of each company utilizing consumer choice health plans. Year-to-year claim activity will vary; annual results will show more volatility if the population is small. For small employers with slightly higher or lower numbers, large claims will have a significant impact.*

E-Prescribing

Doctors write billions of handwritten prescriptions every year, of which more than 150 million require a call from the pharmacist to the doctor for three reasons: the pharmacist cannot read the writing, the drug is not compatible with another drug the patient is taking, or the pharmacist wants to substitute a drug so the patient's insurance will cover it. That is an enormous waste of time and resources on a correctable problem. But more important, written prescriptions kill people—and the evidence is overwhelming. Medication errors contribute to more than 7,000 deaths annually, exceeding those resulting from workplace accidents, yet we have no OSHA-like (Occupational Safety and Health Administration) response. According to a report by the Institute for Safe Medication Practices, medication errors could be cut by 55 percent if physicians switched to electronic prescriptions. This is more than a theory: a computerized physician order entry system at the Metropolitan Hospital Center in New York helped reduce medication errors by more than 40 percent, while incorrect drug orders fell by 45 percent, and illegible orders all but disappeared.

Following the installation of a computer prescribing module in the Oregon Health and Science University Hospital emergency department, prescriptions were three times less likely to include medical errors and five times less likely to require pharmacist clarification than handwritten prescriptions. A survey of four hundred physicians found that 76 percent said electronic-prescribing technology enabled them to deliver better quality care.

Electronic prescriptions are also proven to increase efficiency. A study by Tufts Health Plan found that electronic prescribing saved two hours a day per physician. In addition, the technology helped doctors improve patient safety in several ways: it made prescriptions more legible, it let them know of potential drug interactions, and it let doctors know whether patients had been refilling their prescriptions on time.

A study by the University of Virginia found that e-prescribing devices cut prescription refill times to an average of sixty-nine seconds, down from the fifteen minutes that nurses had to wait on hold before their orders were taken.

Within three months of implementing a new e-prescribing platform and improved training procedures, inbound pharmacy calls fell 36 percent and outbound calls to manage renewals fell 50 percent, according to a recent study on the impact of electronic prescribing technology. Financial savings equated to approximately $3,000 per physician per year.

Temple University Health System primary care physicians saved 10 percent on malpractice insurance premiums after installing an electronic prescribing system. Yet, while nearly all physicians' offices have computers and 75 percent of doctors own a handheld computing device, according to a 2002 Harris survey only 16 percent of office-based physicians were using electronic prescribing tools and only 2 to 3 percent of the more than three billion prescriptions dispensed annually were processed electronically.

E-prescribing and electronic health records are only two areas where we have been slow to adopt health IT, despite the existence of proof that it saves both lives and money. Even bar coding, which has been used in grocery stores for decades, is relatively simple, and has been proven to be dramatically successful in preventing drug errors in hospitals, has been adopted only by about 50 percent of our hospitals.

While some providers resist new technologies and cling to paper records, many would like to use technologies but say that the financial costs often put them out of reach. Furthermore, interoperability, or the inability of various technologies to "talk to each other," or integrate with future technologies, increases buyer hesitancy.

Clearly, our 20th century reimbursement models and the absence of uniform standards of interoperability are roadblocks we must address if we are to create the 21st Century Intelligent Health System we envision. (The congressional testimony in the Appendix provides additional details about the possibilities, the challenges, and the solutions to accelerating the adoption of health IT.)

Component Three: Health, not Healthcare: Prevention, Early Detection, Self-Management, and Best Practices

The need to transform the current system from an acute care–focused system to one of prevention and early detection is evident. Heart disease, the leading cause of death for both men and women in the United States, accounted for nearly 700,000 deaths in 2002. In 2005, heart disease was projected to cost $393 billion. It is the leading cause of death for American Indians, Alaska Natives, blacks, Hispanics, and whites. More than 300,000 people have bypass surgery in the United States each year.

Heart disease and its complications can be prevented. Among people with heart disease, studies have shown that lowering cholesterol and high blood pressure can reduce the risk of dying of heart disease, having a non-fatal heart attack, and needing heart bypass surgery or angioplasty. For people without heart disease, studies have shown that lowering high blood cholesterol and high blood pressure can reduce the risk of developing heart disease in the first place.

A system focused on prevention rather than on acute care would provide the incentives and policies to support lifestyle changes needed to control cholesterol and blood pressure. A culture of physical activity and healthy diet choices would replace the current epidemic of inactivity and "fast food."

The increased incidence of diabetes is another example of the impact of a healthcare system focused on acute care and not prevention. Type 2 diabetes can be prevented. According to Frank Vinicor of the CDC, "Recent studies have shown that people with pre-diabetes can successfully prevent or delay the onset of diabetes by losing 5 to 7 percent of their body weight. This can be accomplished through thirty minutes or more of physical activity most days of the week and by following a low-calorie, low-fat plan, including a diet rich in whole grains and fruits and vegetables."

For those who have developed diabetes, complications can be prevented through control of blood glucose, blood pressure, and blood lipids and by receiving other preventive care practices such as eye exams and foot checks. In fact, every percentage point drop in the results of the A1C blood test (used to measure a person's average blood sugar level over two to three months) reduces the risk of microvascular complications (eye, kidney, and nerve diseases) by 40 percent.

However, our current system, in providing reimbursement for volume of care rather than outcomes, discourages the type of care that prevents diabetes complications and acute episodes. Not long ago there was a news story about a diabetes clinic that managed the health of its patients so well that it was forced to close because it did not receive a high enough level of reimbursement to stay in business. In other words, by keeping its patients healthier, the clinic forced itself out of business. This is further evidence that the 20th century system we have inherited is measuring and rewarding the wrong things.

The same mindset is evident when it comes to the willingness of the system to pay for technologies and discoveries to keep us healthy. Using diabetes again as an example, our tendency is to pay for dialysis or amputations but to refuse to pay for the education, the tools, or often the medications that can prevent these costly and tragic consequences. A system that takes advantage of 21st century opportunities will be able to provide us with a whole new range of technologies, tools, and screening mechanisms that will allow us to stay healthier, avoid or delay many illnesses, and manage illnesses we develop. Yet it must also have the mechanisms to pay for, disseminate, and deliver those solutions if they are to make a difference.

Finally, a 21st Century Intelligent Health System will be able to quickly discern and share knowledge about what approaches, technologies, treatment options, and standards of care are most successful in preventing illnesses and their complications. This is something that is impossible in a 20th century disconnected, paper-based system. Currently, there is a tragic failure to routinely deliver best standards of care. A recent study by Rand showed the significance of the problem.

Why Quality Standards Matter

Condition	What We Found	Potentially Preventable Complications or Deaths (annual)
Diabetes	Average blood sugar not measured for 24%	2,600 blind; 29,000 kidney failure
Hypertension*	Less than 65% received indicated care	68,000 deaths
Heart attacks*	39-55% did not receive needed medications	37,000 deaths
Pneumonia*	36% of elderly received no vaccine	10,000 deaths
Colorectal cancer*	62% not screened	9,600 deaths

Source: Woolf SH, "The Need for Perspective in Evidence-Based Medicine," *Journal of the American Medical Association*, Vol. 282, 1999, pp. 2358-2365.

The Rand study also noted that people with diabetes received only 45 percent of the care they needed. For example, less than one-quarter of diabetics had their average blood sugar levels measured regularly. Poor control of blood sugar can lead to kidney failure, blindness, and amputation of limbs.

The problem is magnified if we consider the impact of the current environment on future possibilities. For example, if Dr. Andrew von Eschenbach is right, we might be able to find a way to eliminate cancer as a cause of death by 2015. But even if we do, if our current 20th century system of delivery has not changed dramatically, it is likely that our own doctor might not adopt the necessary lifesaving practices until 2032. In those seventeen years, how many people would have died needlessly? How many wives or husbands, sisters or brothers, children or grandchildren? It's a potential scenario that gives us a startling glimpse into two possible futures: one in which we cling to the status quo and another in which we save countless lives and millions of dollars by replacing the current system.

The Strategies

We believe there are at least nine key strategies to take us from where we are today to our vision of a 21st Century Intelligent Health System.

1. Create information-rich health savings accounts to both incentivize and empower the individual.

2. Create secure electronic health records with expert systems to maximize accuracy, minimize errors, reduce inefficiencies, and improve care.

3. Develop a new system of health justice that has patient safety as a central component.

4. Create a buyers' market for pharmaceuticals by building a transparent system for individuals, doctors, and pharmacists of price and efficacy information about prescription and over-the-counter drugs. The system would have an open formulary with an "after-pay" rather than a co-pay: a "Travelocity" for drug purchasing.

5. Create a system and culture of rapid adoption of solutions that result in better outcomes at lower cost for both the public and private sector.

6. Establish an intellectually credible, accurate system for capturing the cost and benefits of better solutions, better

technologies, and better outcomes in order to create a technically correct model of return on investment for solutions resulting in better outcomes at lower cost.

7. Develop a real-time continuous research database and discover-develop-disseminate-deliver ability: turning cancer into a chronic disease by 2015 and eliminating preventable complications from diabetes by 2015.

8. Combine these electronic systems into a virtual public health network for health protection against natural outbreaks and a bioshield against deliberate biological attack.

9. By implementing the first eight strategies, turn health and healthcare from a problem into an opportunity, making it the leading creator of high-value jobs and foreign exchange earnings in American society, including as a first step the creation of an undersecretary of commerce for health.

Forging the Path to a 21st Century Intelligent Health System

Moving from where we are today to a 21st Century Intelligent Health System represents a major transformation. Meanwhile, the change will constantly be happening at four levels:
1. The individual
2. The organization or institution
3. The culture or society
4. Science, which dramatically changes everything

These are not sequential or separate levels. Instead, changes at the four levels happen simultaneously, and changes at one level are caused by—and subsequently cause—changes at the other levels. We will have to manage the current dysfunctional system while we are leading the transformation to the new system.

The Watershed
of Fundamental Change

Lead the Transformation

Manage the
Sustaining
System

Manage the
Sustaining
System

Copyright 2006, The Center for Health Transformation.

As the new system is created, we will have to manage it even as we prepare to cross another watershed, because the reality is that transforming health and healthcare will involve crossing a series of watersheds.

Changing a system as large as healthcare cannot be an organized march. Nor is it a sudden leap into a new world. Rather, it is a migration from what currently exists to the system we envision. Migrating to the 21st Century Intelligent Health System is illustrated in the following model:

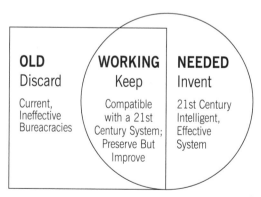

OLD	**WORKING**	**NEEDED**
Discard	Keep	Invent
Current, Ineffective Bureacracies	Compatible with a 21st Century System; Preserve But Improve	21st Century Intelligent, Effective System

(With thanks to Senator Bob Kerrey for helping to develop this model)
©2006 Center for Health Transformation

Transitioning into a 21st Century Intelligent Health System requires us to mix the old and the new. Components of the health system that are working effectively and are compatible with a 21st century system should be preserved and improved. We must learn to discard those elements that are clearly not working and replace them with new solutions.

Growing a Health Transformation Movement

To create and lead a migration this large, we have to grow a movement of citizen leaders dedicated to health transformation. Doing this involves:

- *Communicating the urgency and the vision (including vision-level metrics) of a 21st Century Intelligent Health System, in order to win the argument with the public and with a growing number of allies.* In communicating the need, it's important to remember that moral purpose must precede practicality. We must start by communicating the moral purpose (why it should be done), followed by the practical (data that shows that it can be done), followed by the action (what we should do).

- *Defining the right language and repeating it constantly to get our allies and other people to use it.* We have to talk over and over about a 21st Century Intelligent Health System; we have to talk about "right to know," not transparency; we have to talk about health, not healthcare; we have to talk about saving lives ahead of saving money. Having the right vision, the right solutions, the right language, and then engaging in simple, consistent repetition are the most powerful techniques we have.

- *Constantly acquiring energetic people who will help move us toward our vision through their leadership.* Our goal is to get a legislator here introducing "right to know" legislation, an insurer there moving to accelerate IT adoption, an employer over there implementing HSAs. By every day adding new people doing new things that advance health transformation, the momentum of change will keep building until it simply overwhelms the status quo.

- *Constantly identifying and sharing with others 21st Century Intelligent Health solutions that are proven to save lives and money to show that this is possible and to accelerate the broader adoption or adaptation of those solutions.* This requires a constant listen, learn, help, lead orientation. (Please see Appendix E and visit www.healthtransformation.net to review some of the transforming solutions that we have found, or contact us at info@healthtransformation.net to suggest your own.)

- *Creating an environment where there are hundreds or thousands of decentralized projects that move us toward a 21st Century Intelligent Health System.* Note that this is not a central command and control operation but an environment where we want lots of people with lots of health transformation ideas engaged in managing projects that begin changing the landscape of health and healthcare. They will help us envision the future and understand new opportunities to move toward that future, and they will also help us determine what 20th century roadblocks need to be replaced with 21st century policies and structures in order to accelerate the adoption of projects such as theirs.

Meanwhile, the project created by an employer is likely to be different from the one created by an IT firm, and both are likely to be different from what a collaborative catalyst such as the Center for Health Transformation would undertake. The projects are determined by the mission and the capabilities of each organization. At times, however, various organizations will collaborate in a broader multi-stakeholder project. For example, in Georgia, the Center for Health Transformation is coordinating a project that has brought together more than twenty large employers, including the state government, along with all the major insurers and hundreds of physicians to create a statewide pay-for-performance project designed to improve the quality of care for people with diabetes.

Stakeholders, Coalitions, and a Collaboration of Leaders

To create the new 21st century health system, we need people from all parts of the system involved. Health and healthcare are incredibly complex issues, and changing one part of the system will impact other parts of the system in ways we need to understand. As we deal with the opportunities and roadblocks involved in transformation, we can learn a lot by listening to those in the system describe what is working and what is not. However, we cannot organize ourselves around the wishes and the self-protective stances of stakeholder groups. Instead, we have to constantly ask ourselves, "What is in the best interests of the health of the average American?" We then let the stakeholders reorganize themselves around that.

Nobody got up in 1890 and said, "Gee, I wonder what we should do about transportation? Let's go ask the stagecoach owners!" Instead, the Wright brothers said, "We think we want to invent the airplane." Henry Ford said, "I think I will mass produce cars." They were trying to optimize the range of choices we as citizens have for transportation. We need to do the same thing in health: focus on what would give the average citizen the longest possible life with the highest quality of life with the lowest cost—and then let the stakeholders reorganize themselves around that.

Meanwhile, if we can get those stakeholders to say "yes, if" rather than "no, because" we will have engaged them in helping create a better future—and will have potentially added more energy, ideas, and leaders to the movement we are building. Individuals and organizations involved in the movement will contribute in one of three ways: as individuals working in an entrepreneurial way on individual projects and actions; as part of a temporary coalition to work on a specific project or task; or as a collaboration of leaders dedicated to our shared vision of a 21st Century Intelligent Health System. Many of those we can learn from represent "islands of excellence" in a sea of 20th century mediocrity. They are key to the transformation, as they serve the role of providing models we can replicate, adapt, or expand upon to drive the transformation.

In the new system, the role of the various stakeholder groups will require a new type of collaboration and a new kind of leadership, including:

- **Individuals** will have more rights but also more responsibilities. They will have access to more information and choices but will be expected to become partners in their own health and health-care. Assuming that their health is their doctor's problem and not their own will be a thing of the past. As the wealth of information, knowledge, and scientific breakthroughs rapidly expand, people will have to become their own best advocates, as no doctor will be able to keep up with the constant changes and advances related to every condition and relevant to the personal profile of each patient. In addition, individuals can help drive the transformation and improve their own health and healthcare by selecting providers who embrace the principles and practices of the 21st Century Intelligent Health System and by voting for policymakers who will advance such a system.

- **Healthcare Providers (including physicians, hospitals, nurses, and other healthcare professionals)** will have to embrace and adopt new technologies, new interoperable systems, and a new culture. A future where the individual is at the center, where learning is constant and real-time, and where innovations are much more rapidly driven through the system will require a different culture. There will be more partnering, increased reliance on IT-assisted knowledge and expert systems and a system where (like at the Mayo Clinic) health professionals consult one another.

- **Payers (including insurers and employers)** will be called upon to provide the employees and/or providers they serve with incentives for better outcomes and for the adoption of 21st century solutions, including IT and adherence to best standards of care and health management activities such as prevention and early detection. They will also find themselves engaged in collaborative projects, often with partners who in other settings are considered competitors. As combined databases enrich the intelligence capabilities that strengthen the system, there will be a new transparency and sharing based on the public good that will cross competitive lines. Meanwhile, they will also have to constantly adopt new IT capabilities and create new products to stay in step with the 21st century requirements and trends.

- **Solution Providers and Vendors** will have to embrace an interoperability and level of transparency that will force many of them to change their competitive strategy. They will also have to constantly innovate, as products will evolve and be replaced. They will be called upon to make it easier for their customers to use their solutions and to upgrade or replace them when necessary. As we move toward a more personalized system, vendors will find themselves in the position of having to respond to individualized demands through offering real-time customization and adaptation of their offerings to meet their customers' changing needs. They will often find that their customers become partners in the research, development, and distribution of their products.

- **Government** will be engaged at three levels: as policymaker, as employer, and as provider of healthcare for the poor, the elderly, and the disabled. In each role they must lead by creating and implementing policies and solutions that accelerate the adoption of an individual-centered, IT-rich system focused on prevention, early detection, self-management, and best practices. Because government controls 45 percent of healthcare spending and because the policies it enacts broadly impact the system, the involvement of government in transforming the system is critical. This means that we need to dramatically transform the way government currently works with regard to health and healthcare.

Fifteen Key Health Transformation Projects for Government to Undertake

1. Implement a metrics-based system of management and leadership in all government health and healthcare programs. We must start by having big vision metrics for the entire country, and then making sure that each agency and each program has its own metrics that relate to the overall metrics, and that each person in those agencies and programs has metrics relative to their specific projects. When metrics are not being met, we need to either make changes in a program or eliminate it.

2. Ensure accurate scoring of healthcare spending by the Congressional Budget Office. The CBO has long used outdated models to analyze the costs of proposed legislation. These models ignore the economic growth, efficiencies, and cost savings that result from implementing innovative and transformational policies. When considering health and healthcare opportunities, the CBO must begin to consider cost savings related to improved efficiencies and to the avoidance of illnesses or consequences, and it should also begin to report anticipated outcomes in terms of lives saved and clinical outcomes.

3. Fundamentally reform the reimbursement model to reward quality outcomes. We need to move to a reimbursement model that pays providers for risk-adjusted quality outcomes. Current pay-for-performance and other incentive programs are a first step toward an outcomes-based payment structure.

4. Build a national health information network. A modernized, interconnected healthcare system would electronically link physician offices, hospitals, pharmacies, public health agencies, and other key first responders, providing valuable data to prepare for and respond to an emergency. In an extreme disaster, such as a hurricane, an avian flu pandemic, or a terrorist attack using a weapon of mass destruction, advanced expert systems could perform a variety of essential services. They could electronically track patients' hospital visits, symptoms, and conditions; direct scarce resources to where they are most

> The success or failure of any government in the final analysis must be measured by the well-being of its citizens. Nothing can be more important to a state than its public health; the state's paramount concern should be the health of its people.
>
> *Franklin Delano Roosevelt*

needed; assess the effectiveness of response strategies in close to real time; support contact tracing for appropriate infectious diseases; determine possible origins and causes of an outbreak; and capture other vital sources of data. They could also help us in the aftermath of an extreme disaster, such as Hurricane Katrina, where the ability to care for evacuees was impacted drastically by the fact that nearly all citizens fled the Gulf with no medical histories, no medication lists, no treatment regimens, no lab results—no healthcare documentation of any kind.

When there is no emergency to respond to, a national health information network would be the information highway that every doctor and healthcare provider in the country could use in the course of care. From electronic prescribing and remote patient monitoring to clinical trial applications and medical research, a national health information system would provide the connectivity, efficiency, and improvement that we all aspire to achieve in healthcare.

5. Reimburse hospitals and physicians for using health information technology in the course of care. One way to guarantee better health outcomes is to encourage the use of health information technology such as electronic health records, decision support tools, bar coding, and computerized physician order entry. If we truly want better health at lower costs, the number-one priority of every stakeholder in healthcare should be to get these technologies into the hands of every healthcare professional in the country.

6. Reform Stark and anti-kickback laws to speed health IT adoption and deliver better care. Physician adoption of electronic health records is woefully inadequate, and current Stark and anti-kickback laws are part of the problem. The Stark statutes prohibit physicians from referring their patients to a hospital, urgent care center, laboratory or other facility with which they (or a family member) have a "financial relationship," be it as an investor, contractor, or owner of the facility. While these laws go a long way toward combating fraud and abuse, they pose a significant barrier to widespread adoption of health IT. To break down this barrier, we propose that strong and specific language be enacted to the Stark and anti-kickback statutes to create an exception protecting hospitals and physicians from prosecution for collaborating on HIT. Congress should pass reforms that create straightforward legislative exemptions to these statutes so that hospital systems and other entities can choose to provide community physicians with health information technology, particularly electronic health records. Within these bounds, the forces of health IT could be unleashed and its full promise realized.

7. Reimburse preventive care and health screenings for employees and recipients of government health programs. A 21st Century Intelligent Health System must include much heavier doses of preventive care, wellness check-ups, and incentives to meet individualized health standards. For example, there will not be enough doctors or dollars in our healthcare system to handle the explosion in diabetes alone if current trends are not altered. Regular, appropriate preventive care is the best way to ensure a better quality of life at lower cost.

8. Increase consumer access to information about cost and quality. Allow and facilitate the use of de-identified information about Medicare, Medicaid, and government employee outcomes in order to provide risk-adjusted information to the public about cost and quality of hospital and physicians.

9. Increase the creation and adoption rate of health discoveries and advances through increased metrics-based investment in scientific research and through balancing safety with speed in FDA reforms. We must increase our investment in scientific research, including cancer research, which is at a critically important stage. However, we should also put metrics in place to assure that the money is appropriately directed and managed. In addition, we need to balance safety with speed in FDA reform because a single-minded emphasis on safety can kill when it delays lifesaving advances. For instance, to date the FDA has declined to provide accelerated review for Alzheimer's therapies even though this disease is a dehumanizing and certain killer that robs Americans of their last years. Certainly this is a case where delays for the sake of safety certainly are not safe for those now contracting the disease. Or consider how long the polio vaccine might have been delayed if subjected to today's FDA approval process. What would have been the invisible cost of this delay in death and paralysis? Safety is important, but that concept must include the danger of delay.

10. Use market-based reforms to insure all Americans. Congress should establish a national health insurance marketplace by giving individuals the freedom to shop for insurance plans across state lines; providing low-income families with $1,000 in direct contributions to a health savings account, along with a $2,000 advanced tax credit to purchase an HSA-eligible high-deductible health plan; making premiums for these plans tax-deductible; providing tax rebates to small businesses that contribute to their employees' health savings accounts; allowing 100 percent rollover of funds in flexible spending accounts; and requiring that anyone who earns more than $50,000 a year must purchase health insurance or post a bond.

State governments should remove the barriers to purchasing health insurance by eliminating unnecessary mandates, outdated pricing restrictions, premium taxes, and bureaucratic costs. They should also pass high-risk pool legislation, provide direct subsidies to health savings accounts that supplement the proposed federal subsidies, and make tax-deductible insurance premiums and contributions to health savings accounts.

11. Create a 21st Century Responsible Citizen Medicaid Program. Medicaid is actually three separate programs and should be treated as such: long-term care for the chronically ill, a capabilities program focused on integrating Americans with special needs into the mainstream, and a standard health insurance for the poor. Medicaid must leverage 21st century medicine to provide proactive, high quality healthcare services for individuals and families. Incentive accounts for wellness, competition among plans, and transparency of results are the keys to modernizing Medicaid.

12. Increase choice in Medicare. We have a model for an improved Medicare system that is older than Medicare itself: the Federal Employee Health Benefit Program (FEHBP). It is the system that insures members of Congress, their staffs, and nine million federal employees, their dependents, and retirees. The FEHBP allows beneficiaries to choose their own plan and switch plans every year if they are not satisfied. Two hundred bureaucrats at the Office of Personnel Management run the FEHBP, whereas over 5,000 bureaucrats administer Medicare—a program only slightly more than four times the size. Competing private plans in the FEHBP offer prescription drug coverage and satisfaction rates with the programs are very high. The FEHBP has no administered pricing regime and only loosely regulates the benefit package.

13. Create a new system of health justice. The current system of litigation is too expensive for America, fails to provide justice for Americans, and is being made steadily worse and more expensive by predatory trial lawyers who have more and more resources devoted to gaming the system to enrich themselves at the expense of Americans. This is especially true in the healthcare system. We must devise a much fairer, less expensive, and more timely system of health justice that provides conflict resolution and equity protection that would protect the rights of individual Americans as well as be more effective and less expensive. The key is to ensure that we do what is right for the individual who has a legitimate grievance, for those who help maintain health, and for society. As a beginning step, in order to ensure the availability of doctors it is important to create and/or maintain hard caps on non-economic damages in medical liability cases.

Texas serves as a great example. Between 1996 and 2000, one in every four doctors in Texas was sued. As a result, insurance to protect against lawsuits had risen so dramatically that doctors were leaving the state in droves and nursing homes were closing their doors. In 2003, Texas enacted profound tort reform that included $250,000 caps on non-economic damages for physicians and other providers. Since 2003 Texas has added more than 4,000 doctors, particularly in underserved specialties and counties.

14. Deploy personal health records to all Medicare beneficiaries. By providing a personal health record for every citizen who has Medicare, the government could dramatically impact the adoption of electronic health records, their use by physicians, and our ability to provide improved care for seniors.

15. Create an undersecretary of commerce for health. Health and healthcare represent a vibrant opportunity for economic growth and job creation. To capitalize on this, we need an undersecretary of commerce for health who will be focused on the opportunities rather than the problems associated with health and healthcare. The position should be charged with the task of ensuring that domestic and international policies do not stifle or interfere with the innovation and competitiveness of this increasingly vital sector of the economy.

Conclusion

The challenges and the opportunities inherent in the world today make health transformation not a choice, but a necessity. If we are to create for our children and grandchildren a healthy and prosperous future, we must create a 21st Century Intelligent Health System that saves lives and saves money. This IT-rich, quality-focused system will be one that is centered on the individual and emphasizes prevention, wellness, and best practices.

To migrate to that future, we must understand the various parts of the system, the way the various parts impact one another, and the way those interactions impact the overall outcome. We must also understand where in the system we can make changes that will have the greatest impact. Government, as creator of health policy and as purchaser of approximately 45 percent of healthcare spending, is critical to health transformation.

The movement we are undertaking will require many people working together: individuals working independently on projects or actions; temporary coalitions working together on specific, mutually beneficial projects; and a more lasting collaboration of leaders who share our vision. All are key to creating and implementing projects and solutions that help fulfill the key strategies necessary to make a 21st Century Intelligent Health System not just a vision but a reality.

CONCLUSION

Your Turn to Lead
The Unending Process of Innovation, Creativity, Leadership, and Transformation in the 21st Century

This is not a magic cookbook that you can memorize and apply automatically. Transformation is an extraordinarily complex process. Even though we have been actively studying transformation for decades, we still find ourselves challenged constantly. We find ourselves learning every day. Indeed, we find ourselves having to invent new solutions and new approaches just to meet the new situations, opportunities, and challenges that our efforts at health transformation and in other areas bring to our door.

It seems as though every time we solve one area of transformation there are new developments in technology, new developments in the market, and new complexities in how the world is working. Each of these challenges the patterns that have worked until now and require us to think through new and better ways of transforming.

We have also discovered that, as our process of transformation has attracted more attention and more talent, we are surrounded more and more by people who know a lot more than we do. We find ourselves in a system of learning and teaching in which everyone is learning from each other and teaching each other.

We hope that as you enter into this process of transformation you will recognize that you are as much a pioneer as a student. As you develop your own experiences of transformation you will become a teacher and contributor from whom others will learn. We encourage you to contact us at info@healthtransformation.net to let us know what is working and what needs improving. Let us know what you are inventing that we and others can learn from. Let us know what problems seem so fundamental that we all need help trying to solve them. Remember, as a citizen YOU are the leader in inventing the future.

For four hundred years Americans have been developing new solutions to meet new situations. We have created new social organizations, new commercial organizations, new political organizations, and new voluntary cooperative efforts. We have created the freest, safest, and most productive society in history because we have worked to liberate every American to genuinely pursue happiness and create a better future for themselves and their children.

Now, in the early years of the 21st century, we find ourselves with new challenges and new competitors. If every American takes up the leadership challenge of citizenship, we will drown our problems in solutions and grow our opportunities into new achievements. This will not be the work of a handful of transformational leaders. This will be the work of millions of transformational citizens in economic, cultural, familial, and political roles.

This book was written to launch you on that great adventure and to provide you with an initial handbook for that pioneering journey. With your help and your feedback, over the next few years we will develop even more principles and even better lessons. And with your leadership, we will create a safer, healthier, freer more prosperous future for America—and, in the words of President Ronald Reagan, preserve for our children and grandchildren this, the last best hope of mankind on earth.

APPENDICES

Appendix A: Eleven Key Principles

Move to the sound of the guns	*You get what you inspect; not what you expect*	

Deep, Mid, Near Campaigns

- Design for all three campaigns
- Focus first on the Deep Campaign to learn how to shape the Mid and Near Campaigns

Deep - 10%
Mid - 20%
Near - 70%

Discover

Develop

Disseminate

Deliver

Questions to Ask

1. What do you want to accomplish?
2. Who must say yes?
3. How will you implement if they say yes?
4. When will they listen to you?
5. What are the metrics of success which allow you to know that implementation is occurring?

Connecting Islands of Excellence with Invisible Bridges

The Lion - Chipmunk Antelope Theory

- Leadership must focus on large changes
- Lions cannot hunt chipmunks; they will starve to death. They must hunt antelope to stay alive.
- Define the antelope and don't get distracted by the chipmunks.

Observe

Orient

OODA Loop

Decide

Act

- *"Yes, if"...not "No because"*
- *Cheerful Persistence*
- *Import knowledge; Export work*

277

Appendix B: Example of Mind Mapping used for Project Planning

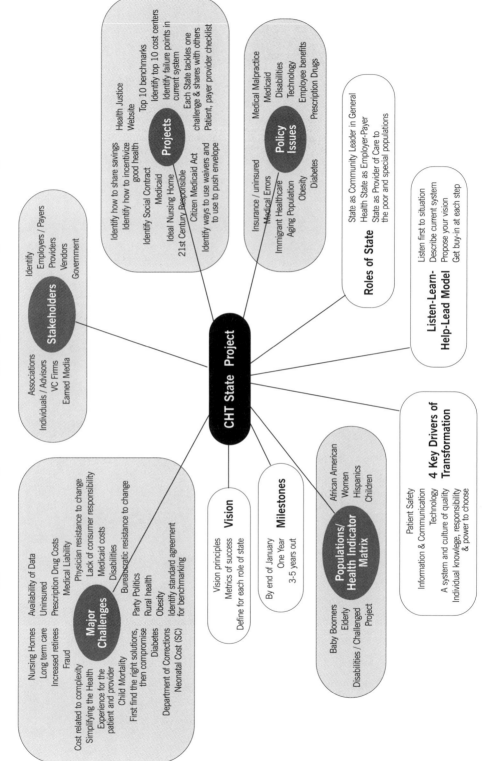

CHT State Project

Stakeholders
Associations
Individuals / Advisors
VC Firms
Earned Media
Identify
Employers / Payers
Providers
Vendors
Government

Projects
Identify how to share savings
Identify how to incentivize good health
Identify Social Contract
Medicaid
Ideal Nursing Home
21st Century Responsible
Citizen Medicaid Act
Identify ways to use waivers and to use to push envelope
Health Justice
Website
Top 10 benchmarks
Identify top 10 cost centers
Identify failure points in current system
Each State tackles one challenge & shares with others
Patient, payer provider checklist

Policy Issues
Insurance / uninsured
Medical Errors
Immigrant Healthcare
Aging Population
Obesity
Diabetes
Medical Malpractice
Medicaid
Disabilities
Technology
Employee benefits
Prescription Drugs

Roles of State
State as Community Leader in General
Health State as Employer-Payer
State as Provider of Care to the poor and special populations

Listen-Learn-Help-Lead Model
Listen first to situation
Describe current system
Propose your vision
Get buy-in at each step

Major Challenges
Nursing Homes
Long term care
Increased retirees
Fraud
Cost related to complexity
Simplifying the Health
Experience for the patient and provider
First find the right solutions, then compromise
Diabetes
Department of Corrections
Neonatal Cost (SC)
Availability of Data
Uninsured
Prescription Drug Costs
Medical Liability
Physician resistance to change
Lack of consumer responsibility
Medicaid costs
Disabilities
Bureaucratic resistance to change
Party Politics
Rural health
Obesity
Identify standard agreement for benchmarking
Child Mortality

Vision
Vision principles
Metrics of success
Define for each role of state

Milestones
By end of January
One Year
3-5 years out

Populations/ Health Indicator Matrix
Baby Boomers
Elderly
Disabilities / Challenged
Project
African American
Women
Hispanics
Children

4 Key Drivers of Transformation
Patient Safety
Information & Communication
Technology
A system and culture of quality
Individual knowledge, responsibility & power to choose

279

Appendix C: Center for Health Transformation Problem Solving Process

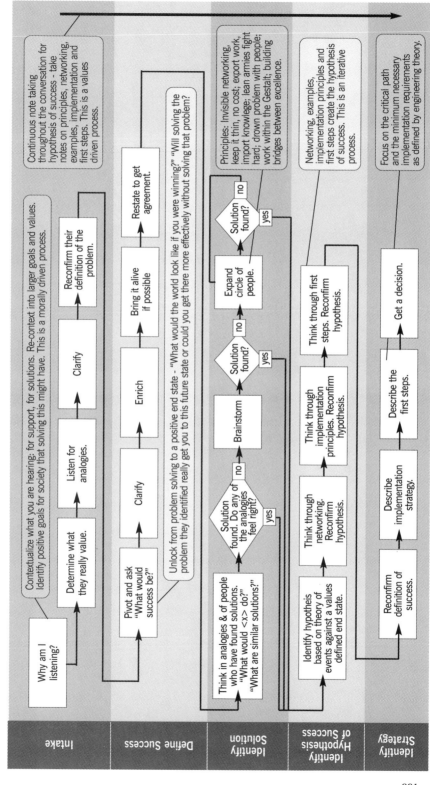

281

Appendix D

Eight Simultaneous Leadership Principles

There are eight simultaneous principles of leadership that transformational leaders must follow, requiring them to constantly ask the following questions:

1. What is our vision-strategies-projects-tasks planning model and the listen-learn-help-lead process which has informed it?

2. What is the center of gravity for our efforts to succeed, and, as we move to each new challenge, what is the center of gravity for its success?

3. What is our deep-mid-near plan? (Always done in that order.)

4. Are there guns whose sounds we have to move to at this minute?

5. As we learn from the sound of the guns, are we using an observe-orient-decide-act loop (the OODA loop)?

6. What are the antelope we are trying to get and what are the chipmunks that are distracting us and need to be delegated?

7. What do we need for our visible and invisible allies to sustain the invisible bridges that hold people together across institutional borders?

8. Above all, since it is the ultimate center of gravity in a free society —how are we leading the information and people efforts to sustain the entire process's legitimacy?

Appendix E

Statement of Former Speaker of the House Newt Gingrich, Founder of the Center for Health Transformation,[1] Before the Senate Commerce Subcommittee on Technology, Innovation, and Competitiveness

Wednesday, June 21, 2006

Chairman Ensign, Senator Kerry, and members of the Subcommittee:

Thank you for the opportunity to testify today about how health information technology is transforming and will continue to transform health and healthcare in America.

We are on the cusp of enormous change. The level of scientific knowledge we will discover over the next twenty-five years will be four to seven times greater than the last twenty-five years. Combine this fact with the economic engines revving in China and India, we know that our current path is unsustainable. Look at the American manufacturing sector, particularly the pain of the automakers, where they spend more dollars per car in healthcare than they do in steel. This is the future of all sectors of the economy if we do not change.

The outlook for the federal government is no better. Healthcare consumes 26 percent of all federal spending and growing, dwarfing every other priority. The looming retirement of the Baby Boomers and their entrance into Medicare will call for painful choices tomorrow if we do nothing today. With continued budget deficits running hundreds of billions of dollars every year, despite the recent "success" of cut-

---

[1] The Center for Health Transformation is a collaboration of leaders dedicated to the creation of a 21st Century Intelligent Health System that saves lives and saves money for all Americans. For more information on the Center and our Health Information Technology project, please contact David Merritt at 202-375-2001.

ting the deficit in half, we will pay a severe price if we do not transform health and healthcare.

Thankfully today we can see the glimmerings of a brighter future. With momentum building for healthcare consumerism, chronic care management tools, and the adoption of health information technology, we know what that brighter future will look like: 100 percent insurance coverage; consumers will be empowered; quality and price information will be readily available; early detection and prevention will create a culture of health; reimbursement will be driven by outcomes; and the use of interoperable technology will be ubiquitous. We will have built what we call a 21st Century Intelligent Health System.

Change of this magnitude is never easy. But the level of difficulty should not dissuade us from progress, because in the end our goal is a 21st Century Intelligent Health System—a fully interoperable, consumer-centered healthcare system that saves lives and saves money for all Americans. This system will improve individual health, reduce costs, and build a brighter future for all Americans.

And to get there, the widespread adoption of health information technology is essential.

In this testimony, there are eleven key messages that I urge this subcommittee, the Congress, and the private sector to act upon. If we act we will modernize healthcare through the adoption of health information technology and help build that 21st Century Intelligent Health System.

1. Build a National Health Information Network as a Vital Part of Our National Security Preparedness and Response Strategies

In 1954 Vice President Richard Nixon called for the federal government to spend "a very substantial sum of money," $500 million at the outset, to build an interconnected interstate highway system.[2] He called for the federal government to make this a national priority because "... our highway network is inadequate locally, and obsolete as a national system." President Eisenhower had seen the wisdom of

---

[2] Richard M. Nixon, Speech to the Governors Conference, Lake George, NY, July 12, 1954.

an interconnected system as early as 1919, when he was on an Army convoy from Washington, D.C., to San Francisco. It took sixty days to complete the journey.

On June 29, 1956, nearly fifty years ago to the day, President Eisenhower signed the Federal-Aid Highway Act. It called for the construction of more than 40,000 miles of interstate highways and appropriated $25 billion over ten years. This was a vast sum of money, considering that total federal spending in 1956 was $70 billion, which made this one of the nation's highest priorities.

It was no mistake that the original highway system was named the National System of Interstate and Defense Highways. The president, the Congress, and the states knew that a national, interconnected system would be a vital tool to properly prepare for and respond to a national emergency. In fact legislation required that one mile out of every four be built in a straight line so that military aircraft could land in case of a national emergency. As Vice President Nixon said, an interconnected system was necessary because of the "appalling inadequacies [of the current system] to meet the demands of catastrophe or defense, should an atomic war come."

Fifty years later another national, interconnected system is needed: this time we must build a national health information system because it, too, is a national security necessity.

A modernized, interconnected system could electronically monitor and automatically alert officials in an extreme disaster such as Hurricane Katrina, an avian flu pandemic, or a terrorist attack using a weapon of mass destruction. Advanced expert systems could electronically track patient visits, their symptoms, and their conditions; direct scarce resources to where they are most needed; assess the effectiveness of response strategies in close to real time; support contact tracing for appropriate infectious diseases; determine possible origins and causes of an outbreak; and capture other vital sources of data. The earlier we can detect a public health crisis, the better the chance of containing and managing it—and the better chance we have of saving lives and properly caring for those who need it.

Our most recent extreme disaster, Hurricane Katrina, provided many lessons for us to learn. The most important lesson is that bureaucratic systems do not and cannot work. In Katrina we witnessed bureaucratic failure at every level: the city of New Orleans failed, the state government of Louisiana failed, and the government of the United States failed.

Current bureaucracy is best described as a box, be it state government, the federal government, or a local school board. They are inefficient, incompetent, and arrested in time. "Reforms" within the box are nothing more than attempts to appear relevant in today's world, when in fact the box was created by the Civil Service Acts of the 1880s and has not been modernized since the 1930s. Modernization to them is transitioning from quill pens and longhand to manual typewriters and carbon paper.

In the real world we have seen the advent of the radio, television, computers, and the Internet. This world is best described as a circle. It is highly efficient, intelligent, and extremely innovative. We use examples of the circle every day through services like UPS, FedEx, Google, Amazon, and electronic ticketing. These organizations are centered upon and at the service of the individual, not the system and its mindless processes.

To truly transform we must migrate to this new system over time. We must discard the hopeless parts of the current system, incorporate what does work, and build the rest.

Transforming bureaucracy is the only way we will avert a repeat of the Katrina debacle. For further detail on this subject, please see

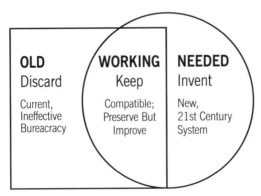

OLD	WORKING	NEEDED
Discard	Keep	Invent
Current, Ineffective Bureacracy	Compatible; Preserve But Improve	New, 21st Century System

(With thanks to Senator Bob Kerrey for developing nthis model)
©2006 Center for Health Transformation

Appendix II of this testimony, which is a working paper entitled 21st Century Entrepreneurial Public Management: Getting Government to Move at the Speed and Effectiveness of the Information Age.

Because of bureaucratic failures, survivors of Hurricane Katrina had to rebuild much of their lives, but unfortunately they have had to rebuild their healthcare history as well. One million, one hundred thousand paper medical records were destroyed in Katrina's fury and the subsequent floods. Most survivors fled the Gulf with no medical histories, no medication lists, no treatment regimen, no lab results— no healthcare documentation of any kind.

When citizens made their way to emergency shelters, how did healthcare professionals properly care for them with no information? Think of the AIDS patients who were taking an intricate drug cocktail to prolong their lives. Think of the Medicare beneficiaries who were taking multiple prescriptions to treat a host of chronic conditions. What about the cancer patients who were in the middle of radiation treatment—what happened to them after their paper medical records were destroyed?

M.D. Anderson in Houston, one of the premier cancer treatment centers in the world, treated hundreds of evacuees in the aftermath of Hurricane Katrina. For those Gulf residents who were in clinical trials with the National Cancer Institute, their data was electronic and available immediately at M.D. Anderson, and their treatments were resumed exactly where they left off. For those who were not in a clinical trial and did not have their records stored electronically, doctors scrambled to quickly redo tests and recreate intricate treatment regiments. Intuitively we know that many people died as a result. Their cancer ultimately killed them—but the lack of information most assuredly did as well.

In the wake of Katrina, the Department of Veterans Affairs (VA) demonstrated the power of electronic health records in action. As the hurricane barreled towards the Gulf Coast, the VA made final backup copies of tens of thousands of electronic health records for their veterans in the region. Unlike the hundreds of thousands of citizens who received care with no documented history, when veterans arrived at VA facilities across the country, their full medical histories were intact and available immediately.

A generation ago our leaders made a national, interconnected highway system a national priority, and today we have the most modernized transportation infrastructure in the world. It changed the face of America forever. It released the power of interstate commerce, created a national sense of community, connected rural America with urban cities, and drove innovation from coast to coast. The benefits, both economically and socially, are incalculable.

A national, interconnected health system would have the same effect. When there is no emergency, this network could be leveraged in innumerable ways in the routine care of patients. This could be the information highway that every healthcare provider in the country could use in the course of care. From electronic prescribing and transmitting images to clinical trials and medical research—this could be the technical infrastructure that allows for the connectivity, efficiency, and improvement that we all aspire to achieve. Networks like the World Wide Web and network application platforms, such as Internet2, hold such explosive potential that it would be tragic to not leverage them in healthcare.

The Congress must make the construction of a national health information network a top priority. In such a dangerous world, it should be an integral part of our national security strategy. I urge the Congress to take action on this priority now. It is an investment in the health and security of our country.

2. Transform the Reimbursement System to Reward Quality Outcomes and Drive Adoption of Health Information Technology

We get what we pay for. We have designed an acute-care system that is based on the myth of the fifteen-minute cure...just go see your doctor, and he will make you better. Today we are doing a wonderful job if our measures of success are inefficiency, high costs, and poor patient health. If we are satisfied with these outcomes, with its needless deaths and waste, then we should maintain the status quo. But if we truly want an intelligent, modernized health system that delivers more choices of greater quality at lower cost, then we must enact real change—starting with the reimbursement structure.

Our current payment system is not based on the quality of care that is delivered. Instead it pays providers for simply delivering care, regardless of outcome. Hospitals and providers that deliver better care are for the most part reimbursed at the exact same rate as those who provide poorer care.

Additionally, the payment system encourages the overutilization of resources. Like any contracted professional, be it a plumber or a builder, doctors are paid for performing their craft, which in this case is treating patients. They are not paid for keeping their patients healthy and out of their office or hospital—they are paid when they treat their sick patients in their office or hospital. This approach is so perverse that many argue that medical errors actually reward a hospital or physician because they can then bill for additional services.

We need a new model. Reimbursement drives adoption, be it a new test, device, or treatment, and we need a reimbursement model that takes into account the quality of the care that is delivered, not simply that it was delivered.

Current pay-for-performance and other incentive programs are a first step toward an outcomes-based payment structure. The Centers for Medicare and Medicaid Services (CMS) and many private insurers are partnering with their physician and hospital networks to pilot new financing and delivery models based on outcomes, from the Leapfrog Group and Integrated Healthcare Association to Blue Cross Blue Shield plans and Bridges to Excellence. All of them know that reimbursement drives adoption.

In Georgia the Center for Health Transformation is leading the nation's largest Bridges to Excellence diabetes program. Led by UPS, BellSouth, and Southern Company, all members of the Center for Health Transformation, there are currently fourteen major employers, including the state of Georgia, participating in the program. The state medical society and hospital association are actively participating as well. Serving in the role of administrator are Blue Cross Blue Shield of Georgia, Humana, Aetna, CIGNA, Kaiser Permanente, and UnitedHealthcare. Physician recruitment efforts are ongoing, with WellStar Health System and the Morehouse Community Physicians' Network leading the way.

The program, like other pay-for-performance initiatives, pays incentives to physicians who practice best standards of diabetes care. The program encourages individuals with diabetes to see these physicians to improve their quality of life and avoid the long-term complications of the disease. In the process, physicians are rewarded for providing high-quality care, individuals with diabetes are healthier, and employers save money. A recent actuarial analysis of the program by Towers Perrin reports an estimated savings of $1,059 per individual if blood pressure, Hemoglobin A1C, and LDL control measures are met. By saving lives and saving money, this Bridges to Excellence module should be the minimum standard of diabetic care throughout the country.

CMS will soon roll out an innovative initiative called the Medicare Health Care Quality Demonstration Program, also known as the 646 demonstrations. A major focus of these five-year demonstrations will be to improve the delivery of care in ambulatory offices by testing significant changes to payment and reimbursement, as well as performance measures and the practice of evidence-based medicine. Health information technology, and reimbursing for its use, will be front and center.

Reimbursement drives adoption. One example is telemedicine. This is an innovative and cost-effective approach that allows hospitals, clinics, and physicians without technology to partner with those that do. Videoconferencing with experts, transmitting images and records for second opinions, remotely monitoring patients, and virtual emergency rooms and tele-pharmacy services are some of its uses. Particularly for rural facilities, telemedicine improves patient care by increasing access to specialists, and it also saves money by delivering better care and reducing expensive services.

Most insurers reimburse their network providers for telemedicine, which drives adoption, because they know it will save lives and save money. Colorado is poised to become the 39th state to reimburse its Medicaid providers for telemedicine services. Unfortunately this means that eleven states still do not reimburse providers for using this technology. This shortsighted perspective, most likely based on perceived budget savings, is blind to the financial savings that technology can bring, and, more importantly, the improved health outcomes.

One way to guarantee better health outcomes—which in the system of the future should bring higher reimbursement rates—is to encourage the use of health information technology, such as electronic health records, decision support tools, barcoding, and computerized physician order entry. Please see the attached appendix to this testimony for documented clinical results and operational efficiencies that health information technology can bring.

If we truly want better health at lower costs, the number one priority of every stakeholder in healthcare should be to get technology into the hands of every provider in the country. And the surest way to accomplish this is to reimburse hospitals and physicians for using health information technology in the course of care. Reimbursement indeed drives adoption.

Insurers—especially Medicare and Medicaid—should incentivize the purchase of health information technology through higher reimbursement rates. From electronic prescribing tools to electronic health records, even nominally higher rates will drive the adoption of technology because providers want long-term, predictable revenue streams. Consider the Hospital Compare site, www.hospitalcompare.hhs.gov. CMS reimburses at a slightly higher rate those hospitals that electronically report their quality data. With an incentive of only .45 percent, nearly 99 percent of hospitals electronically submit their data. Organized properly, the broad adoption of technology would be no different.

Health insurance giants Aetna and CIGNA Healthcare recently announced that in select markets they will reimburse physicians for conducting electronic or web-based consultations with their patients. Studies have shown that utilizing technology this way decreases administrative time for providers and their staffs, increases patient satisfaction, and decreases office visits and utilization. Every other insurer, including Medicare and Medicaid, should follow their lead.

The real question boils down to this: if a provider endangers their patients' lives by delivering care through a paper record, should we pay them the same as a provider that delivers better care because they invested thousands of dollars in technology? A rational reimbursement system would pay more for the latter.

Representative Nancy Johnson introduced H.R. 3617, the Medicare Value-Based Purchasing for Physicians' Services Act, which begins the transformation to a new system. Congress should lead by holding hearings on this vital topic and begin the necessary process of building a new and rational payment system.

3. Create Legislative Exemptions to Stark and Anti-Kickback Laws to Speed Health IT Adoption and Deliver Better Care

Physician adoption of electronic health records is woefully inadequate, and current Stark and anti-kickback laws are part of the problem. Congress should pass reforms that create new exemptions to these statutes so that hospital systems and other entities can choose to provide community physicians with health information technology, particularly electronic health records. These reforms will speed the widespread adoption of health IT, quickly close the "adoption gap" between large and small physician practices, and, most importantly, improve the lives and healthcare of millions of Americans.

With tens of billions of dollars lost every year due to fraudulent claims and payment abuses, Stark and anti-kickback laws seek to protect the system—and patients—from criminal providers and suppliers. The anti-kickback laws prohibit hospitals, home health providers, nursing homes, and other providers from giving or receiving "remuneration," or financial incentives, to physicians and others in exchange for referring patients to their facilities. The Stark statutes prohibit physicians from referring their patients to a hospital, urgent care center, laboratory, or other facility with which they (or a family member) have a "financial relationship," be it as an investor, contractor, or owner of the facility.

Unfortunately these laws are also barriers to the widespread adoption of health information technology. Even the Government Accountability Office concluded as much:

> "[These laws] present barriers by impeding the establishment of arrangements between providers—such as the provision of IT resources—that would otherwise promote the adoption of health IT… Healthcare providers are uncertain about what would constitute violations of the laws or create a risk of litigation. To the extent there are uncertainties and ambiguity in pre-

dicting legal consequences, healthcare providers are reluctant to take action and make significant investments in health IT."[3]

Representatives Nancy Johnson and Nathan Deal introduced H.R. 4157, which, among other things, creates new exemptions to these statutes that will permit hospitals, doctors, and other organizations to drive adoption of health information technology at the physician level. Representatives Lacy Clay and Jon Porter introduced H.R. 4832, which also provides clear, concise, and workable reforms. Under these exemptions hospital systems and other entities, such as pharmaceutical manufacturers and clinical laboratories, could utilize their existing IT infrastructure to provide the hardware, software, connectivity, and support to their community physicians, clinics, and rural hospitals.

A hospital executive told us at the Center for Health Transformation that if the Congress were to pass straightforward legislative exemptions, his system would wire 6,000 physicians within twelve months. That is dramatic progress that is blocked by current law. By preventing the rapid adoption of health information technology, the current Stark and anti-kickback statutes are not protecting patients—they are endangering them. It is time the Congress enacts exemptions to these statutes before even more American lives are lost.

4. Modernize the Congressional Budget Office to Ensure Accurate Scoring and Encourage Transformational Legislation

Financing the adoption of health information technology could be rapidly expedited with reimbursement reform at HHS and reforming Stark and anti-kickback statutes. But it might be expedited even more quickly by modernizing the scoring processes at the Congressional Budget Office (CBO). Ensuring more accurate scoring at the CBO will lead to a dramatic improvement in American health and healthcare. Doing so will literally save thousands of American lives and billions of their tax dollars.

Today, we spend billions of dollars on government programs that are financial black holes, while at the same time the CBO will not prop-

---

[3] GAO-04-991R, August 13, 2004, HHS's Efforts to Promote Health Information Technology and Legal Barriers to Its Adoption

erly score legislation that would actually reap dramatic improvements—both financially and socially. The CBO ignores the economic growth, efficiencies, and cost savings that result from implementing innovative and transformational policies.

The following results were documented by real hospitals and real physicians who every day see the benefits of their investments in health information technology. But the CBO refuses to score these kinds of savings:

- The Indiana Heart Hospital in Indianapolis built a new facility that is totally paperless, which reduced medication errors by 85 percent. If we could achieve the same results nationwide, we would save more than 6,000 Americans every year, since medication errors kill nearly 7,500 citizens annually, according to the Institute of Medicine.[4]

- PeaceHealth is a billion-dollar hospital system with facilities in Alaska, Washington, and Oregon. With the help of GE Healthcare, a member of the Center for Health Transformation, PeaceHealth built a sophisticated electronic health record that helped triple its patients' compliance rate with diabetic guidelines, thanks to a combination of online disease management tools and the involvement of diabetes educators. As a result, hemoglobin A1C levels of less than 7, the target level for diabetes control, improved from 44 percent in 2001 to more than 60 percent last year.

Diabetes was the sixth leading cause of death in the U.S. in 2000 and costs the system $132 billion every year.[5] If the results that PeaceHealth documented with its diabetics were seen nationwide, we would save thousands of lives and billions of dollars every year.

- The Health Alliance Plan and Henry Ford Health System in Southeastern Michigan partnered with the Big Three automakers, which are all members of the Center for Health Transformation, to implement electronic prescribing in the

---

[4] Institute of Medicine (IOM), "To Err Is Human: Building a Safer Health System," 2000.

[5] Centers for Disease Control and Prevention National Diabetes Fact Sheet, http://www.cdc.gov/diabetes/pubs/factsheet.htm

region. In the first 12 months of the program, the technology electronically caught more than 85,000 prescriptions that generated drug-interaction or allergenic alerts. According to the Henry Ford Health System, the $1 million start-up investment generated a $3.1 million savings, primarily due to increased generic drug utilization. Generic use jumped by 7.3% because of the automatic alerts that physicians receive when they begin to prescribe a branded drug if a comparable generic is available.

If federal legislation were introduced to wire the nation's physician offices for electronic prescribing, the savings would be breathtaking. With more than three billion prescriptions written every year[6], studies have concluded that universal electronic prescribing could save an estimated $27 billion every year.[7]

• Within the year the state of Tennessee will deploy to every Medicaid beneficiary an electronic health record filled with their personalized medical history. Tennessee officials project that for every $1 spent on the new technology in its first years of operation, the state will save $3 to $4—from reductions in duplicate tests, adverse drug effects, and unnecessary inpatient admissions. Some estimate that the savings from this investment could grow to as much as 9-to-1, as the number of doctors using the system increases.

CBO refuses to score these kinds of savings. From their perspective a similar federal approach would result in a net loss against the federal budget, even though such ubiquitous technology would have a dramatic net gain in revenue because it would help deliver better care.

With the search under way for a new CBO director, this is the perfect time for the Congress to modernize the office. Representative Jim Nussle, chairman of the House Budget Committee, and Senator Judd Gregg, chairman of the Senate Budget Committee, should immediately hold hearings on this vital issue and push the CBO to modernize and ensure accurate scoring.

---

[6] Agency for Healthcare Research and Quality. MEPS Highlights #11: Distribution of healthcare expenses, 1999.

[7] eHealth Initiative, Electronic Prescribing: Toward Maximum Value and Rapid Adoption, April, 2004.

5. Pass Federal Legislation on Health Information Technology Now

For the last year the Congress has played games on health information technology. More than a dozen bills have been introduced, but still nothing has become law. It is time for the Congress to act.

The Senate passed S. 1418, the Wired for Health Care Quality Act. This bill, among other things, directs the Secretary of Health and Human Services (HHS) to develop uniform quality measures to be used to assess the quality of care a patient receives, including elements of a qualified health IT system. It also contains grant funding for connecting physicians and creating community networks, authorizing $652 million from 2006 through 2010.[8]

Last week H.R. 4157 was passed by the House Ways and Means Committee, and key provisions were also passed by the House Energy and Commerce Committee. The bill, most notably, creates clear and workable exemptions to Stark and anti-kickback laws; complements current federal activities to develop interoperable data standards; lays out a roadmap to create a consistent and common framework of state and federal privacy laws; and requires HHS to move to ICD-10 coding.

The House and Senate should see immediately pass legislation that:

- Drives adoption of health information technology and spells out the federal government's role in developing interoperability standards, including deadlines for action;

- Provides meaningful grants or an innovative loan program to spur adoption, in the absence of reimbursement reform;

- Creates clear, concise, and straightforward exemptions to Stark and anti-kickback statutes so that hospital systems and other entities can choose to provide community physicians with health information technology, particularly electronic health records;

---

[8] Notwithstanding the overwhelming evidence that health information technology dramatically improves the quality of care while saving money, the CBO score did not incorporate any macroeconomic savings in its analysis. The CBO provided a four-page overview of the federal dollars that would be spent, but not a word on the anticipated savings.

- Begins the process of harmonizing the wide discrepancy between state and federal privacy laws, while ensuring consumer confidentiality;

- Directs HHS to move to ICD-10 coding, despite its complexity, to ensure that technology captures accurate information, and;

- Makes uniform quality measures and reporting a vital part of this bill.

There has been enough posturing on this issue by both chambers and both parties. Now it is time for leadership. When the Congress does send a bill to President Bush, I urge Members to avoid checking this issue off your list. To truly build a 21st Century Intelligent Health System, this must be the first of many legislative initiatives, from reimbursement reform to its role in national security, health information technology should be a priority for years to come.

6. Solve the Interoperability Issue by Developing Data Standards for Health Information Technology

Interoperability means that every stakeholder in healthcare will have the ability to securely exchange electronic data in the course of patient care. This may sound impossible, considering that we hope to connect hundreds of thousands of doctors; thousands of hospitals; tens of thousands of pharmacies; hundreds of insurers; 300 million patients; all fifty state governments; Medicare; public health agencies; long-term care facilities; and dozens of other entities.

While this does appear daunting, technology is the easy part. Through the Internet, fiber-optic cables, high-speed connectivity, and the continued innovation of technology companies, the technology exists today to build a national, interconnected system.

The private sector, particularly those companies that develop health information technology products and those that use them, should take the leading role in developing data standards that will enable the electronic exchange of information from one system to another.

Data standards of interoperability have been achieved in other industries. Tom Friedman, in his book *The World is Flat*, provides an excellent summary of how the private sector collectively agreed upon data standards for the Internet, so that every system spoke the same language. They gave up competing over who could build the best island of isolation, fit with its own language, platforms, and applications. Instead they agreed to a common framework where they would compete on service, functionality, and quality. This common playing field gave rise to the modern Internet and all of its marvels. Healthcare should follow this model.

The Electronic Health Record Vendors Association (EHRVA) is doing just that. EHRVA is a group of more than forty technology companies, lead by industry innovators like Siemens, GE Healthcare, and Allscripts, all of which are members of the Center for Health Transformation. The EHRVA recently released an updated Interoperability Roadmap that outlines workable and pragmatic approaches over the next few years to achieve a common framework where all systems can exchange information. The vendor community (which creates most of the health IT products) and hospitals and doctors (who actually use these products) must actively partner together for us to move ahead. These efforts should be mindful of or in conjunction with any federal efforts on data standards and interoperability, such as Secretary Leavitt's American Health Information Community.

7. Support Community Efforts to Build RHIOs and Health Information Exchanges

Building the system of tomorrow requires action today. From adoption and interoperability to consumer engagement and data research, innovators at the local and regional level are not waiting for others to lead. Hospitals, doctors, technology vendors, health plans, state and local governments, employers, and consumers are collaborating in hundreds of communities from coast to coast to build regional health information organizations (RHIO) for the betterment of individual health.

The federal government sees the value in these efforts as well. Last year the Department of Health and Human Services awarded four contracts worth nearly $20 million to build prototypes for a national health information network. Technology leaders such as Microsoft, Cisco, IBM, CSC, and Sun Microsystems will work with RHIOs from across the country. These demonstrations will provide key lessons that communities can learn.

The characteristics of RHIOs differ greatly from one to the next, just as communities themselves differ from one to the next. Differences abound in geographic location, size, scope, sophistication, and stakeholder involvement. There is no single recipe for success. However, the experiences of health information exchanges from across the country will be invaluable as we progress toward building the national health information network. While there are significant differences between RHIOs, there are four crucial areas all efforts must address if they are to succeed: financing, health management, privacy and security, and interoperability.

Financing is critical to every business—local and regional healthcare networks are no different. These initiatives must bring value to their communities, participating organizations, and perhaps most importantly, they must bring value to the consumer. But to build such a network, proper funding is needed. Many health information exchanges have relied on grant funding as their primary revenue stream. In the long run, with little hope for large federal investments, this business model is not viable. Health information exchanges must be independent and self-sustaining, and their operating costs must be borne by all participating stakeholders. If the value of a RHIO is demonstrated to its community, the market will ensure its financial viability.

The key promise and payoff from a connected healthcare community is improving the quality of care that all patients receive—from reducing medical errors to monitoring chronic conditions to discovering new treatments. RHIOs must be designed so that clinicians exchange patient data in real time for use at the point of care. Changes of this magnitude are always disruptive. That is why RHIOs must be designed to complement workflow rather than complicate it. By data-mining patient health information, we will yield new breakthroughs in treatments, therapies, and understanding of disease that will transform the practice of medicine.

Health information exchanges must make privacy and security a top priority. If personal health information is not secure, if consumer privacy is not adequately protected, the network is doomed to fail. A uniform patient identifier is part of this process, be it a common algorithm or a unique number. By ensuring that the right patient's information is pulled at the right time, both clinicians and patients will have confidence in the RHIO, and the public can be convinced that their electronic information is accurate, confidential, and secure. One step in the right direction is to dramatically toughen the penalties for hacking into electronic medical files and making slander laws applicable to publishing or posting online any personal health information. The Congress should closely examine possible changes to Title 18 of the U.S. Code of Criminal Procedures that would harshly punish the malicious use of personal health information.

Connecting a healthcare community means developing technologies so that all stakeholders can share information in real time: hospitals, pharmacies, physicians, nurses, long-term care facilities, health plans, and consumers. This is daunting—but it can be done. The technical architecture will differ from one RHIO to another, but the use of common data standards will not. Through their experiences and successes, RHIOs can push the industry to reach consensus and convergence upon common data standards that will help achieve interoperability. This must be done with existing systems in mind. Data standards must be designed so that current technologies can be upgraded to meet new requirements, rather than forcing providers to replace current systems and start from scratch.

As industry stakeholders come together in communities across the country, the Congress—as well as state and local governments—must actively engage these efforts. From funding and regulatory reform to building networks and Medicaid engagement, these projects are laboratories of innovation. Many will likely fail, but some will likely succeed, and they could provide a guidepost for the rest of the nation to follow.

8. Empower Consumers with Personal Health Records, a Significant Step in Building a 21st Century Intelligent Health System

Personal health records are a significant step forward in building a 21st Century Intelligent Health System. Hospital admissions, physician office visits, diagnosis codes, procedure codes, pharmacy orders, and other valuable pieces of information are often electronically captured by a health plan through the claims process. Laboratory and other clinical data is even more valuable. Combine these two data sets with other information such as family history, allergies, and medication history; we have a powerful foundation on which to build a personal health record that will help improve individual health and healthcare.

Insurers, providers, and technology vendors are actively building and deploying interfaces that consumers can securely use for decision support, education on chronic conditions, and email with their providers. Using claims data, health plan personal health records are often personalized with an individual's medical history, contact information for their physicians, and tailored information for their health conditions. Representatives Jon Porter and Lacy Clay introduced the Federal Family Health Information Technology Act of 2006 (H.R. 4859), which complements many of the existing efforts already under way in the health plan community to deploy consumer-centric personal health records. CMS should also move quickly to deploy personal health records to all Medicare beneficiaries.

Consumers will be an integral part of any national health information network because it will be designed around them. At the end of the day we are talking about the health of each individual American, and personal health records are an innovative and important way to engage them to proactively take responsibility for their health.

9. Ensure Consumer Confidentiality by Protecting Privacy and Strengthening Security

Individuals have the right to control—and must have the ability to control—who can access their personal health information. All health information technology should be deployed to improve individual health, not to protect the status quo of proprietary claims to data. Each stakeholder should be given equal access to the record—by the consumer—in the course of delivering care. At the same time consumer privacy protections at the state and federal levels should be consistent. Health information technology and the sharing of medical data must not be constrained simply because it moves from one state to another. An integrated regulatory and statutory framework should complement technology, not complicate it. H.R. 4157 lays out a reasonable roadmap to accomplish this.

10. *Uphold the Individual's Right to Know Price and Quality of Health Services*

Every American has the fundamental right to know the price and quality of health and healthcare services before making a purchasing decision. Sites like www.myfloridaRx.com and www.floridacompare-care.gov must become the norm in a consumer-centered system. CMS is moving in this direction, by posting prices for 30 common procedures in Medicare, and every state should follow Florida's lead.

An individual's right to know price and quality goes hand-in-hand with health information technology. Electronic physician offices, wired long-term care facilities, and modernized hospitals can easily capture and report price and quality information. But they must first have the capability to capture information. This is yet another reason why the adoption of health information technology is so vital.

For more information on this important issue, please see my testimony I provided on this subject to the House Energy and Commerce Committee Subcommittee on Health on March 15, 2006. This is available at www.healthtransformation.net.

11. *Create an Undersecretary of Commerce for Health to Drive Innovation, Economic Growth, Competition, and Quality Care*

Most policy debates frame healthcare as a problem—whether a matter of financing, provision, equity, or quality. While important, these discussions ignore that the health sector is not only the largest sector of the U.S. economy, but it is a vibrant and quickly growing sector as well.

The position of undersecretary of commerce for health should be created within the Department of Commerce, and should be charged with ensuring that domestic and international policies do not stifle the innovation and competitiveness of this increasingly vital sector of the economy. The undersecretary would be charged with ensuring that: (1) regulations do not place unwarranted burdens on healthcare companies; (2) foreign governments protect the intellectual property rights of U.S. companies and allow these companies fair access to their domestic markets; and (3) the U.S. government enthusiastically and meaningfully promotes the U.S. health sector in the international marketplace.

The undersecretary of commerce for health would be the sole undersecretary within Commerce charged with representing the interests of a specific sector of the U.S. economy. This attention is warranted for two reasons. First, the healthcare sector is subject to greater government regulation than any other leading sector of the U.S. economy. Thus, it follows that at least one senior official within the U.S. government be explicitly charged with ensuring that these domestic and international regulations do not place an undue burden on the sector. Second, the healthcare sector is of vital importance to all Americans, as the following points make clear:

- Economic Engine. The healthcare sector is the largest component of the U.S. economy, accounting for one-seventh of U.S. economic activity. Composed of 8,500 firms (mostly employing fewer than 50 people), the U.S. medical technology industry already sustains 350,000 high-value manufacturing jobs paying an average of 49 percent more than those in other manufacturing sectors and accounts for roughly half of the $175 billion global production of medical products and supplies.

- Job Creation. The healthcare industry is the largest high-value job-creating sector in the United States—in 2002, health services accounted for 12.9 million American jobs. The Department of Labor projects that by 2012, one out of every six new jobs will be created within the healthcare sector. A 2003 New England Health Care Institute study showed that every job in the medical technology sector generates another 2.5 jobs elsewhere in the economy.

- International Competitiveness. Boasting the world's leading pharmaceutical companies, medical device manufacturers, and treatment facilities, the U.S. health sector holds tremendous potential for significantly reducing the U.S. current account deficit. However, the $3 billion trade surplus the United States has historically enjoyed in this sector has recently vanished, prompting serious questions about the fairness of overseas markets.

• Quality of Life. The most significant output of the U.S. health sector—increased quality of life for Americans, as well as for beneficiaries of U.S. innovation throughout the world—is not captured by conventional economic measures. Yet it is of fundamental importance to all Americans.

Health information technology and the undersecretary of commerce for health go hand-in-hand: without technology, there will be little innovation, and the delivery of care will continue to lag behind other nations. Technology, innovation, and better quality care will be a magnet for people from all over the world to visit our country and utilize our system.

The creation of this position is another way for the federal government to take a lead role in promoting the adoption of technology and innovation. I urge the Congress to hold hearings on this issue and quickly create this vital position.

Looking Ahead

If healthcare in America is to survive and transcend the challenges of the future, we must build a 21st Century Intelligent Health System that saves lives and saves money for all Americans.

In a 21st Century Intelligent Health System, every American will have the tools to maximize their health, happiness, and security. Every American will have insurance coverage and access to the care that they need when they need it. Every American will be empowered to make responsible decisions about their own health and healthcare. Every American will own their health records. Every American will have a right to know the price and quality of medical services.

In a 21st Century Intelligent Health System, the focus will be on prevention and wellness. Innovation will be rapid, and the dissemination of health knowledge will be in real time and available to all. And reimbursement will be a function of quality outcomes, not a function of volume.

This will require fundamental changes, but they are changes that are absolutely necessary. I know that this will indeed improve consumer health, reduce costs, and build a brighter future for America.

Appendix I

The following success stories document the progress that the private sector has made deploying health information technology, from real clinical improvements to conclusive efficiency gains. These serve as a small sample of what is happening in communities across the country where transformational leaders are coming together to implement technology that saves lives and saves money. While I cannot vouch for the accuracy of the case studies, I applaud each of the success stories that were forwarded to us. I urge the Congress to examine them in more detail, seek out other successes that are happening in your states and districts, and actively support them.

Allscripts
www.allscripts.com

We are fortunate to have a healthcare IT industry that has consistently provided innovative solutions to all sectors of healthcare. From saving lives to saving money, the healthcare IT industry is working closely with doctors, nurses, technicians, administrators, and patients to change the paradigm of waste and inefficiency to one that promotes quality, efficiency, and a return on investment. In California the Brown & Toland Medical Group implemented health information technology including electronic health records and personal health records. The group received $3.2 million in 2004 and 2005 from a major pay-for-performance program, scoring in the top 10 percent of all California medical groups and IPAs enrolled. In the District of Columbia, in just thirty days, physicians at George Washington University Medical Faculty Associates, a non-profit, academic multi-specialty DC-based medical group practice decided that they couldn't afford to wait any longer on technology. In an impressive show of teamwork, GW implemented the EHR for 100 physicians in only thirty days.

America's Health Insurance Plans and Blue Cross Blue Shield Association
www.ahip.org and www.bcbsa.com

America's Health Insurance Plans and the Blue Cross Blue Shield Association, both members of the Center for Health Transformation, are partnering in the area of personal health records (PHRs).

Patient-centered PHRs hold the potential to transform the healthcare system. They will empower both consumers and their caregivers with information; help promote the use of effective, evidence-based treatments and procedures; help improve the safety and effectiveness of healthcare quality; and ultimately; decrease healthcare costs. However, AHIP and BCBSA recognize to realize these objectives, PHRs must be both portable and interoperable. As an individual moves through the healthcare system, from plan to plan, employer to employer, or into the Medicare program, the information in the PHR should be readily available. AHIP and the BCBSA are developing a standardized minimum PHR data content description, the processing rules, and standards required to ensure data consistency, record portability, and PHR interoperability. These standards will be made publicly available later this year.

Last November, AHIP released an in-depth report on health insurance plans' latest IT solutions in areas such as e-prescribing, digital radiology, online decision support, electronic health records, and personal health records. A useful, one-page summary is available at: http://www.ahipresearch.org/pdfs/AHIP_InvHealthIT_05.pdf

Bridges To Excellence
www.bridgestoexcellence.org

Bridges To Excellence has created innovative programs that are, through financial incentives and public recognition, encouraging physicians and physician practices across the country to adopt and use better systems of care, in particular EHRs. This technology, as well as following best practices, is helping to deliver better care for patients with chronic conditions. During its pilot phase, more than 1,000 physicians in the Boston area and Albany have significantly changed the way they practice medicine, adopted EHRs, and are delivering better clinical and financial outcomes for all their patients—Medicare, Medicaid, and private sector employers. As a result of the efforts, the employers participating in BTE have saved over $3 million in direct medical costs and their employees are getting better care.

CareScience, A Quovadx Company

www.carescience.com

With the help of CareScience™ Quality Manager, St. Vincent Indianapolis Hospital has dramatically improved its approach to blood utilization and management. By analyzing and comparing blood usage practice patterns, St. Vincent Indianapolis Hospital has increased the safe utilization of blood, improved patient outcomes, and reduced blood utilization costs. In fact, the organization has reduced total blood use by 30 percent, decreased iatrogenic blood loss in critical care settings by 86 percent, and documented $4.4 million in blood acquisition cost savings over five years with an estimated $35 million in total cost savings when fully accounting for labor, supplies, and reduction in adverse event—all as a direct result of improvements in blood management.

Utilizing CareScience Quality Manager and the philosophy of "care-based management of cost," North Mississippi Medical Center was able to thoroughly investigate their trauma & neurosurgery patient populations, identify root causes, and engage a team of clinicians across departments to improve processes and treatment protocols. The end results included improved patient outcomes, increased staff satisfaction, reduced length of stay, and a savings of over $1.4 million for Medicare patients alone.

Citizens Memorial Healthcare, Bolivar, Missouri

www.citizensmemorial.com

Citizens Memorial Healthcare is an integrated rural healthcare delivery system with 1,538 employees and 98 physicians serving a population of 80,000 in Southwest Missouri. The system includes one hospital, five long-term care facilities, 16 physician clinics and home care services. Citizens' electronic medical record crosses the continuum of care and is used by every admitting physician.

Ninety-two percent of registered patients are "known to the system" and therefore not asked to repeat demographic information. 20,000 bar-coded express registration cards have been issued. More than one-half of radiology exams are scheduled directly by a physician office. 64,860 patient records have been created. A unique EMR identification number links visits together. Physicians are able to view individual visits, multiple visits, or all visits in one comprehensive online chart. Over $1,000,000 in supply and procedure charges are captured per month as a byproduct of care documentation. "Yellow-sticker-charging" has been eliminated from hospital inpatient floors. Citizens has also experienced an improvement in the revenue cycle through a decrease in accounts receivable for the Citizens physician clinics, an increase in supply charges per patient day, and a decrease in claim denials. Because of its efforts, CMH was awarded a Nicholas E. Davies EHR Recognition Program, sponsored by the Healthcare Information and Management Systems Society (HIMSS). The program recognizes healthcare provider organizations that successfully use EHR systems to improve healthcare delivery.

Clearwave
www.clearwaveinc.com

Clearwave, a member of the Center for Health Transformation, is the ATM network of healthcare. Clearwave is implementing technology within physician offices that will allow the real-time identification of patient benefits, create a network for the delivery of Individual Health Records (IHR, PHR, VHR) to the physician, as well as allow patients to do a self pay as it relates to copays, outstanding balances, and high deductible amounts. For too long, physicians have not been in control of real-time benefit determination and/or obtaining payment at the time of service, and with the advent of consumer directed health plans, the physicians, financials are at serious risk. The Clearwave network via its self-service kiosk will ensure physicians get paid in a more timely manner with real-time data support. The Clearwave network is not just for the large or financially viable practices. The Clearwave network is priced so that all physicians can participate whether in Atlanta or Vidalia because it's not driven by the installation of costly hardware but by an Internet connection. Clearwave is currently rolling out hundreds of kiosks in the Georgia and Florida markets, with thousands to follow in the near future.

Covisint, a subsidiary of Compuware Corporation
www.covisint.com

Led by North Carolina State Medicaid, BCBSNC and WakeMed Health & Hospital's Raleigh Campus, healthcare providers and payers across the state coalesced around Covisint's web-based technology environment to exchange patient information. More than 57 hospital systems and 317 post-acute and ancillary providers within the state are managing external patient communications through this secure online environment.

By expediting communications with nursing homes and the state Medicaid program—combined with a commitment to quality case management—WakeMed Raleigh reduced the average length of stay for patients being transferred to nursing homes by 1.35 days. Advanced Home Care, one of the largest privately held home medical equipment companies in the region, reduced Medicaid prior approval turnaround time to less than ten days, where the average for the industry is 83 days. The company attributes this improvement to rapid, online physician signature collection and e-form communication with Medicaid—enabled through the Covisint environment. Other results included increased employee productivity, management oversight, and accountability into external communications, as well as increased patient satisfaction. Expanding throughout the southeast to Louisiana, South Carolina, Georgia, Virginia, and Florida, Covisint's technology environment has now more than 6,000 users.

DaimlerChrysler Corporation
www.daimlerchrysler.com

DaimlerChrysler Corporation, along with General Motors and Ford Motor Company, all members of the Center for Health Transformation, partnered with Medco Health Solutions and RxHub to form the Southeast Michigan e-Prescribing Initiative (SEMI). The goals of the initiative are to actively promote the adoption of electronic prescribing standards and practices by the Southeast Michigan prescriber community, reduce medication errors and associated costs, and improve the quality of care. Also partnering in the initiative are Health Alliance Plan and Henry Ford Health System. Participating in the initiative are Blue Cross Blue Shield of Michigan and PharmaCare. This initiative is also supported by the United Auto Workers.

To date, more than 800 physicians have enrolled in the SEMI program. In 2005, SEMI was awarded a grant by the Centers for Medicare and Medicaid Services to study the results of the initiative on seniors.

Henry Ford Health System and Health Alliance Plan were awarded the Health Information Technology Award by the Greater Detroit Area Health Council in part because of their success in enrolling over 60 physicians into the SEMI program. In Feb. 2006, the Henry Ford physicians reached the milestone of 500,000 prescriptions placed via e-prescribing. From a quality of care standpoint, e-Prescribing messages alerted doctors to 6,500 potential allergic reactions. From a cost standpoint, 50,000+ prescriptions were changed or cancelled due to formulary alerts, which increased the use of generic drugs. Additionally, e-Prescribing helped improve overall generic use rate by 7.3 percent, which will save $3.1 million in pharmacy costs over a one-year period.

DaimlerChrysler has also been working with Ford Motor Company and General Motors to transform health and healthcare through the use of best practices and health information technology. Working together with Covisint, a division of Compuware and member of the Center for Health Transformation, the three automakers have engaged employers, hospital systems, physician groups, and healthcare payer organizations to join an eight-week pilot project that will gather input for a long-term healthcare IT solution in southeastern Michigan. The goal is to increase patient safety by reducing medical errors and reducing healthcare costs. Electronic health record technology will also provide patients with greater control of their information, empowering individuals as healthcare consumers. The three autos are also working with the State of Michigan's Health Information Network (MI HIN) Conduit to Care project to promote connecting healthcare communities across the State of Michigan.

Electronic Health Record Vendors Association
www.ehrva.org

HIMSS EHRVA is a trade association of Electronic Health Record (EHR) vendors who have joined to lead the accelerated adoption of EHRs in hospital and ambulatory care settings. Representing an estimated 98 percent of the installed EHR systems across the country, our industry contributions are founded in a competency to recognize the diverse needs of our combined provider clients—and a capacity to respond with a unified voice relative to core challenges within today's healthcare environment. The association focuses on issues surrounding standards development, the EHR certification process, interoperability, performance and quality measures, and other EHR issues subject to increasing government, provider and payer-driven initiatives and requests.

The Certification Commission for Healthcare Information Technology (CCHIT) process for certificating EHRs was greatly advanced through EHRVA contributions and involvement. In addition to thousands of hours dedicated to providing detailed feedback to the Commission, the association has provided a commissioner and work group-level representation to the CCHIT since its inception. While continuing to engage the Commission in dialogue related to process transparency, achievable certification targets, and improving the cost effectiveness of the certification process, EHRVA members remain engaged in CCHIT efforts through participation in the certification process for ambulatory EHRs and in representation in current and new work groups.

Geisinger Health System, Danville, Pennsylvania
www.geisinger.org

As her father was slowly dying of liver disease, Carol agonized over his condition. Even though she lived in New Jersey, far from her father, she took an active role in his care. With her father's permission, Carol used the Internet to securely view portions of his electronic medical record from Geisinger Health System in Danville, Pennsylvania. MYGeisinger.org allowed Carol to check her father's lab results, view his medications, order prescription refills, and make appointments. From New Jersey Carol noticed unusual fluctuations in his temperature and alerted his doctor in Pennsylvania. Her vigilance, even from hundreds of miles away, was able to forestall the possible onset of pneumonia.

Another Geisinger patient was visiting her son in Bar Harbor, Maine, when she suddenly saw double. Her son immediately took her to the local emergency room, where doctors reviewed portions of her Geisinger medical record online. With her permission, they reviewed her vital signs and previous test results and compared them to her current status. Fortunately, her vision returned to normal and she was soon released from the hospital. Her online medical record allowed her to avoid a series of uncomfortable, unnecessary, and expensive tests.

HCA (Hospital Corporation of America)
www.hcahealthcare.com

HCA, a member of the Center for Health Transformation with more than 170 hospitals in the U.S., has created and recently completed implementation of eMAR (electronic medication administration record), the largest hospital barcode system to help prevent medication errors. The system uses handheld scanners and mobile laptop computers to read barcode labels on medications and patient armbands. An HCA nurse scans the barcode labels and the system checks the patient's electronic medication record to help ensure the right patient receives the right dose of the right drug at the right time through the right route. In 2005, more than 116 million doses of medication were scanned using eMAR, and HCA estimates it helped prevent more than 2 million medication errors. According to the American Society of Hospital Pharmacists, only 10 percent of U.S. hospitals are using barcode systems like HCA's eMAR.

HealthTrio
www.healthtrio.com

HealthTrio, a member of the Center for Health Transformation, has developed a PHR/EHR which consists of a combination of personal entry data and an ambulatory electronic health record. The foundation of the HealthTrio PHR/EHR is clinical information collected from claims data residing in the various health plans, which then ensures that the list of encounters between the consumer and the provider is a complete irrespective of the number of providers and facilities visited by the patient. The PHR/EHR is supplemented by the consumer's own direct personal entries. Initial input is done by completing a "Health Risk Assessment" and appropriate surveys. The patient could enter their progress and history through free text. This record is further supplemented by electronic import or download of the information from pharmacy benefit managers, providing a medication list and history, as prescribed by all the providers interacting with the patient. Selected clinical information, which is necessary for continuing care of the patients from the labs, outpatient facilities, and hospital EMRs, is imported into the PHR/EHR by using HL7 or customized interfaces. This record then allows for better coordination of care and prevents duplication of tests and medications. In addition, SNOMED has been deeply integrated in the technology, so the information in the PHR/EHR is all encoded.

The integration of SNOMED into the PHR/EHR is going to produce a transformational change in the practice of medicine by allowing electronic analysis of very large population-based studies and would provide criteria for evidence-based practice of medicine, profiling of the providers, allowing transparency of the cost and quality of care provided by the providers. Care management and disease management could be done more effectively at a fraction of the cost.

Henry Ford Health System, Detroit, Michigan
www.henryford.com

At Henry Ford Health System (HFHS) in Detroit, Michigan, information for more than 3.5 million patients has been recorded electronically and made available to Henry Ford providers throughout SE Michigan since the 1980s. Henry Ford physicians have not seen a paper chart at hospital bedside or clinic since 2001. Everything is electronic.

HFHS is currently committing approximately $90 million to convert its vast electronic data repository into a fully automated and interactive system. HFHS estimates a 100 percent return on investment within four years. They expect an 8 percent to 10 percent savings in operational efficiency. This savings is measured by the number of physician or other provider hours expended per patient day. The savings increase capacity and allow the same number of physicians, nurses, and allied health professionals to provide care to more patients. HFHS expects a 10 percent savings on patient throughput. Rework, readmissions, and hospital discharge inefficiencies (resulting in longer lengths of stay) are a common source of cost that can be eliminated through the fully automated and interactive medical record. They expect a 2 percent to 7 percent savings in billing recovery. Savings accrue primarily through better capacity to bill for services provided, but not captured or adequately documented without the Automated Medical Record improvements. HFHS is deploying more than 1,500 end-user devices in 2007, including computers on wheels, TabletPCs, laptops, and handheld devices at a cost of about $8 million. This investment supports the full spectrum of clinicians (physicians, nurses, therapists, pharmacists) engaged in entering and reviewing patient information at the point of care in a wireless environment.

Humana and BCBS of Florida
www.humana.com and www.bcbsfl.com

Blue Cross Blue Shield of Florida and Humana, a member of the Center for Health Transformation, have partnered to roll out a statewide personal care profile based on health plan claims data to share information that may be useful to physicians in treating plan members. Using the existing Availity infrastructure, which all network physicians with Humana and BCBS of Florida currently use to check eligibility, a button will be added that will allow physicians and nurses to print a simple two-page summary with a patient's medication history, lab order history, diagnosis codes, and provider information. This effort lays a foundation upon which both health plans and healthcare providers can add on functionality to make the technology more sophisticated with the ultimate state being achieved with increased quality of care.

In a future phase of this program, a consumer who currently has coverage with Humana changes plans and selects BCBS of Florida, their personal care profile will still be available to their physician transcending the plan to plan data barrier. This multi-plan approach is the only one of its kind in the country. It is the beginning of a permanent personal care profile that follows the consumer wherever they go. Nearly a third of Floridians are covered by Humana and BCBS of Florida, and these two plans are actively recruiting other insurers to join the effort, including Medicaid. By adding Medicaid beneficiaries to the project, more than half of the state's population will be involved.

IBM
www.ibm.com/us/

Prospective healthcare involves collaborating with employees in a coordinated fashion to improve health—in effect, heading problems off before they occur. IBM, a member of the Center for Health Transformation, is developing patient-centric programs that are doubly proactive: they both reach out to a wider range of employees, and are more able to help them anticipate and manage health risks.

The personal health records that IBM is providing to its U.S. employees are a prime example of this patient-centered approach. When an IBMer first goes to the Web site for their personal health record, they are offered a financial incentive to complete an employee health risk appraisal, develop a personal preventive care action plan, and identify quality hospitals in their area. Based on the results, an IBMer can subscribe to receive expert information, articles, and advice on how to reducing their risks. It identifies eligibility for additional benefits and services such as disease management and refers employees to those resources. Decision support tools for drug comparison and interactions, hospital quality and Leapfrog results (from the Leapfrog Group's performance measurement system) provide individual support for optimizing benefits quality and costs.

For IBM, the risk assessment tools and the personal health records provided to its workforce are an investment that is recouped through improvements in employee health and the significant cost savings that result. As a result of our consumer-centric health programs for employees, IBMers are healthier and have lower health expenses than others in our industry. We have demonstrated that information-rich, patient-centric wellness programs aren't marginal benefits. They are very good business: IBM's employee injury and illness rates are consistently lower than industry levels; IBM has documented significant decreases in the number of health risks among its workforce as a result of participating in wellness initiatives; IBM's disease management programs have demonstrated a 9 to 24 percent reduction in emergency room visits and a 13 to 37 percent reduction in hospital admissions resulting in an overall 16 percent reduction in medical and pharmacy costs adjusted for medical trend over a 2-year period. IBM has also had significant success in improving the management of care for employees with chronic problems such as asthma and diabetes.

With the health improvements, IBM has seen cost benefits. IBM healthcare premiums are 6 percent lower for family coverage and 15 percent lower for single coverage than industry norms. IBM employees benefit from these lower costs as well—they pay 26 to 60 percent less than industry norms. In total, these well-being programs deliver more than $100 million in annual savings.

Inland Northwest Health Services
www.inhs.org

Inland Northwest Health Services (INHS), a 501(c)(3) in Spokane, Washington, and member of the Center for Health Transformation, is a shared services organization providing centralized information technology and clinical systems across the continuum of care covering thirty-four hospitals and numerous physician clinics in Washington, Idaho, and Alaska. Four new hospitals are in progress in southern California. This network is significant because of its size (2.7 million patient records), breadth of clinical data and images available, and because competitive healthcare facilities have been collaborating successfully on the governance and technology infrastructure for more than nine years. Facilities are contributing to a regional data repository, with standardized data and a common Master Patient Index, which allows healthcare providers to access needed patient data from any hospital in the region. The repository also includes data from reference laboratories and imaging centers, providing a single source of comprehensive information about any patient. Providers can either view the data via a secure web portal, download it wirelessly to a personal digital assistant, or have the data transferred as a standard electronic message to their clinic's electronic medical record system. INHS not only makes data available when and where it is needed, the standardized approach to hospital information systems saves money. Further, the centralized data repository provides a ready source of information on the health of the population, for use in public health and bioterrorism surveillance.

INHS is also implementing a centralized approach to physician office electronic medical record systems. In this model, INHS serves as an Application Service Provider, housing EMR systems for physicians on central servers. This helps physicians implement and maintain EMR systems at a lower cost than individual physicians would pay on their own. Further, the centralized approach assures that INHS can readily develop interfaces between the hospital system and the EMR system, allowing bi directional electronic transfer of data between the two systems. The result will be a comprehensive electronic health record, with healthcare providers able to access ambulatory care, emergency room, and inpatient data from wherever care is delivered. Because of this simplified approach to EMR adoption and utilization, INHS anticipates that 40 percent of physicians in the Spokane area will be using EMRs by the end of 2006.

InterComponentWare (ICW)
www.us.icw-global.com or www.us.lifesensor.com

ICW is a leading international e-health provider founded in Germany with transforming market entry strategies for the U.S. ICW delivers components for interoperability solutions for healthcare stakeholders, utilizing "connector" technology and the patient-centered and patient-owned LifeSensor®, a true interoperable Personal Health Record. ICW interoperability can enable bidirectional autopopulation of data to and from the LifeSensor PHR. Continued technology expansion includes recent integration of the CHILI web-server into the ICW hospital networking solution, now allowing access to DICOM image data, permitting viewing of digital images and videos, magnetic resonance tomographies, and x-ray and ultrasound images in a virtual patient record.

ICW has played vital roles in the national e-health card (eCard) program in Germany and Austria. Current ICW projects in Europe include: 1) a physician's network enabling interoperable connectivity, which has been recognized as a leading RHIO in a study by the University of Erlangen; 2) a privately funded implementation of a regional eHealth network, which delivers interoperability to providers, practitioners and pharmacies, and via LifeSensor, patients; 3) an interoperability project at Rhön Hospitals connects existing, but until now, isolated information systems without requiring the replacement of existing software. ICW is also involved with hospital and clinical projects including the "Partnership for the Heart" program at Charité hospital, for patients with chronic heart failure, utilizing remote patient monitoring. ICW is also leading a breast cancer project at University of Tubingen, which enables authorized medical personnel outside the University system to view and add treatment information, resulting in better patient management, improved care, and better health outcomes.

McKesson Corporation
www.McKesson.com

For more than 170 years, McKesson has led the industry in the whole-sale delivery of medicines and healthcare products. Today a *Fortune* 16 corporation, McKesson delivers vital pharmaceuticals, medical supplies, and healthcare IT solutions that touch the lives of more than 100 million patients each day in every healthcare setting. As the world's largest healthcare services company with a customer base that includes more than 200,000 physicians, 25,000 retail pharmacies, 5,000 hospitals and 600 payers, McKesson is well positioned to help transform the healthcare system.

Today more than 4 million care providers use McKesson's Horizon Clinicals® solutions to process more than 22 million orders per week. More than 500,000 full time equivalent registered nurses rely on McKesson solutions to deliver safe, high-quality care. The company's bar-code medication administration solution issues more than 649,000 alerts weekly. Its interdisciplinary documentation solution automates chart audits required for regulatory purposes, reduces documentation time by up to 35 percent, and in combination with bar-coded medication administration, improves nursing satisfaction by up to 45 percent. McKesson currently records over 3 million logins each month to its Web-based physician portal. This online gateway lets community-based physicians, hospitalists, and other caregivers log on once to gain single-source access to the patient's virtual EHR, no matter where the data resides.

McKesson offers a medication administration system that features barcode technology to support the hospital team and protect the patient by verifying the "five rights" of medication administration: right patient, right drug, right dose, right route and right time. The barcode technology used in McKesson's solution suite has been shown to reduce medication administration errors by as much as 87 percent.

M. D. Anderson Cancer Center, Houston, Texas
www.mdanderson.org

The University of Texas M. D. Anderson Cancer Center has enabled its health transformation through the development of ClinicStation, its in-house developed electronic medical record system. This year, more than 74,000 people with cancer will receive care at M. D. Anderson, and about 27,000 of them will be new patients. Approximately one-third of these patients come from outside Texas seeking the research-based care that has made M. D. Anderson so widely respected. With the ClinicStation EMR, M. D. Anderson's caregivers initiate over 1.5 million patient queries a month reviewing digitally available information such as images (240,000 studies reviewed/month), transcribed clinical documents (3.3 million/month), radiology reports (658,000/month), as well as pathology and laboratory reports (1.8 million/month). M.D. Anderson caregivers access the EMR system via both wired and wireless access in the hospital, out-patient clinics, offices and even remotely from home or while traveling. When outside M.D. Anderson, caregivers have remote access to their patients' records via a virtual private network (VPN) connection. The ClinicStation EMR allows caregivers to simultaneously review and consult on patient records regardless of where they are located (access is available anywhere with an Internet connection). While there is universal access to patient records, access is restricted to authenticated users. Every accession of patient data is permanently recorded in audit record databases.

Most patients referred to M.D. Anderson have their diagnosis of cancer revealed on diagnostic imaging studies prior to their arrival. Patients bring these "outside" studies on film or ever more commonly on compact disks (CD-R). M.D. Anderson informatics personnel have developed diagnostic image importation software to allow images obtained throughout the country and world to be imported directly onto the M. D. Anderson Picture Archiving and Communications (PACS) system and then made instantly available for caregivers to deliver expert diagnostic oncology opinions. In the past year, over 33,000 "outside" studies were imported into M.D. Anderson's PACS system. Of the 77 million images available on PACS from the past 12 months, over 5.6 million images (7.3 percent) originated from "outside" studies. Currently, over 190 million images representing the past 5 1/2 years of diagnostic study information is available for instant review. As filming of M.D. Anderson studies is no longer routinely performed, upon request, patients are provided CD-R disks of images from their M.D. Anderson studies. This technology improves patient health because radiologists are better able to diagnose current cancer status by comparing the current study to imaging studies obtained months or in some cases years before.

Methodist Medical Center of Illinois, Peoria, Illinois
www.methodistmedicalcenter.org

Methodist Medical Center has been at the forefront in implementing electronic systems to reduce medical errors and improve physician access to patient records and test results. The 353-bed facility has not only reduced medication errors by 50 percent using barcode scanning at the bedside, but it uses technology to provide network physicians anytime, anywhere access to information on 18,000 inpatients and more than 300,000 outpatients each year. When a medication is scanned at a patient's bedside, it is verified against the physician order and screened for allergies, interactions, and therapeutic duplication by pharmacists using the pharmacy system. Two of Methodist's 15 nursing units have achieved the targeted 90 percent rate for medication barcode verification. For its efforts, Methodist achieved the National Patient Safety Goals with zero violations.

Methodist also achieved an almost-perfect score from the Joint Commission on Accreditation of Healthcare Organizations—ranking it in the top 4 percent of all U.S. hospitals. But that was not enough for this hospital, which also supports 30 clinics and physician practices. Using McKesson's ambulatory EHR many redundant, inefficient paper-based processes in ambulatory settings were eliminated. Methodist practitioners now write more than 40,000 electronic prescriptions monthly, and paper charts for medication-related issues have been virtually eliminated. In addition, chart pulls related to medication refills were reduced by 93 percent. Methodist also estimates it will save $300,000 in external transcription fees.

MinuteClinic
www.minuteclinic.com

MinuteClinic, a member of the Center for Health Transformation, is the pioneer and largest provider of retail-based healthcare in the United States, with 82 MinuteClinic healthcare centers in 10 states and 150–200 additional centers planned by the end of 2006. MinuteClinic has managed approximately 500,000 patient visits using an electronic medical record system that guides diagnosis and treatment, generates patient education materials and builds diagnostic records that are sent to primary care providers. The EMR embeds nationally established clinical practice guidelines from the Institute for Clinical Systems Improvement, the American Academy of Family Physicians and the American Academy of Pediatrics. This system provides a foundation for generation of Continuity of Care Records (CCR) and HL7 patient encounter reports. MinuteClinic actively seeks and supports ways to improve the secure, appropriate exchange of patient care information by electronic methods.

North Carolina Disease Event Tracking and Epidemiologic Collection Tool (NC DETECT), Chapel Hill, North Carolina
www.ncdetect.org

NC DETECT is a secure, Web-based system that provides access to emergency department data (ED) in a timely manner to authorized users at the local, regional and state level. NC DETECT receives ED data from disparate hospital information systems across the state electronically on a daily basis. Aggregated and standardized based on CDC's Data Elements for Emergency Department Systems (DEEDS), the data are immediately available to authorized users via a secure, database-driven, Web-based portal. The portal provides reporting on disease and injury conditions and utilizes both diagnostic data and syndrome-based data. Emergency department data, and the other sources soon to be loaded into production, are also instrumental in monitoring the public's health after natural disasters. Hurricanes especially have had a huge effect in North Carolina in recent years, and NC DETECT will greatly reduce the burden on data providers when it comes to reporting on disaster-related illness and injury. Because of its efforts, NC DETECT was awarded a Nicholas E. Davies EHR Recognition Program, sponsored by the Healthcare Information and Management Systems Society (HIMSS). The program recognizes healthcare provider organizations that successfully use EHR systems to improve healthcare delivery.

Northwest Physicians Network, State of Washington
www.npnwa.net

The Northwest Physicians Network is comprised of nearly 400 providers representing primary care and more than thirty different specialty disciplines in two Washington state counties. NPN incorporated in January 1995 and is now the largest IPA in the state. The foundation of its success is based on the belief that patient centered, physician driven care, coupled with solid data, responsible use of resources, and active disease management programs are imperative components to the successful delivery of care.

NPN has sponsored the South Sound Health Communication Network, linking patients to their doctors and their clinical data. Approximately 75 independent community doctors, nurses, and office managers are online. Quest Diagnostics and Medical Imaging Northwest now push lab data and imaging results into the Network for real-time consultations and complete patient data storage. One seven-physician clinic in Pierce County, Washington, implemented the Network to complement their existing EHR system. A line-item audit of the previous twelve months versus the twelve months after implementation reveals impressive savings: savings from administrative supplies, $7,142; savings from FTE reduction, $19,600; savings from dictation reductions, $7,525. Total workflow net savings per physician was $4,098, for a total net savings per year of nearly $30,000.

Partners HealthCare, Boston, Massachusetts
www.partners.org

Partners HealthCare is an integrated health system founded by Brigham and Women's Hospital and Massachusetts General Hospital in 1994. In addition to its two academic medical centers, the Partners system also includes community hospitals, specialty hospitals, community health centers, a physician network, home health and long-term care services, and other health-related entities. Computerized physician order entry will be completely implemented in all Partners acute care hospitals by the end of 2006. Electronic medical records are being used or implemented by ~85 percent of physicians at the academic medical centers and 52 percent of community primary care physicians in our Network. We have roughly 6,000 physicians in our Network of which 4,300 are targets for ambulatory EMR (excluding pathologists, anesthesiologists, radiologists and other specialists who would be unlikely to use an ambulatory EMR).

Partners IT executives, who are members of the College of Health Information Management Executives, are implementing a "fail safe" system for medication ordering and administration, including computerized physician order entry, "smart" pumps, electronic medication administration record software, and bar-coding of patients, staff, and drugs.

PeaceHealth
www.peacehealth.org

PeaceHealth is a billion-dollar hospital system with 1.4 million patient records with six facilities in Alaska, Washington, and Oregon. With the help of IDX (now GE Healthcare), a member of the Center for Health Transformation, PeaceHealth built the Community Health Record. The Community Health Record contains all the information a provider needs to care for a patient—from lab results to MRI images to cardiology charts. It is secure, HIPAA-compliant, and totally online. Patients can access their records from anywhere via a secure connection—individuals are able to refill prescriptions, correspond via email with doctors, check lab results, schedule appointments, and request referrals. Every stakeholder has access to these records, including doctors, nurses, case managers, health plans, and independent physician groups.

Adverse drug events have been reduced by 83 percent, as documented by a pilot study in Eugene, Oregon. Allergy lists are close to 100 percent complete, thanks to an expert technical rule that flags missing information. Compliance with diabetic guidelines has tripled in three PeaceHealth facilities, thanks to a combination of online disease management tools and the involvement of diabetes educators. Hemoglobin A1C levels of less than seven, the target level for diabetes control, improved from 44 percent in 2001 to more than 60 percent last year. And LDL levels of less than 100, the target range, jumped from 28 percent in 2001 to 52 percent last year.

Per-Se Technologies
www.per-se.com

In the U.S. approximately 20 percent of new prescriptions and as many as 30 percent of refillable prescriptions are never filled. The adoption of technology in the prescribing process provides a way for physicians to know when a patient is not taking his medication. Ensuring patients take their medication as prescribed significantly reduces healthcare costs by avoiding situations where patients arrive sicker at a healthcare provider than if they had taken their medication. To help reduce medical errors and the cost of healthcare, Per-Se Technologies began an electronic prescribing initiative in early 2006 to help physicians electronically obtain a complete picture of a patient's medication history and plan coverage before issuing a new prescription.

Through partnerships as well as Per-Se's extensive customer base, Per-Se is connected to more than 20 percent of U.S. physicians, more than 50 percent of U.S. hospitals, more than 90 percent of U.S. pharmacies, and all of the nation's insurance companies. Per-Se's ePrescribing offering provides functionality during the prescribing process to a physician at the point of care. This functionality includes patient medication history to assess drug allergies and drug-to-drug interactions, and checks benefit plan drug formularies to facilitate less expensive generic drug use. Per-Se's goal is to increase ePrescribing adoption of the nation's physicians from today's 2-3 percent to more than 30 percent by 2010.

Presbyterian Healthcare Services, Albuquerque, New Mexico
www.phs.org

A true end-to-end medication management system drives out errors at every stage where they can occur—ordering, transcribing, dispensing, and administering. Presbyterian Healthcare Services has been building such a system since 1999, beginning by automating pharmacy operations to support barcode point-of-care medication administration, or "BPOC." Results of a three-year study showed a 77.9 percent drop in medication administration errors. In 2004, PHS integrated BPOC with a pharmacy information system that enables nurses and pharmacists to share information regarding patient allergies, schedule changes, and missing doses. Via pharmacy-laboratory system integration, the pharmacist is notified of abnormal values. A nursing electronic documentation system incorporates the updated medication administration record in the patient's chart after every med pass. And a secure portal gives clinicians anywhere, anytime access to patient information. More than 1,000 physicians and other caregivers use it today.

Most recently, PHS introduced a computerized physician order entry system with clinical decision support (CPOE/CDS) to its hospitalists, with other physician groups scheduled a month apart throughout the year. Two-way communication with the pharmacy system simplifies the verification process, eliminates transcription errors and enables physicians and pharmacists to share a common drug knowledge base, formulary and allergy information. As a result of this large technology deployment, between 2002 and 2005 the mortality index at Presbyterian Hospital dropped from 1.2 to 0.9. Harm rate has also continued to decline to a current low of 0.48 (number of adverse drug events per 1,000 doses), which is within the top 10th percentile for harm rate nationally.

Quality Improvement Organizations
www.ahqa.com

Under a performance-based contract with Medicare, Quality Improvement Organizations (QIOs) in every state and territory in the U.S. are supporting healthcare transformation by giving free hands-on assistance with health IT adoption to more than 3,500 doctors. To help these doctors avoid simply automating our current system of care, QIOs are providing valuable support with the redesign of care processes to improve quality and efficiency. And QIOs are not just working with practices in affluent areas—nearly one-quarter of the practices receiving QIO assistance are those that treat underserved patients.

Medicare's investment in health IT adoption assistance through the QIOs holds significant promise for achieving higher quality of care for Americans. Policymakers should examine the approach QIOs are taking to help physicians effectively use health IT and consider how this strategy could also help the increasing number of long-term care providers pursuing the use of IT for better quality care for the frail and elderly. QIOs in at least forty-two states are also supporting local health information exchange efforts, many in leadership roles. QIOs are helping accelerate the formation of these efforts by serving as neutral conveners, bringing together diverse stakeholders—including home health agencies and nursing homes—to build consensus around governance structures, sustainable business plans, and policies for data use and information sharing.

Quest Diagnostics
www.questdiagnostics.com

Quest Diagnostics, a member of the Center for Health Transformation and the nation's largest clinical reference laboratory, has developed its Care360 patient-centric physician portal for small to mid-size physicians and physician practices. Care360 allows a medical practice to easily collect, review, and seamlessly communicate vital clinical aspects of a patient's medical history, including laboratory and medication information. Care360 is positioned as an affordable alternative to expensive and complex EHR systems for ambulatory physician practices that are seeking clinical information technology solutions. Care360 gives the physician a convenient way to order laboratory tests and prescriptions online; an effective and integrated view of a patient's laboratory and medication history at the point of care; and the ability to share information securely with other physicians and other caregivers within and beyond their office for treatment and other appropriate purposes in a truly interoperable fashion. Additionally, Care360 provides physicians with the tools for participating in pay for performance programs.

By virtue of its national network of Care360 and other systems and a clinical transaction infrastructure supporting over 80,000 physicians nationwide and over 1,000,000 clinical transactions daily, Quest Diagnostics is playing a leadership role in the growing number of community initiatives focused on healthcare information technology adoption and interoperability.

Quovadx
www.quovadx.com

Quovadx, a member of the Center for Health Transformation and a worldwide supplier of healthcare interoperability solutions, has enabled the Florida Department of Health (FDOH) to transform a manual set of data collection processes and disparate applications into an integrated system for reporting and analysis of critical information for public health and safety. Utilizing Cloverleaf® Integration Services from Quovadx, the FDOH now provides managers and policy makers with access to critical data residing in various counties and application systems across the state.

These vastly improved capabilities enable the FDOH to immediately distribute alerts as soon as lab reports are processed by the Cloverleaf engine for the early detection and intervention of impending healthcare risks. Laboratory data needed for disease surveillance programs can now be accessed within 48 hours compared to the previous average of ten days. Additionally, on a federal level, the department can now make connections between diseases and infected persons or populations in multiple locations, enabling the FDOH to respond to national biohazard security threats, such as smallpox or anthrax, quickly identify and respond to regional outbreaks and environmental hazards, and securely transmit data from their Immunization Registry to the CDC.

Southeast Texas Medical Associates, Beaumont, Texas
www.setma.com

SETMA began in 1995 as a single-location, primary-care practice with five providers utilizing transcription for documenting medical records. In 1997, SETMA had grown to a 10-provider practice and realized that future growth and development was limited by the paper-based medical record. Today, SETMA has three clinical locations and 36 clinical personnel, including 23 full-time-equivalent physicians. In 2005, SETMA was located directly in the eye of Hurricane Rita, however, no medical records were lost as a result of SETMA's EHR and back-up process. Because of its efforts, SETMA was awarded a Nicholas E. Davies EHR Recognition Program, sponsored by HIMSS. The program recognizes provider organizations that successfully use EHR systems to improve healthcare delivery.

Patients can request prescription refills online, with requests automatically routed for physician approval and transmission to a pharmacy. Prior to implementing the EHR, SETMA had a 20 percent immunization compliance rate. Post EHR, it exceeds 80 percent. Comprehensive electronic disease management efforts have been launched, with over 5,000 patients assessed through a comprehensive program each month. SETMA has established a continuum of care model of healthcare delivery by tying the clinic to the hospital, to the physical therapy clinic, to the home, to the hospice, to the home health agency, etc. The full continuum of care is captured electronically.

Decreases in medical transcription costs saved more than $340,000; increases in average billable charges generated more than $150,000 in revenue; overall average charge per patient visit increased 20 percent and the average collection increased 30 percent; administrative staff required to handle the patient's chart decreased by 76.7 percent, saving more than $120,000 per year; the average man-hour cost to establish a chart decreased 85 percent, an annual savings of more than $22,000; average cost for administrative supplies decreased more than 87 percent; the practice saved more than $380,000 in paper and supply costs; amount of time required to handle phone call inquiries that required the chart has been reduced by 73 percent; number of tasks decreased from 18 down to 2, total annual savings exceed $103,000; and number of claim denials has decreased 26 percent, reduced days in accounts receivables by 7 days, thus increasing actual revenues by $102,000.

Southwest Medical Associates, a subsidiary of Sierra Health Services, State of Nevada
www.smalv.com

The largest medical group in Nevada, Southwest Medical Associates, a subsidiary of Sierra Health Services, is changing the way doctors practice medicine. SMA successfully deploying Allscripts Electronic Health Record, TouchWorks™ to its nearly 250 medical providers, and is providing electronic prescribing to all of the physicians in the State of Nevada—for free.

It has worked. In 2005, Nevada physicians wrote more than one million electronic prescriptions for their patients, making them a leader in electronic prescribing practices with a growing body of data proving a reduction in medical prescription errors and a significant improvement in utilization of generic prescription drugs. Electronic prescribing ensures that physicians write safe, clean prescriptions for their patients, and helps them select medication alternatives that are covered by their patients' insurance plans, thereby reducing the out-of-pocket cost of prescription drugs for their patients.

More than $5 million saved. After three years of using electronic prescribing, SMA's generic fill rate (GFR) had achieved a 4.8 percent lead over a controlled group of physicians in other SHS network groups that do not use electronic prescribing. Because every one point increase in GFR equals a cost savings to the organization of 1.5 percent, SMA's increased generic utilization saves $4.75 million each year, or 7.2 percent of its 2005 drug spend of $66 million. TouchWorks, which is a full electronic health record, also greatly streamlines the process of approving prescription refills, in the process creating indirect financial savings to SMA of $208,640 a year through increased nurse productivity. Taken together, the EHR's annual financial savings of $4.96 million has netted SMA a reduction in costs of $5.17 per prescription on average. SMA's solution also has increased formulary compliance for the group's physicians, and enhanced patient safety. Thanks largely to its eRx initiative, SMA now has a generic utilization rate of 73.2 percent, one of the highest rates in the country.

SureScripts
www.surescripts.com

SureScripts was founded in 2001 by the National Association of Chain Drug Stores and the National Community Pharmacists Association to improve the quality, safety, and efficiency of the overall prescribing process through electronic prescribing. The SureScripts Electronic Prescribing Network is the largest network to link electronic communications between pharmacies and physicians, allowing the electronic exchange of prescription information. Through the SureScripts Network, providers can send and receive new prescription information, renewal requests, other messages related to prescriptions, medication history, and formulary/eligibility information. SureScripts' system helps to ensure neutrality, patient choice of pharmacy, and the provider's choice of the best therapy. The pharmacy industry has been a leader in implementing information technology in healthcare, resulting in cost savings, efficiency in the delivery of care, and better healthcare.

Virtua Health
www.virtua.org

Virtua Health is a community-based four-hospital system in Southern New Jersey. While in the process of installing EHR and other ancillary technology in their hospitals, they are using the opportunity to streamline clinical workflows, reduce duplication and waste, and improve patient care. Virtua has brought in a clinical informaticist from PriceWaterhouseCoopers (PwC) to assist in realizing these opportunities. An early adopter of Six Sigma methods in healthcare, Virtua has been able to realize savings of several million dollars in operations. Simultaneously, Virtua is piloting a physician practice based EHR which will ultimately be integrated with the hospital EHR. Through this process, Virtua hopes to improve communications with the community physicians as well as provide better continuity of care.

Along the continuum, Virtua has implemented an electronic record for their home care division. Patient discharge information is automatically passed to the home care agency. Appointments scheduling is accomplished electronically before the patient leaves the hospital. Homecare nurses carry tablets or laptops to the patient's home where all of the necessary information is available. Nurses travel from home to the clients and transmit information to the main office each evening. Productivity has increased, patients are seen in a more timely fashion, and cost savings have been close to $1 million by implementing technology simultaneously with streamlining workflow.

Appendix II

21st Century Entrepreneurial Public Management as a Replacement for Bureaucratic Public Administration:
Getting Government to Move at the Speed and Effectiveness of the Information Age

By Newt Gingrich

December 12, 2005

It is simply impossible for the American government to meet the challenges of the 21st century with the bureaucracy, regulations, and systems of the 1880s.

Implementing policy effectively is ultimately as important as making the right policy. In national security we have an absolute crisis of ineffective and inefficient implementation which undermines even the most correct policies and risks the security of the country. In health, education, and other areas we have cumbersome, inefficient, and ineffective bureaucracies which make our tax dollars less effective and the decision of representative government less capable. People expect results and not just excuses.

To get those results in the 21st century will require a profound transformation from a model of Bureaucratic Public Administration to a model of 21st Century Entrepreneurial Public Management.

As Professor Philip Bobbitt of the University of Texas has noted: "Tomorrow's [nation] state will have as much in common with the 21st century multinational company as with the 20th century [nation] state. It will outsource many functions to the private sector, rely less on regulation and more on market incentives and respond to ever-changing consumer demand."

It is an objective fact that government today is incapable of moving at the speed of the information age.

It is an objective fact that government today is incapable of running a lean, agile operation like the logistics supply chain system that has made Wal-Mart so successful or the recent IBM logistics supply chain innovations which IBM estimates now saves it over $3 billion a year while improving productivity and profits.

There is a practical reason government cannot function at the speed of the information age.

Modern government as we know it is an intellectual product of the civil service reform movement of the 1880s.

Think of the implications of that reality.

A movement that matured over 120 years ago was a movement developed in a period when male clerks used quill pens and dipped them into ink bottles.

The processes, checklists, and speed appropriate to a pre-telephone, pre-typewriter era of government bureaucracy are clearly hopelessly obsolete.

Simply imagine walking into a government office today and seeing a gas light, a quill pen, a bottle of ink for dipping the pen, a tall clerk's desk, and a stool. The very image of the office would communicate how obsolete the office was. If you saw someone actually trying to run a government program in that office you would know instantly it was a hopeless task.

Yet the unseen mental assumptions of modern bureaucracy are fully as out of date and obsolete, fully as hopeless at keeping up with the modern world as that office would be.

Today we have a combination of information age and industrial age equipment in a government office being slowed to the pace of an agricultural age mentality of processes, checklists, limitations, and assumptions.

This obsolete, process-oriented system of bureaucracy is made even slower and more risk averse by the attitudes of the Inspectors General, the Congress, and the news media. These three groups are actually mutually reinforcing in limiting energy, entrepreneurship, and creativity.

The Inspectors General are products of a scandal and misdeed-oriented mindset which would bankrupt any corporation. The Inspectors General communicate what government employees cannot do and what they cannot avoid.

The emphasis is overwhelmingly on a petty dotting of the i's and crossing the t's mentality which leads to good bookkeeping and slow, unimaginative, and expensive implementation.

There are no Inspectors General seeking to reward imagination, daring risks, aggressive leadership, over achievement.

Similarly, the members of Congress and their staffs are quick to hold hearings and issue press releases about mistakes in public administration but there are remarkably few efforts to identify what works and what should be streamlined and modernized.

Every hearing about a scandal reminds the civil service to keep its head down.

Similarly, the news media will uncover, exaggerate, and put the spotlight on any potential scandal but it will do remarkably little to highlight, to praise, and to recognize outstanding breakthroughs in getting more done more quickly with fewer resources.

Finally, the very nature of the personnel system further leads to timidity and mediocrity. No amount of extra effort can be rewarded and no amount of incompetent but honest inaction seems punishable. The failure of the system to reinforce success and punish failure leads to a steady drift toward mediocrity and risk avoidance.

**Building a 21st Century Intelligent, Effective,
Limited Government Versus Marginally Reforming
Current Ineffective Bureaucracies**

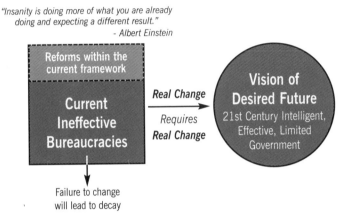

*"Insanity is doing more of what you are already
doing and expecting a different result."*
- Albert Einstein

Rather than change, most bureaucracies prefer the comfortable routine of explaining failure

Of course, it is not possible to reach the desired future in one step. It will involve a series of transitions, which can also be illustrated.

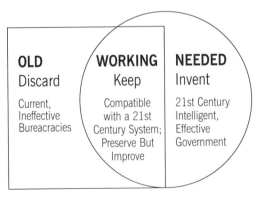

(With thanks to Senator Bob Kerrey for helping to develop this model)
©2006 Center for Health Transformation

The difference in orientation between what we are currently focused on and where we should be going can be illustrated vividly.

Without fundamental change, we will continue to have an unimaginative, red tape–ridden, process-dominated system which moves slower than the industrial era and has no hope of matching the speed, accuracy, and agility of the information age.

The Wal-Mart model is that "everyday low prices are a function of everyday low cost." The Wal-Mart people know that they cannot charge over time less than it costs them. Therefore if they can have the lowest cost structure in retail they can sustain the lowest price structure.

This same principle applies to government. The better you use your resources the more things you can do. The faster you can respond to reality and develop an effective implementation of the right policy the more you can achieve.

An information age government that operated with the speed and efficiency of modern supply chain logistics could do a better job of providing public goods and services for less money.

Moving government into the information age is a key component of America being able to operate in the real time 24/7 worldwide information system of the modern world.

Moving government into the information age is absolutely vital if the military and intelligence communities are to be capable of buying and using new technologies as rapidly as the information age is going to produce them.

Moving government into the information age is unavoidable if police and drug enforcement are to be able to move at the speed of their unencumbered private sector opponents in organized crime, slave trading, and drug dealing.

Moving government into the information age is a key component of America being able to meet its educational goals and save those who have been left out of the successful parts of our society.

Moving government into the information age is a key component of America being able to develop new energy sources and create a cleaner environment with greater biodiversity.

Moving government into the information age is a key component of America being able to transform the health system into a 21st Century Intelligent Health System.

This process of developing an information age government system is going to be one of the greatest challenges of the next decade.

It is not enough to think that you can simply move the new developments in the private sector into the government. The public has a right to know about actions which in a totally private company would be legitimately shielded from outside scrutiny. There will inevitably be congressional and news media oversight of public activities in a way that would not happen in the purely privately held venture.

As Peter Drucker warned thirty years ago in *The Age of Discontinuities*, the government is different. There are much higher standards of honesty and fairness in government than in the private sector. There are legitimately higher standards for using the public's money wisely. There are legitimate demands for greater transparency and accountability. The public really does have a right to know about actions which in a totally private company would be legitimately shielded from outside scrutiny. There will inevitably be congressional and news media oversight of public activities in a way that would not happen in the purely privately held venture.

There are also legitimately higher expectations of accuracy. In early July, in yet another adjustment to an earlier estimate, the Congressional Budget Office revised its budget deficit projections for this fiscal year. In less than six months, the CBO was off by nearly 12 percent. If the Office of Management and Budget agrees with the new CBO projection, its estimate will have missed the mark by nearly 24 percent—an error of more than $100 billion. How can our elected officials make informed policy decisions with such faulty analysis? We deserve honest answers.

The House and Senate Budget Committees should hold hearings to reform the current CBO scoring processes because modernizing government starts with open and accurate budget projections. These projections must include the impact that proposed legislation will have on the private sector, not just its impact on the federal budget.

For instance, federal spending that promotes health information technology or medical innovation has the potential to save countless lives and billions of dollars in the private sector. But without scoring these benefits CBO and OMB will never be able to distinguish between legislation as an investment and legislation as a cost.

All of these factors require us to develop a new model of effective government and not merely copy whatever the private sector is doing well. That new model can be thought of as 21st Century Entrepreneurial Public Management.

21st Century Entrepreneurial Public Management

The term 21st Century Entrepreneurial Public Management was chosen to deliberately distinguish it from Bureaucratic Public Administration. We need two terms to distinguish between the new information age system of entrepreneurial management and the inherited agricultural age system of bureaucratic administration.

The one constant is the term *public*. It is important to recognize that there are legitimate requirements of public activity and public responsibility which will be just as true in this new model as they were in the older model. Simply throwing the doors open to market oriented, entrepreneurial incentives with information age systems will not get the job done. The system we are developing has to meet the higher standards of accountability, prudence, and honesty which are inherent in a public activity.

We have to start with a distinguishing set of terms because we are describing a fundamental shift in thinking, in goals, in measurements, and in organization. Changes this profound always begins with language. People learn new ideas by first learning a language and then learning a glossary of how to use that new language. That is the heart of developing new models of thought and behavior.

Shifting the way we conceptualize, organize, and run public institutions will require new models for education and recruitment as well as for the day to day behavior.

We must shift from professional public bureaucrats to professional public entrepreneurs. We must shift from administrators to managers. The metrics will be profoundly different. The rules will be profoundly different. The expectations will be profoundly different.

A first step would be for Schools of Public Administration to change their titles to Schools of Entrepreneurial Public Management. This is not a shallow gimmicky word trick. Changing the name of the institutions that attract and educate those who would engage in public service will require those schools to ask themselves what the difference in curriculum and in the faculty should be.

The president, governors, mayors, and county commissioners should appoint advisory committees from the business community and from schools of business to help think through and develop principles of 21st Century Entrepreneurial Public Management.

Principles of 21st Century Entrepreneurial Public Management

This topic is just beginning to evolve. Over the next few years it will lead to books, courses, and even entire programs. Obviously it can only be dealt with briefly in this paper. For more information and for developments since the date of this paper, go to www.newt.org and click on 21st Century Entrepreneurial Public Management.

The following are simply an introductory set of principles:

1. Every system should define itself by its vision of success. Unless you know that a department or agency is trying to accomplish (and has been assigned to accomplish by the president and the Congress), you cannot measure how well it is doing, how to structure the agency, how to train the employees so they can be an effective team. Definition of success precedes everything else.

2. Planning has to always be in a deep-mid-near model. For government deep is probably ten years, mid is about three years and near is next year. Unless the agency plans back from the desired future it is impossible to distinguish between activity and progress. In Washington and most state capitals far too much time is spent on today's headline and today's press conference and not nearly enough time is spent preparing for tomorrow's achievement.

3. Every agency and every project has to be planned with a clear process of:

  a. defining the vision of success;

  b. defining the strategies which will achieve that vision;

  c. defining the projects (definable, delegatable achievements see below) necessary to implement the strategies;

  d. defining the tasks which must be completed to achieve the projects;

  e. defining the metrics by which you will be able to measure whether the project is on track; and

  f. turning to the customers, the experts, and the decision makers and following a process of listen-learn-help-lead to find out whether your definition of success and definition of implementation fits their understanding. This process properly used turns every person into a consultant helping improve your planning and your execution.

4. Every significant system requires a reporting process comparable to the ComStat and TEAMS reporting instituted by Mayor Giuliani in the New York City Police Department and the prisons. Giuliani's leadership is a good introduction to the concept of ComStat and similar reporting and managing tools. The key is for senior leadership to constantly (weekly in key areas, monthly in others) review the data and make changes in a collaborative way with the team charged with implementing the system. Every significant strategy requires an Assessment Room in which the senior leadership can see all the key data and review the totality of the strategy's implementation in one sweeping overview. Determining what metrics should be used to define success and maintaining those metrics with accuracy is a major part of this process. The absence of ComStat systems, the absence of assessment rooms, and the absence of routine review is a major factor in the ineffectiveness and inefficiency of the federal government in almost every department. "You get what you inspect not what you expect" is an old management rule. If no one knows what is going to be inspected and if no data is available for inspection it should not surprise us that the current system also does not function very well.

5. When a strategy is not working well senior leaders need to ask

the following tough-minded questions:

a. Is the strategy the right one (this suggests a courageous reexamination of external realities to see if we have simply tried to do the wrong thing)?

b. If it is the right one then is the problem resources?

c. If we have the right strategy and the right resources then do the people implementing it need more training?

d. If we have the right strategy, the right resources, the right training, do we have the wrong people in charge?

e. If everything looks like it should be working, is there something inherently wrong with the structure and the system which needs to be changed so we can achieve our goals?

f. If everything is in place but it still is not working, are there regulations which are slowing us down and making us ineffective and if there are, who is drafting up the replace ment regulations to be issued by the president or whatever authority is required?

g. If everything is in place that the Executive Branch can control, is the problem with the law and should the president send to Congress proposed changes to enable the strategy to be implemented?

h. Can these seven steps be undertaken on a weekly or at most monthly basis so the rhythm and tempo of government can begin to match the requirements of the information age?

6. The process of defining and managing projects will require profound changes in the laws governing personnel, procurement, etc. Projects are the key building blocks of Entrepreneurial Public Management. They permit the senior leader to delegate measures of accomplishment rather than measures of activity. A simple distinction is between asking bureaucracies to engage in cooking and asking someone to prepare dinner for twelve people at 8 o'clock tomorrow night for $11 a piece and making it Mexican food. The Bureaucratic Public Administration request for cooking allows the bureaucracy to report on activities (we are cooking every day, we are studying cooking, we are having a cooking seminar) without any metric of achievement. The process of defining achievements and delegating them is virtually impossible under today's personnel, procurement, and spending laws. A clear

example of the difference can be found by studying the division commanders' use of emergency money in Iraq with the Coalition Provision Authority process. One division commander told me they could use the emergency money to order cars from a local Iraqi and that Iraqi could procure the cars in Turkey and drive them to the local town faster than they could process the paperwork in Baghdad to begin the process of purchasing through the CPA. The Congress and the president agreed to spend $18 billion rebuilding Iraq and ten months later $16 billion was still tied up in paperwork. Only the commanders' emergency money was being spent in a timely, effective way. The same experience happened in Afghanistan where the United States Agency for International Development could not process the paperwork fast enough to meet the requirements of rebuilding Afghan civil society. One commander said that in rebuilding a society after a war "dollars are to rebuilding what ammunition is to a firefight." If the ammunition for the war were as constrained and slow as the dollars in reconstruction we would lose every war. Getting the system to move at the speed of wartime requirements and at the speed of information age processes requires a totally new model of delegating massively to project managers who are measured by their achievements, not by the details of process reporting. This will be the most profound change in shifting from Bureaucratic Public Administration to Entrepreneurial Public Management and it will require substantial change in law, in culture, and in congressional and executive leadership expectation. To be sustained it will also have to be understood by reporters and analysts so the news media is focused on the same metrics as the leadership.

7. At every level leaders have to sift out the vital from the nice. In the information age there is always more to do than can possibly get done. One of the keys to effective leadership and to successful projects is to distinguish the vital from the useful. A useful way to think of this is that lions cannot afford to hunt chipmunks because even if they catch them they will starve to death. Lions are hyper-carnivores who have to hunt antelope and zebras to survive. Every leader has to learn to distinguish every morning between antelope and chipmunks by focusing on success as defined in a deep-mid-near time horizon then

allowing that definition of success to define the antelope that really have to be achieved in order for the project to work.

8. An effective information age system has to focus on the outside world and "move to the sound of the guns." In the Bureaucratic Public Administration model which was developed at the cusp of the shift from an agrarian to an industrial society the key to focused achievement was to define your silo of responsibility and stick within that silo. As long as you were doing your job within that system of accountability you were succeeding even if the larger system were collapsing or failing. In the information age this internally oriented approach is doomed to fail. There are too many things happening too rapidly for people to be effective staying focused only on their own system. As Peter Drucker pointed out in his classic, *The Effective Executive*, effective leaders realize that all the important impacts occur outside the organization and the organization exists for the purpose of achievements measured only by outside occurrences. Since the world is so much larger and so much faster-moving than our particular activity we have to constantly be paying attention to the outside world. The military expression of this is the term OODA loop. In the modern military the winning side observes a fact, orients itself to the meaning of that fact, decides what to do, acts and then loops back to observe the new situation faster than its competitor. The winning team is always more agile and agility is a vital characteristic for winning systems in the information age. This process is characterized by Dr. Andy von Eschenbach of the National Cancer Institute as the ability to discover-develop-deliver as rapidly as possible. However you describe these capabilities, they are clearly not the natural pattern of Bureaucratic Public Administration. They have to become the natural rhythm of Entrepreneurial Public Management if government is to meet the requirements of the information age.

9. When dealing with this scale of complexity and change people have to be educated into a doctrine so they understand what is expected and how to meet the expectations. We greatly underestimate how complex modern systems are and how much work it takes to understand what is expected, what habits and patterns work, how to relate to other members of

the team. The more complex the information age becomes and the faster it evolves, the more vital it is to have very strong team-building capabilities so people can come together and work on projects with a common language, common system, and common sense of accountability. Developing this kind of common understanding is what the military calls doctrine. Every system has to have a doctrinal base and the team members will be dramatically more effective if they have a shared understanding of the doctrine of their team.

10. The better educated people are into doctrine, the simpler the orders can be. The less educated someone is into the common doctrine, the more complete and detailed the orders have to be. With a very mature team that has thoroughly mastered the doctrine and applied it in several situations, remarkably few instructions are required. In a brand new team the orders may have to be very detailed. The Entrepreneurial Public Management system has to have the flexibility to deal with the entire spectrum of knowledge and capability this implies.

11. The information age requires a constant focus on team building, team development, and team leadership. It is the wagon train and not the mountain man that best characterizes the information age. People have to work together to get complex projects completed in this modern era. It takes a while to build teams. There should be a lot more thought given to changing personnel laws so leaders can arrive in a new assignment with a core team of people they are used to working with. Admiral Ed Giambastiani of the Joint Forces Command (which has responsibility for pioneering information age transformation in the military) has captured the distinction in modern sophisticated team requirements. He has a single chart that shows the growth in maturity towards truly interdependent teams. These teams are integrated, collaborative, inherently joint, capabilities-based and network-centric. Entrepreneurial Public Management will require similar standards of sophisticated organization and teamwork for it to work at its optimum.

12. Information technology combined with the explosion in communications (including wireless communications) create the

underlying capabilities that should be at the heart of transforming government systems from Bureaucratic Public
Administration to Entrepreneurial Public Management. The
power of computing and communications to capture, analyze, and convey information with stunning accuracy and
speed and at ever declining costs creates enormous opportunities for rethinking how to deliver goods and services. These
new capabilities have been engines of change in the private
sector. They are the heart of Wal-Mart's ability to turn "everyday low price is a function of everyday low cost" into a realis-
tic implementation strategy. They are at the heart of the revolution in logistics supply chain management. They are this
generation's most powerful reason for being sure we can
expect more choices of higher quality at lower cost. We have
only scratched the surface of the potential. The Library of
Congress now has a digital library with millions of documents
available 24 hours a day 7 days a week for free to anyone in the
world who wants to access them through the Internet. It is
possible for every school in the country to have the largest
library in the world by simply having one laptop accessing the
Internet. This is a totally different kind of system for learning.
NASA is now connecting to schools to allow students to actually direct telescopes and search for stars from their classroom. This is an extraordinary extension of research opportunities to young scientists and young explorers. The potential
to use the computer, the Internet, and communications
(again including wireless) has only begun to be tapped. The
more rapidly government leaders study and learn the lessons
of these new potentials the more rapidly we will invent a 21st
century information age governing system which uses
Entrepreneurial Public Management to produce more choices of higher quality at lower cost.

13. The agrarian-industrial model of government saw the citizen
    as a client of limited capabilities and the government employ-
    ee as the center of knowledge, decision, and power. It was a
    bureaucrat-centered model of governance (much as the
    agrarian-industrial model of health was a doctor-centered
    model and the agrarian-industrial school was a teacher-cen-
    tered model. The information age makes it possible to develop
    citizen centered models of access and information. The

Weather Channel and Weather.com are a good example of this new approach. The Weather Channel gathers and analyzes the data but it is available to you when you want it and in the form you need. You do not have to access all the weather in the world to discover the weather for your neighborhood tomorrow. You do not have to get anyone's permission to access the system 24 hours a day 7 days a week. Google is another system of customer centric organization that is a model for government. You access Google when you want to and you ask it the question that interests you. Google may give you an answer that has over a million possibilities but you only have to use the one or two options that satiate your interest. Similarly Amazon.com and E-Bay are models of systems geared to your interests on your terms when you want to access them. Compare these systems with the current school room, the courthouse which is open from 8 to 5, the appointment at the doctor's office on the doctor's terms, the college class only available when the professor deigns to show up. Government is still mired in the pre-computer, pre-communications age. A key component of Entrepreneurial Public Management is to ask every morning what can be done to use computers, the Internet, CDs, DVDs, teleconferencing, and other modern innovations to recenter the government on the citizen.

14. A customer centered, citizen centered model of governance would start with the concept that as a general rule, being online is better than being in line. It would both put traditional bureaucratic functions on the Internet as is happening in many states (paying taxes, ordering license tags, etc.) but it would also begin to rethink major functions of government in terms of the new Internet-based system. The information age makes possible a lot more citizen self-help as defined by the citizen's needs. If learning is individually centered and adapted to the needs of each person, and available when they need it and on the topics of skills they need, then how would that learning system operate? If prisoners out on parole were monitored by wireless information age technology to ensure they were going to work, taking their classes, staying out of off-limits areas, etc., then how would the new model parole system operate? If migrant children could be connected to an online, videoconferencing and teleconferencing learning system so

they had a continuity of learning experience how would that process operate? These are just some examples of how a citizen centered new model would be different from using information systems to improve the existing agrarian and industrial era delivery systems.

15. One of the key side effects of information technology and ubiquitous communications is the development of much flatter hierarchies and much greater connectedness across the entire system. In private business, the military, and in customer relationships, there is a much flatter system of information flow. The power of knowledge is to some extent driving out the power of the hierarchy. A networked system seems to operate very differently than the pyramid of power which has been dominant since the rise of agriculture with a few at the top giving orders to the many at the bottom. Increasingly, who knows is defining who is in charge. Entrepreneurial Public Management will have a much more fluid system for shifting authority based on expertise and on identifying what knowledge needs to be applied so the right informed person can be brought in to make the decision as accurate and effective as possible. Bureaucratic Public Administration defined who was in the room by a system of defined authority without regard to knowledge. Entrepreneurial Public Management will define participation in the decisions by a hierarchy of knowledge and experience rather than a hierarchy of status and defined authority.

16. There will be a radical shift toward online learning and online information. In the information age people need to know so much in so many different areas (while the knowledge itself keeps changing in a rapidly evolving world) that it is impossible for the traditional classroom based continuing education system to keep up with modern reality. The combination of videoconferencing, online learning, mentoring, and apprenticeships will presently create a totally different system of professional development and continuing education. Governments will shift from flying people to conferences and workshops toward having videoconferences. They will also shift from courses built around the teacher's convenience and occurring inconveniently in time and place toward on going

learning opportunities that can be accessed 24/7 so people can learn when they need, what they need, and at their own convenience. This will increase the learning while decreasing the cost in both time and money.

17. Personnel mobility will be a major factor in the information age and will require profound changes in how we conceptualize a civil service. The information age creates career paths in which the most competent people move from challenging and interesting job to challenging and interesting job. A government civil service that required a lifetime commitment was both guaranteeing that it would not attract the most competent people and guaranteeing that it would not have the flexibility to bring in specialists when they are needed. A new system of allowing people to move in and out of government service, to move from department to department as they are needed, to accumulate and take with them health savings accounts and pension plans, to build up seniority with each passing assignment, and to be able to rise without continuous service as long as their experience and knowledge has risen will be necessary for an Entrepreneurial Public Management system to attract the kind of talent it will need in the information age. It may also make sense for different governments to agree to count the experience in other governments in assigning status and pension eligibility so people could move between governments as well as within them.

18. Outsourcing is inevitably going to be a big part of the information age. Virtually every successful private sector company uses outsourcing extensively. The ability to create competitive pressures and shift to the best provider is inherent in the outsourcing model. Applying these principles to the public sector will both save the taxpayer money and improve substantially the quality and convenience of services provided to the citizens. It is also simply a fact that in many of the most complex developments of the information age the public sector bureaucracy simply cannot attract the expertise and build the capability to manage the new systems effectively. In these cases outsourcing is the only way to bring new developments into the government.

19. Privatization needs to be readdressed in Washington and in the states. At one time the United States was a leader in privatization but now we have fallen far behind many foreign countries. There are a number of opportunities for privatization which would help balance the budget, increase the tax rolls of future contributors to government revenue, and increase the efficiency of the services delivered to the citizen. The Thatcher model of selling some of the stock to the beneficiaries of the services dramatically reduced resistance to privatization in Britain. A similar strategy of developing an economic incentive for those most likely to object to conclude that privatization was a good thing for them personally would lower the resistance and increase the opportunity to move naturally market oriented entities off the government payroll and into the market where they belong.

20. For activities where privatization would be wrong there is a pattern of public-private partnerships which should be examined. The Atlanta Zoo was on the verge of being disaccredited because the city of Atlanta bureaucracy simply could not run it effectively. Mayor Andrew Young courageously concluded that the answer was to create a public-private partnership with the Friends of the Zoo. The city would continue to own the zoo and would provide some limited funding but the Friends of the Zoo would find additional resources and would provide entrepreneurial leadership. The Friends of the Zoo then recruited Dr. Terry Maples, a brilliant professor from Georgia Tech and a natural entrepreneur and salesman. With Terry's leadership and the Friends of the Zoo's enthusiastic backing, he rapidly turned ZooAtlanta into a world-class research institution and a wonderful attraction both for the families of the Atlanta area and to visitors from around the world. ZooAtlanta went from being an almost disaccredited embarrassment to an extraordinary example of a public-private partnership. Other zoos around America have had similar experiences with new entrepreneurial leadership bringing new ideas, new excitement, and new resources to what had formerly been government-run institutions. The government retains ownership of the zoo but the daily operations are under the control of the entrepreneurial association that raises the money and provides strategic guidance. The result is far

more energy and creativity and a great deal of flexibility of implementation than could ever be achieved with the purely public bureaucracy. This is the model that should be applied to creating a truly national zoo in Washington, where the National Zoo has suffered from the problems of a neglectful bureaucracy. This is also the model of the kind of activities which could be used in many other areas. When something can't be privatized or outsourced the next question should be whether there's a useful public-private partnership that might be used to accomplish the same goals with fewer tax payer resources and more creativity, energy, and flexibility.

21. As a general principle, proposals that (i) dramatically improve applying logistics supply chain management, go paperless, adapt a quality-metrics system and/or (ii) outsource or privatize, should be viewed by third-party independent experts with no financial interests as well as by the agency to be changed. As a general rule government agencies or department leaders faced with improvements that will shrink their work force or shrink their budget will be reluctant to say yes. There are no incentives and rewards in government for downsizing and modernizing. The senior leader and the legislative branch need third-party opinions as well as the in-house review and the vendor's proposal to ensure that the maximum improvements are being implemented.

22. Create pressure for modernizing government at all levels by requiring federal and state governments to benchmark best practices every year and agree to pay no more than 10 percent above the least expensive, most effective programs. This approach would create a continuous pressure to have government programs in each state constantly adapting toward better outcomes at lower cost. This approach also might entail providing a bonus to the state which has the best program in the country. It would also create an annual rhythm of benchmarking and data gathering which would revolutionize how we think about government. Benchmarking would also make very visible the cost of recalcitrant government unions and the cost of bureaucratic resistance to modernization.

23. This system of Entrepreneurial Public Management requires profound changes in the analytical assumptions of the Congressional Budget Office (CBO) and the Office of Management and Budget (OMB). Today neither office has a model for distinguishing between investments which increase productivity and lower cost and pure costs. Neither system has a model for offsetting future savings against innovation and technological breakthroughs. Neither system has a model for the impact of incentives on behavior. The result is both systems are essentially reactionary and premodern in their assessment of proposed policies. In many ways the CBO-OMB reactionary models are the greatest single roadblock to sound investment in an incentivized, technologically advanced, dramatically more productive future. Their scoring systems reinforce current spending on obsolete bureaucracies and inhibit investments in profound change.

These twenty-three principles are examples of the kind of thinking which will be required to move from a system of Bureaucratic Public Administration to a system of Entrepreneurial Public Management. It is one of the most important transformations of our lifetime and without it government will literally not be able to keep up with the speed and complexity of the information age.

The Legislative Role in 21st Century Entrepreneurial Public Management

The Congress and state legislatures should begin holding hearings on the difference between a government run according to the information age principles of Entrepreneurial Public Management from a government run according to the principles of Bureaucratic Public Administration. For the legislative branch the changes will include:

- Replacing the current civil service personnel laws with a new model of hiring and leading people including part-time employees, temporary employees, the ability to shift to other jobs across the government, the ability to do training and educating on an individualized 24/7 Internet based system;

- Radically simplifying the disclosure requirements which have become a major hindrance to successful people coming to work for the federal government;

- The Senate adopting rules to minimize individual senators holding up presidential appointments for months. The current process of clearing and confirming presidential personnel should be a national scandal because it disrupts the functioning of the Executive Branch to a shocking degree. There should be some time limitation (say 90 days) for every appointment to reach an up or down vote on the Senate floor (this is separate from judicial nominations, which is a different kind of problem). The current Senate indulgence of individual senators is a constant wound weakening the Executive Branch's ability to manage;

- Creating a single system of security clearances so once people are cleared at a particular level (e.g., secret, top secret, code word) they are cleared throughout the federal government and do not have to go through multiple clearances;

- Writing new management laws that enable entrepreneurial public leaders to set metrics for performance and reward and punish according to the achievement level of the employees;

- Within appropriate safeguards, creating the opportunity for leaders to suspend and when necessary fire people who fail to do their jobs and fail to meet the standards and the metrics;

- Working with the major departments to reshape their education and training programs and their systems of assessment so they can begin retraining their existing work force into this new framework;

- Transforming the General Accounting Office, the Congressional Research Service, and the Congressional Budget Office into institutions that understand and are implementing the principles of Entrepreneurial Public Management;

- Developing a system for educating new members of Congress and new congressional staff members into these new principles;

- Creating an expectation that within two years every current congressional staff member will have taken a course in the new method of managing the government in an entrepreneurial way;

- Rethinking the kind of hearings that ought to be held, the focus of those hearings, and the kind of questions that government officials ought to be answering;

- Designing a much more flexible budget and appropriations process that provides for the kind of latitude entrepreneurial leaders need if they are to be effective;

- Establishing for confirmation hearings the kind of questioning that elicits from potential office holders how they would work in an Entrepreneurial Public Management style and apply these questions with special intensity to people who come from a long background of experience in the traditional bureaucracy.

With this set of changes the legislative branches will have prepared for a cooperative leadership role in helping the executive branch transform itself from a system dedicated to Bureaucratic Public Administration into one working every day to invent and implement 21st Century Entrepreneurial Public Management.

INDEX

The Art of Transformation

by Newt Gingrich and Nancy Desmond

If you would like to purchase copies of this book in quantities of 100 or more, please contact us at

THE CENTER FOR HEALTH TRANSFORMATION

1425 K Street, NW
Suite 450
Washington, DC 20005

(202) 375-2001

www.healthtransformation.net